ESRI

The Economic and Social Research Institute

T   -profit
c   nomic
F   This book is due for return on or before the last date shown below.   ted by
g   erned
b   tive of
b   encies,
u

Victims of Recorded Crime in Ireland

Results from the 1996 Survey

Dorothy Watson

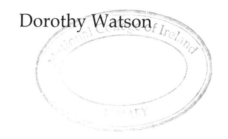

Oak Tree Press

Dublin

in association with
The Economic and Social Research Institute

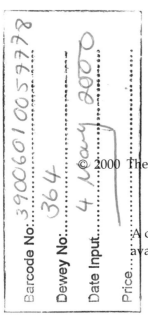
Oak Tree Press
Merrion Building
Lower Merrion Street
Dublin 2, Ireland
www.oaktreepress.com

© 2000 The Economic and Social Research Institute

A catalogue record of this book is
available from the British Library.

ISBN 1 86076 160 7

This study forms part of The Economic and Social Research Institute's
General Research Series, in which it is Paper No. 174. It has been subject
to the normal internal and external refereeing procedures employed for
that series and accepted for publication by the Institute, which is not
responsible for either the content or the views expressed therein.

Printed in the Republic of Ireland
by Colour Books Ltd.

Contents

Tables and Figures

About the Author

Dr Dorothy Watson is a Research Officer at the Economic and Social Research Unit. Her research interests include the study of social inequality, crime, values and belief systems, and survey methodology.

Acknowledgements

Research is always a communal endeavour, and I am very conscious that this report would not have been possible without the contributions of a number of people, to whom I would like to express my thanks.

Kieran O'Dwyer of the Garda Research Unit has been involved in the project since the beginning, contributing significantly to the research design, the development of the sampling frame from which the final sample of victims was selected, the design of the questionnaire, and providing detailed comments and suggestions on early drafts of the report. To Kieran, the staff at the Garda Research Unit and the members of the Garda Síochána who were instrumental in the development of the sampling frame, my sincere thanks.

My colleagues at the ESRI also deserve thanks. The organisation and development of the report benefited significantly from the comments of Tony Fahey and Edgar Morgenroth. Brendan Whelan provided important support and encouragement, both at the early stages of the project and in bringing it to a conclusion.

Dave Rottman, now at the National Centre for State Courts, gave encouragement, suggestions, and also inspiration through the high quality of his earlier work on crime in Ireland.

I am also grateful to the anonymous external reviewer, to Dr Ian O'Donnell of the Irish Penal Reform Trust, the Combat

Poverty Agency and the Department of Social, Community and Family Affairs for comments on earlier drafts of the report.

The staff at the Survey Unit of the ESRI — Sylvia Blackwell, Maura Cagney, Pat Devlin, Pauline Needham, Fergal Rhatigan, Bernadette Ryan and James Williams — dealt ably and cheerfully with a very complex questionnaire. A special thanks also to the interviewers who worked on the project, and to the respondents who were willing to answer the detailed questions we put to them. I hope that the results presented here faithfully reflect their experiences.

Sarah Burns and Kevin Dillon at the ESRI library were able to obtain quickly the large number of books and articles needed. Pat Hopkins prepared the questionnaire for printing, provided important advice on layout and formatting, and capably managed the printing and binding of early drafts of the report.

My thanks also to Brian Langan of Oak Tree Press for thoughtful comments on the manuscript and the considerable job of proofing and formatting the text, tables and charts for publication.

The results presented here, their interpretation and any remaining errors or omissions, are the responsibility of the author.

General Summary

Background

The Garda Síochána Annual Report is the primary ongoing source of crime statistics for Ireland, particularly given the absence of periodic victimisation surveys. In view of the reliance on these figures, it is important to explore the "reality" behind them: the nature of the incident itself, the characteristics of the victims, their experience with the criminal justice system, their interaction with the Gardaí, and the impact the crime had on them. The goal of the present study is to present such an in-depth analysis in order to provide insight into the patterning of crime in Ireland and to inform policy on services to crime victims, crime prevention, and the development and interpretation of crime statistics in Ireland.

The study analyses the results of the *Survey of Victims of Recorded Crime* carried out in 1996 by The Economic and Social Research Institute for the Garda Research Unit. Data was collected on the experience of crime victimisation from a sample of 959 victims drawn from the Garda records of those reporting a crime in the year from November 1994 to October 1995. As such, it is a sample of victims of crime that was both *reported to* and *recorded by* the Gardaí. The main strengths of the research design are the inclusion of crimes against businesses or other organisations as well as those against individuals and private households; the use of a stratified sample so that sufficient cases were included in the "rarer" crime categories to permit detailed analyses; and the collection of detailed information on the circumstances of the incident and the characteristics of victims.

For sampling and analysis purposes, the crimes were divided into ten categories, based on (a) whether the incident involved violence or threat; (b) whether the incident involved theft of property; and (c) broad features of the setting. The categories are: theft of vehicle, theft from a vehicle, fraud, assault, burglary, aggravated burglary, theft from the person, aggravated theft from the person, other theft, and vandalism. Crimes in these categories accounted for 97 per cent of all indictable crime in Ireland in 1995. Non-indictable crimes in related categories (vehicle takings, assault, criminal damage) were also included.

This report is not intended to cover all crime. Rather, it is designed to provide insight into the nature, patterning and seriousness of the main categories of crime with identifiable victims recorded in the Garda statistics. This is warranted given the centrality of Garda statistics as the sole regular source of information on crime trends and patterns in Ireland. Unlike classic victimisation surveys, the study cannot provide a comprehensive account of the much-disputed "dark figure" of unreported and unrecorded crime. Nor can we provide the kind of data that would be needed to form the basis of a multivariate analysis of the risk of crime victimisation.

New Insights into Recorded Crime in Ireland

Recorded Crime in Context

The recently published figures from the 1998 Quarterly National Household Survey (QNHS) crime victimisation module provide a context for the interpretation of the recorded crime figures for private households and individuals.[1] Victimisation surveys give

---

[1] Crimes against business and other organisations were not covered in the QNHS crime module.

much higher estimates of the extent of criminal victimisation in a population than police crime statistics, because they "capture" incidents that are not *reported* to the police as well as incidents that may not be *recorded* in the published police statistics. Across seven categories of crime[2] where comparisons were possible, the QNHS crime victimisation results gave a count which was about five times the Garda published statistics for the corresponding period, or 3.3 times if vandalism and bicycle theft are excluded. The biggest differences in Ireland occur for those crime categories where the corresponding non-indictable crimes may not appear in the statistics if no proceedings are taken (vandalism and bicycle theft).

Compared to figures from the 1998 British Crime Survey, the gap between police and victimisation survey counts is slightly smaller in Ireland for vehicle theft, theft without violence and theft with violence; slightly higher for burglary and theft from a vehicle; and considerably higher for vandalism and bicycle theft.

The gap between the two figures should not be used to conclude that the Garda figures are "wrong" or that victim survey counts represent the "true" extent of crime. Instead, the two types of data give alternative accounts of the extent of crime. Both sources have their own strengths and weaknesses. The gap does, however, point to the need to interpret the recorded crime figures in the light of the way in which they are collected and compiled, and points to the importance of regular victimisation surveys, which would permit an assessment of the extent of unreported and unrecorded crime.

The results of the present study also highlight the difficulties involved in comparing the categories used in victim surveys and those used in the Garda statistics. Police and victims may classify the same incident in different ways. In particular, there were dif-

---

[2] The categories were vehicle theft, theft from a vehicle, burglary, vandalism, theft with violence, theft without violence and bicycle theft.

ferences in interpretation between victims and the Gardaí with respect to whether the incident involved assault or threat.

Victims and Incidents: the Implications of Repeat Victimisation

An important finding in the report concerned the implications of repeat victimisation (the extent to which victims had experienced other criminal incidents in a given period) for counts of the number of distinct victims behind the recorded crime figures. Repeat victimisation is quite extensive and is greater for institutions than for individuals. Four out of five of the businesses and organisations in the survey were victims of at least one other criminal incident of any type in a three-year period, compared to about half of the individual victims. Repeat victimisation was particularly common in the case of burglary, other theft, and fraud. It was also found, however, that repeat victimisation more often involved a *different type* of crime than a repeat of the *same type* of incident.

These results have clear implications for counts of victims of crime. The findings suggested that the number of recorded incidents is considerably higher than the number of distinct victims affected: for every 100 incidents across all ten categories, there are about 62 separate victims. The discrepancy is much less for crimes where a repeat of the same type of incident is less common, such as vehicle theft (96 victims per 100 incidents) and theft from the person (98 victims per 100 incidents). The gap between the number of victims and the number of incidents is greatest for other theft (the category that includes shoplifting: 70 victims for each 100 incidents). Since institutions face a higher level of repeat victimisation than individuals, the gap between the number of victims and the number of incidents is greatest for crimes targeted against institutions.

Crimes against Businesses and Other Organisations

A second important contribution of the present study was the information it provided on crimes against businesses and other organisations. The present study provided information that was not previously available in Ireland on the proportion of recorded criminal *incidents* that are directed against institutions (one-third) and the proportion of *victims* of recorded crime that are institutions (one-fifth). The proportion of incidents targeted against institutions is higher than the proportion of victims that are institutions because they experience a higher level of repeat victimisation than individuals and households.

Over one-third of institutional victims were retail establishments, and two-fifths had between one and five employees, probably reflecting the numbers of small-scale and retail outlets in the population. Crimes against institutional targets differ in a number of respects from those targeted against individuals or households. First, the type of crime tends to be different: crimes against institutions account for over nine out of ten cases of recorded fraud, nearly three-quarters of aggravated burglaries, over half of the "other theft" category and over two-fifths of burglary and vandalism incidents. Second, recorded crime against institutions does not show the same "Dublin concentration" as crime against domestic or individual targets: 46 per cent of recorded crime against institutions took place in Dublin, compared to 63 percent of the incidents against individuals. An important exception is aggravated burglary of institutions, with 84 per cent of recorded incidents taking place in the Dublin area.

There were also indications that institutions differed from individuals and private households in the reporting of crime. We were able to examine reporting rates for other incidents experienced by the sample in the three-year period from mid-1993 to mid-1996. While these figures may not be fully representative of overall reporting rates, since we could only look at reporting rates for the subset who had experienced more than one incident in a three-year period,[3] they suggested that institutions were only about half as likely to report a crime (34 per cent) as individual victims (63 per cent). Reporting rates by the two groups were very similar for vehicle crime and burglary and a little higher among institutions for crimes involving violence. However, reporting rates for one of the largest categories of crime directed against institutions — other theft — was particularly low, at only 19 per cent, and rates were also very low for fraud (21 per cent).

Significantly, the results suggested that reporting by institutions of crimes such as "other theft" and fraud is quite selective. A number of findings lead to the conclusion that it is primarily those incidents where the offender is "caught in the act" that are reported to the Gardaí. This has two important implications for the representativeness of recorded crime figures in these categories: they will overstate the total proportion of cases where the offender is apprehended, and they will understate the loss to businesses and other organisations from these types of crime.

The Setting of Crime

We knew from previous studies in Ireland and from the published Garda Statistics that crime tends to be more concentrated in urban areas, particularly in the Dublin region. However, there are large differences between types of crime in the extent of this concentration. The "Dublin concentration" was particularly marked for certain categories of violent crime involving theft: over 80 per cent of aggravated burglaries against institutions and of aggravated theft from the person took place in Dublin city or county. Theft from the person and theft from a vehicle were also particularly concentrated in Dublin.

The study also underlined the link between crime and everyday routines. Almost three-quarters of incidents occur in what

---

[3] The target incident, on the basis of which the victim was selected into the sample, was reported by definition, and had to be excluded from this analysis.

individual victims consider to be their "own area", with more than half occurring at, or near, the home. The greater number of incidents taking place in or near the home is understandable, given that this is where people are likely to spend most of their time. The link between crime and everyday routines was also evident in the timing of incidents. Crimes associated with businesses and their customers tend to take place by day: aggravated burglary, aggravated and non-aggravated theft from the person, other theft directed against businesses, and, to a lesser extent, theft from a vehicle. On the other hand, assault, vandalism, non-domestic burglary and vehicle thefts are more likely to take place at night. About half of domestic burglaries take place during the day, particularly on weekdays when the home is most likely to be empty.

Material gain is clearly a major motivation for crime, with property stolen in over four-fifths of recorded criminal incidents across the categories covered in this study. Cash is stolen in over one-quarter of incidents directed against individuals and nearly one-third of those directed against institutions, and the figure is over two-thirds for personal theft and aggravated burglary. Personal accessories, vehicles, tools or equipment, and retail or manufacturing stock are among the kinds of property taken in over ten per cent of all criminal incidents. The most common forms of recorded fraud — the use of stolen cheques or credit cards and cashing a cheque made out to someone else — suggest connections to the theft where these items were originally stolen.

One recorded incident in six involves some element of violence or threat, from the victim's perspective, with the proportion being similar for individual and institutional victims. This most often takes the form of being pushed, dragged, kicked or punched. The threat or use of a weapon is most common in aggravated burglary (nearly three-quarters of the cases) and occurs in nearly one-third of the incidents of aggravated theft from the person and assault cases. The weapon is usually a "blunt instrument" in assault cases, and either a knife or a gun in aggravated burglaries. A syringe was used to assault or threaten the victim in about one in eight cases of aggravated theft from the person and aggravated burglary.

The evidence does not support the image of assault as involving a lone victim. Only one in six victims of recorded assault were alone with the offender, and half of the assault victims were accompanied by someone they knew (apart from the offender) at the time. This may be an artefact of the reporting and recording process, however. Witnessed assaults are probably more likely to be reported, and the presence of a witness increases the credibility of the victim's complaint. On the other hand, aggravated burglary against individual targets and aggravated theft from the person are more likely to involve a lone victim.

Victimisation Risk

We were able to make an assessment of the risk of criminal victimisation for individuals by comparing the profiles of crime victims in our sample to those of the general adult population, using other data sources. The risk referred to here is the risk of being a victim of a crime that is both *reported* and *recorded*: to the extent that there are differences in reporting by victims, or in recording by the Gardaí, associated with victim characteristics, the "true" distribution of risk may be different.

Victims of recorded crime do not tend to be the most vulnerable members of society. The person reporting the crime is more likely to be male than female for most types of crime, and particularly in the case of assault. An exception is theft from the person — both aggravated and non-aggravated — where victims are more likely to be female. More victims are people in their middle-years than are elderly, with those in the 35–49 age group over-represented in most categories. The risk pattern by age group is largely driven by rates of vehicle ownership and being a head of household. The risk of assault, on the other hand, is greatest for those under age 35, while the risk of aggravated burglary — a very small category numerically but particularly distressing to victims in its impact — is greatest for those over age 65. Finally, those in the higher social classes appear to be at a higher risk of crime than those in the manual social classes, although there were some indications that this may partly reflect reporting differences by social class, particularly for vehicle crime and other theft.

Victim and Offender

In half of the crimes against individuals and about three-quarters of those against institutions, the victim was able to provide some information on the offenders. This information needs to be treated with caution, however, since offenders who are seen, or later identified, may not be representative of all offenders. Where victims had some information on the offender, it emerged that crimes against individual victims were more likely to involve multiple offenders (nearly two thirds of cases) than a lone offender; the offender was more likely to be male (nearly nine out of ten cases) than female; and over two-fifths of the offences were committed by teenagers or children, rather than adults. In crimes directed against institutions, a somewhat higher proportion of incidents involved a lone offender (about two-fifths), female offenders (15 per cent), and a slightly lower proportion involved teenagers or children.

Assault is the only crime where the victim knew the offender (prior to the incident) in more than half of the cases. In assaults of male victims, the offender tended to be less closely linked to the victim than in assaults against females. Only about one-quarter of female assault victims had been assaulted by a stranger (compared to nearly half of male victims); and in just under a quarter of cases involving female victims, the assault was perpetrated by the spouse of the victim. Since domestic violence is known to have a low reporting rate, however, this figure understates the overall proportion of assaults on women perpetrated by a spouse or partner.

In one-quarter of the cases directed against individuals and half of the cases against institutions, the offender had been apprehended. As noted above, the apparently higher "detection rate" of offenders who target institutions may be an artefact of differential reporting: offences such as fraud and other theft, in particular, tend to be reported by institutions only when the offender can be identified.

Victim Satisfaction with Garda Service and Outcome

The general level of satisfaction with the Garda service at the time of reporting the crime was high among victims, but levels of satisfaction with follow-up information on the progress and outcome of the case were low. Only about two-fifths of victims were contacted by the Gardaí after reporting the crime. Institutional victims of recorded crime seemed to be better-informed overall, but this may reflect the more selective reporting of incidents where the offender is "caught in the act", as noted earlier.

Levels of satisfaction with the outcome of the case were also low. About one-quarter of the individual victims and one-third of the institutional victims felt either "fairly satisfied" or "very satisfied" with the outcome. The main reasons for satisfaction or dissatisfaction tended to centre on the arrest and/or conviction of the offender in the case of violent crime, and the recovery/non-recovery of property for non-violent crimes involving theft. At least some stolen property was recovered in about one-third of the thefts targeted against individuals and about two-fifths of those directed against institutions.

Impact on Victim

The survey data analysed in this report allowed us to examine three aspects of the seriousness of the crime, from the victim's perspective: the physical injury involved, the financial costs, and the emotional impact on the victim. The proportion of all recorded crime leading to physical injury is low: seven per cent of the crimes against individual targets resulted in injuries requiring medical attention, with three per cent leading to permanent or recurring problems. The figures were even lower, at two per cent and one per cent, respectively, for crimes targeting institutions. The crimes most likely to result in injuries leading to permanent or recurring problems for the victim were assault (one-fifth), aggravated burglary directed against individuals (six per cent), and aggravated theft from the person (eight per cent).

We measured the direct costs of the crime, such as the value of property stolen or damaged, or out-of-pocket medical expenses. The highest net cost (after insurance) to the individual victims was found for aggravated burglary, with nearly one-quarter of the incidents resulting in losses of £1,000 or more. Theft from the person and aggravated theft from the person had the lowest costs among the property crimes, rarely resulting in losses over £300. Recorded crime against institutions tended to be more polarised, with both a higher proportion of incidents involving no financial cost (often because the offender was caught) and a higher proportion involving costs over £1,000. Burglary was the most expensive type of incident for institutions, with net losses of £1,000 or more in over one-third of the cases.

The third dimension to the seriousness of crime is the emotional impact on the victim. At the time of the interview, which took place between eight months and two years after the incident, one-quarter of the individual crime victims and one-fifth of the institutional victims continued to experience psychological distress (increased anxiety, trouble sleeping, trouble concentrating). This persistent psychological distress was greatest for victims of violent crime: assault, aggravated burglary and aggravated theft from the person.

An analysis of factors associated with distress for individual victims showed that victims are most affected by whether the incident involved assault, threat, or injury. Being present at the time (even when not assaulted or threatened), and suffering a financial loss over £500 also tended to increase distress, but these effects were smaller. Characteristics of the victim also made a difference: those who are likely to feel most vulnerable — women and the elderly — experienced greater levels of distress than men or younger adults. The intervention of the criminal justice system was less important on the whole than aspects of the incident itself. There was some increase in distress associated with the offender being apprehended, but this was reduced where the victim was satisfied with the outcome of the case. Satisfaction or dissatisfaction with the service provided by the Gardaí had no additional impact on distress.

Implications

Services to Victims of Crime

The study pointed to four distinct areas where services to crime victims needed improvement. The first of these involved a clear need to provide follow-up information to victims on the progress and outcome of the case. Contact between police and victims after the crime is reported can be an important component of police–community relations, encouraging greater co-operation between the public and the Gardaí. Even if there is no progress to report in terms of detecting the offender, it sends a clear message that the problems of victims are important to the Gardaí.

The second area is that of support for victims during the court procedure. For the minority of cases where the victim goes to court, half of the individual victims felt that special court services for crime victims were (or would have been) useful to them, with higher figures for victims of assault, burglary and aggravated burglary.

A third recommendation concerns the need for a review of services for victims of assault. Assault victims were the only group where a substantial fraction experienced intimidation by the offender; one-third of those experiencing intimidation felt that the protection provided to them by the Gardaí was not adequate; and one-fifth would have appreciated more protection in court. Assault victims also emerged as having the highest proportion (one-third) who said they would be less likely to report a similar incident in the future. There is clearly a need to review the follow-up services provided to victims of assault after the crime has been reported.

The fourth area identified in the report concerned the need to help victims, especially victims of violent crime, to cope with the emotional trauma associated with the incident. The empowerment of victims — and of those who restrict their lifestyle out of fear of crime — needs to be approached on two fronts. One is to tackle the very real problem of crime itself. But the second element is equally important. This involves a direct attack on the fear of crime. Great care must be taken not to overdramatise the problem of crime in order to make political points or advance commercial concerns. The main way in which crime is overdramatised is the juxtaposition of high numerical figures, which include many less serious incidents, with images and descriptions drawn from the much rarer, very serious and threatening incidents. The problem of crime needs to be put in perspective and the risks weighed alongside the other threats which people face in their everyday lives, such as road safety, illness, job loss and so on.

Some more specific strategies to help crime victims cope with the emotional impact of the incident would include help with crime prevention, providing information on strategies to reduce risk, and enhancing a sense of community involvement in crime prevention, through such programmes as Neighbourhood Watch and Community Alert. Finally, where it seems that a crime victim is overemphasising the level of risk, he or she can be helped by Victim Support to place the level of risk in perspective.

The effectiveness of the changes promised in the revised Victims Charter (Department of Justice, Equality and Law Reform, 1999) and in the Garda Policing Plan (Garda Síochána, 1998b), particularly as regards victim satisfaction with information on progress and outcome of the case, and the provision of protection and support to victims of violent crime, needs to be evaluated and assessed on an ongoing basis. It is significant that a central role in providing support to crime victims — both counselling and the provision of assistance in court — is to be played by Victim Support, a voluntary agency. It is important to ensure that Victim Support has the resources necessary to meet this role, on the one hand, and that there is continuing evaluation of its effectiveness in meeting the needs of crime victims, on the other.

Strategies for Crime Prevention

One finding in the report with broad implications for crime prevention strategies concerns the extent of repeat victimisation, particularly for institutional crime victims. Repeat victimisation has become an international focus of criminological research in recent years, and has been targeted for specific action in the Garda Policing Plan (Garda Síochána, 1998b). Given the present findings, and those from the QNHS crime module, that repeat victimisation is quite extensive, crime prevention strategies directed towards helping victims of reported crime could be a very good use of Garda resources. Contact with the victim following the incident could be used to target crime prevention measures onto those whose risk of re-victimisation is greatest. As well as alleviating the victim's distress, a focus on repeat victims can give a pay-off in terms of reduced crime and increased detections.

A second area of intervention concerns the link between drugs and crime in the Dublin area. Despite the difficulty in specifying precisely how much crime can be attributed to drug users, there is general agreement on the link between certain categories of crime and heroin addiction in the Dublin area (e.g. Rottman, 1989;

Keogh, 1998; Medico-Social Research Board, 1984; Korf and Wiersma, 1996). This link may account for the concentration of specific types of crime in Dublin, and the relatively high proportion of identified offenders who are teenagers in crimes such as aggravated theft from the person and theft from a vehicle.

In addressing the drugs-crime relationship, equal emphasis should be on "target hardening" and on the rehabilitation of offenders. To the extent that obtaining drugs, or the money to buy them, can be made more difficult, we would simultaneously increase the enthusiasm with which (former) drug abusers take advantage of treatment and training schemes. An acknowledgement of the need for such a multi-faceted strategy and the involvement of specialist agencies in dealing with drugs-related crime is contained in the Policing Plan 1998/99 (Garda Síochána, 1998b, p. 23).

Crime Statistics and the Study of Crime in Ireland

In the course of interpreting and contextualising the results of this study, it was clear that there is a dearth of relevant, ongoing research on the overall level and nature of crime in Ireland. The comparison of the results from the 1998 QNHS crime module and the Garda statistics on crime revealed that the two sources could provide a very different picture of the extent of crime in Ireland. This points to the risk involved in drawing conclusions from the recorded crime statistics when we do not know how reporting rates or recording practices may be changing over time, or may vary between different groups in the population. Further, the clear suggestion emerging from the present study that several types of crime against institutions tend to be reported only when the offender is caught, point to the need for a fuller understanding of the range of factors affecting the reporting of crime. Such an understanding can only come from regular victimisation surveys. Periodic crime victimisation surveys, including surveys of businesses and other organisations, are needed to provide an independent source of information against which to assess crime levels and patterns and to evaluate progress in crime prevention.

Apart from victimisation surveys, the production of more detailed statistics on recorded crime has the potential to provide a large increment in value-added in terms of our understanding of crime in Ireland, with a relatively small additional cost. The new system for computerisation of Garda records should simplify the process of producing statistics with a small number of additional breakdowns which would greatly enhance the usefulness of the crime statistics. The results of this study suggest that the following additional pieces of information would be most useful:

- Breakdowns by Garda Division and the five major cities that clearly distinguish crimes involving violence, and the major situational characteristics of the incident (perhaps along the lines of the ten categories used in this report).

- Separate statistics for crimes against individuals or private households and crimes against businesses or other organisations, such as the breakdowns that have been provided for burglary in the 1998 Annual Report (Garda Síochána, 1999).

- For non-indictable crimes with identifiable victims, provide the total number of reported incidents — as has been done for stolen vehicles in recent years — not just those where proceedings are taken. In many cases, the reason that proceedings are not taken has as much to do with whether the offender is apprehended as with the nature of the incident.

- Greater transparency with respect to the recording and counting of incidents. This would include information on the counting of complex incidents involving violation of several different laws; the counting of a series of related incidents, and information on how the classification and counting of incidents may be modified where the case goes to court.

- Increased clarity as to the classification of crimes. This would include details on what is counted as "aggravated" burglary and on the distinction between larcenies from the person described as "pickpocket" and those classified as "mugging".

Chapter 1

Introduction

Background

> If their limitations are fully recognised, crime-related statistics
> offer an invaluable aid to understanding and explanation. On
> the other hand, not only can they be highly misleading if used
> incorrectly, but, if presented in mechanical fashion, without
> any deeper comprehension of their relationship to the reality
> they purport to represent, they can grossly distort the social
> meaning of events as understood by those experiencing or
> witnessing them. Ultimately, indeed, one may ask whether
> "crime" (or any particular category of crime) is a phenomenon
> which can sensibly be described merely by adding up totals of
> diverse actions and incidents. (Maguire, 1994, p. 237)

Research on crime in Ireland has been hampered by a lack of data
on the extent of victimisation, its nature and its impact on the victims (Brewer et al., 1997; McCullagh, 1996; Breen and Rottman,
1985). The only regular source of information has been the Garda
Síochána Annual Reports, providing summary data by category
of recorded crime. This is the primary source of information used
to draw conclusions about changes in the rate and pattern of
crime over time (McCullagh, 1996; Rottman, 1989; Brewer et al.,
1997), and about crime rates in Ireland compared to elsewhere
(Adler, 1983; Brewer et al., 1997).

In other jurisdictions, such as Britain and the United States, regular large-scale "criminal victimisation" surveys provide a supplementary source of information which allows important insights into the nature and extent of unrecorded crime. The "classic" victimisation survey approaches a large sample of adults, asks whether they have experienced each of a set of criminal incidents in a period (usually a year), and collects details on the incidents in question (see, for example, Mirrlees-Black et al., 1998; Rand, 1999). This type of data has not been regularly available in Ireland. The fourth quarter of the 1998 Quarterly National Household Survey (QNHS) contained a module on crime victimisation, but prior to that the only large-scale survey of victimisation was one carried out in the early 1980s (Breen and Rottman, 1985). Although a number of smaller-scale surveys have provided valuable information in the intervening period (O'Connell and Whelan, 1994; Murphy and Whelan, 1995), the total number of cases has been too small to permit detailed analyses. As such, there has been no regular source of data to supplement the information contained in the annual Garda crime statistics.

Given the reliance on statistics available in the Garda Síochána Annual Reports, it is important to explore the "reality" behind them. This reality has a number of dimensions: the nature and details of the incident itself; characteristics of the victims, including whether they were also victims of other crimes; their experience of the criminal justice system, including their interaction with the Gardaí; and the impact of the crime on the victim in terms of injury, financial loss and psychological distress.

The goal of the present study is to provide such an in-depth analysis, by presenting the results of a sample survey of victims of recorded crime. The research was commissioned by the Garda Research Unit in order to examine the quality of service provided by the Garda Síochána to the victims of crime, and to provide information of use in crime prevention. The survey is rich in detail on the nature of the incident, characteristics of the victims — including businesses and other organisations — the experiences of victims in their contact with the criminal justice system, and the impact the crime has had on them. Unlike the classic victimisation studies, these data cannot provide a comprehensive picture of unrecorded crime, or the kind of data which would be needed to form the basis of a multivariate analysis of the risk of crime victimisation. Data on crime from the 1998 QNHS (Central Statistics Office, 1999a) has been crucial in filling in these gaps in our understanding of crime in Ireland, at least as it affects individuals and private households. The present study seeks to provide a detailed examination of the types of incidents that are recorded as crimes in the official Garda statistics in Ireland: both those targeted against businesses and other organisations and those targeted against individuals and private households.

This introductory chapter begins with an overview of the concept of crime, with particular reference to the circumstances in which a single index or a more complex set of measures is desirable. The second section reviews the two main sources of statistics on the overall level and pattern of crime — police statistics and crime victimisation surveys — and locates the present study in the context of the strengths and weaknesses of each approach. The figures emerging from the recently published crime victimisation module of the QNHS are compared to those from the Garda Síochána Annual Reports for the corresponding period in order to place recorded crime in context.

In the third section, details of the design and execution of the survey which forms the main source of data for this report are provided and a typology of crime is proposed, distinguishing between criminal incidents in terms of whether they involve theft of property, whether violence or threat is used, and the broad context in which they occur. In the fourth section, trends since 1982 in the recorded crime statistics for different types of crime in Ireland are explored. The argument here is that a single index of crime would obscure much of importance in recent crime trends. The final section provides an outline of the structure of the report.

The Concept of Crime

For a crime to occur, all that is needed is a law and someone to break it. However, as a characterisation of a social phenomenon that has exercised the minds of theorists, analysts and policy-makers, this definition leaves much to be desired. Crime is something we worry about, and not all laws induce the same level of concern in their breach: compare road tax violations to muggings, for instance. The crime that is the stuff of public anxiety and political discourse consists of incidents that have identifiable victims whose life, welfare or property are threatened by deliberate acts that go beyond the bounds of what is considered socially acceptable behaviour.

One feature of public discourse about crime is the tendency to treat it as a unitary concept. The term "crime" is used as if it were a single phenomenon, whose meaning is clearly understood. A single figure tends to be quoted — typically in Ireland the total number of recorded indictable crimes — as evidence that crime is increasing or decreasing. A unitary concept of crime tends to assume a single major causative factor, on the one hand, and that some important conclusions can be drawn from the overall level of crime, on the other.

Within the field of criminology, the utility of a single concept of crime depends on the general paradigm within which the theorist is operating. Few criminologists would argue that there are not important differences between burglaries, assaults, muggings and vandalism in terms of the impact on the victim or the settings in which they occur. However, depending on the paradigm, the similarities may be more important than the differences. Much work in criminology has sought to relate the overall crime rate, or, more usually, the overall property crime rate, to broad social phenomena such as the level of wealth in society (Shelley, 1981; Field,

1990; Pyle and Deadman, 1994; Deadman and Pyle, 1997; but see Alvazzi del Frate, 1998[1]), inequalities in opportunity (Box, 1987; Wolpin, 1978; Hale and Sabbagh, 1991; Hale, 1998; with roots in the "anomie" theory of Merton, 1968), variations in family structure (Toby, 1979; Nettler, 1978; Hirschi, 1969, 1983) or the rate of social change more generally (the "social disorganisation" perspective with roots in the work of Emile Durkheim, 1984). Such approaches tend to emphasise factors which increase the probability that norms will be violated (the social disorganisation perspective), or factors in the background or experience of particular sub-groups of individuals which make it more likely that they will engage in crime. From this point of view, the similarities among different types of crime are more important than the differences, and the overall crime level has some validity as an index of the extent of rule-breaking in society. These approaches have emphasised the explanation of trends over time, or differences between societies or between groups within a society in the crime rate. The focus is on crime as "rule-breaking" or "norm-violation" and this common element of the diverse activities that make up the overall crime rate is more important than their differences.

On the other hand, the "situational" perspective places more emphasis on the social setting in which crime takes place: the immediate "opportunity structure" of a situation, rather than the motivations or disposition of potential offenders. This attention to the opportunity structure of crime has arisen largely out of the concern to develop effective crime prevention strategies. Traditionally, according to Weisburd (1997), crime prevention research has assumed that efforts to understand and control crime must

---

[1] Alvazzi del Frate notes that when official statistics on recorded crime are used, property crime rates are positively correlated with level of development (as measured by GDP per capita). However, victimisation surveys have shown that property crime is more frequent in developing countries than in the rest of the world. Alvazzi del Frate attributes the different results to an association between the level of development and the reporting and recording of crime (1998, pp. 131–138).

begin with the offender, so that the emphasis is on people and their involvement in crime. Weisburd and others have called for a shift in focus in crime prevention research away from the causes of criminal behaviour to the context in which crime occurs. The concept of the opportunity structure of the crime situation is at the core of this approach, and crime prevention strategies arising from it would emphasise target hardening, or access control, rather than interventions with potential or actual offenders. This does not mean that the offender is ignored: just that he (or, more rarely, she) is moved from the centre of attention to become just one of the many aspects of the crime context. Weisburd argues that the situational approach has the advantage of avoiding the difficulties involved in predicting criminality so as to target interventions at potential offenders, and that situations are more stable and predictable as targets for intervention (Weisburd, 1997).

Two of the earliest proponents of what has been variously termed the "situational", "routine activities" or "opportunity structure" approach were Ronald Clarke and his colleagues at the Home Office in Britain and Marcus Felson and his colleagues in the United States (Clarke, 1980; Mayhew et al., 1976; Cohen and Felson, 1979; Felson and Cohen, 1980, 1981).

Clarke (1980) argued that traditional criminological theories had a "dispositional" bias, where the main object was to show how some people are born with, or come to acquire, a "disposition" to behave in a consistently criminal manner. As an alternative to this, Clarke advocated a "situational" approach, which views crime as the outcome of immediate choices and decisions made by the offender. Clarke emphasises three features of the situational approach: first, explanation is focused more directly on the criminal incident; second, the need to develop explanations for separate categories of crime is made explicit; and, third, the individual's current circumstances and the immediate features of the setting are given considerably more explanatory significance than in "dispositional" theories (Clarke, 1980). Clarke argued that the situational approach is a much richer source of hypotheses than the dispositional perspective.

Closely related to this is the "routine activities" theory (Cohen and Felson, 1979; Felson and Cohen, 1980, 1981; Felson 1998), which also stresses the context in which crime takes place, and the links between patterns of crime and the patterns of routine activity in everyday life. Felson and Cohen (1980) used time series data on crime, and demographic and family indicators to show how changes in one section of society can influence the opportunity structure of crime. The routine activity approach emphasises the spatial and temporal aspects of interactions of every day life, such as where and when people converge. The argument is that specific types of targets are found in particular situations, and the type of criminal activity that emerges in these settings is linked to both the nature of the "guardianship" of those targets and the nature of the offenders that converge within them.

Associated with the "routine activities" or "situational" approach is an emphasis on the rationality of the decisions made by offenders, within the limits of the time and information available to them. Cornish and Clarke argue that:

> . . . even in the case of offences that seemed to be pathologically motivated or impulsively executed, it was felt that rational components were also often present and that the identification and description of these might have lessons for crime control policy. (Cornish and Clarke, 1986, pp. 1–2)

An example of the application of a rational choice perspective to offences which might seem to be primarily impulsive or compulsive in nature is Trevor Bennett's work on opioid addiction. In a study of 135 opioid users in Cambridge, Bennett found that users often consciously decided to begin taking opioids before they had an opportunity to do so; that the decision to try the drug had both a meaning and a purpose; and that there was little evidence of compulsion or inevitability in the development from first use to addiction. There was also evidence of control in the variable nature of drug consumption once the user was addicted. For some users, both becoming addicted and abstaining from addiction were intentional and planned.

> Permanently ceasing opioid use often had less to do with successful withdrawal — which addicts achieved on a regular basis during their periods of voluntary abstinence — than with complementary changes in their lifestyle which made non-addiction both feasible and desirable. (Bennett, 1986, pp. 97–98)

This is not to deny the compulsive element of the addiction itself, but it does emphasise the operation of decision-making in the process.

Much recent criminology has adopted a middle-range approach, eschewing explicit attempts to link crime patterns generally to broader aspects of social structure or social change and focusing on the middle-level opportunity structure within which crime takes place. By its nature, this approach is characterised by an awareness of the specificity of different types of criminal incidents. The emphasis has tended to be on the immediate elements of the crime setting — the flow of potential victims and offenders, the type of property available and how well it is guarded — rather than the broader opportunity structure of society within which potential offenders operate. The assumption is that much crime is opportunistic in nature, so that the motivation of the offender is treated as of secondary importance. In this approach, the "norm-violation" or "rule-breaking" aspect of crime tends to receive attention only to the extent that it is associated with the risk of being caught and punished.

Police Crime Statistics and Crime Victimisation Surveys

Two types of data are generally used in discussions of the overall rate and nature of crime.[2] The first type consists of the figures produced by the police. These provide summary statistics on incidents reported to or discovered by the police and which are deemed to be criminal in nature. The second type of information comes from victimisation surveys: surveys of the general population that ask whether the respondent was a victim of each of a set of incidents in a given period, usually a year, and collect details on the nature of any criminal incidents experienced by the victims. Each type has its own strengths and weaknesses, and they should be seen as complementary sources of information rather than as competing measures of the same phenomenon (see Maguire, 1994, and O'Connell and Whelan, 1994, for a more complete discussion of the differences between the two sources of data).

Police statistics are generally based on information collected at, or close to, the time of the incident, thus avoiding some of the recall problems associated with victimisation surveys. The information is screened more carefully than can be accomplished in a survey to ensure that it actually meets the legal definition of a crime. Police statistics include crimes against businesses or other organisations and crimes against children — which are almost always excluded from victimisation surveys — and crimes with no obvious victim, such as carrying burglary tools.

On the other hand, victimisation surveys provide information on incidents which are unreported or unrecorded. Both the proportion of incidents that are not reported and the proportion of reported incidents not actually recorded can be quite high. Crime victimisation surveys universally result in estimates of the overall crime rate that are considerably higher than those derived from

---

[2] A third data source, although used less frequently, consists of self-reported delinquency studies and offender studies. These are not generally used to assess the overall level of crime, but can be an important source of insight into how offenders weigh the risks and benefits of criminal activity.

police statistics (Maltz, 1999; Mirrlees-Black et al., 1998). The 1998 British Crime Survey, for instance, arrived at a count of comparable incidents that was four times higher than the figure for police-recorded crime (Mirrlees-Black et al., 1998). Later in this chapter, we compare the results of the 1998 QNHS to the Garda figures on recorded crime for the corresponding period, to give an indication of the size of the gap between the two sets of figures in Ireland.

Apart from providing information on the "dark figure" of unrecorded crime, crime victimisation surveys provide data on the distribution of risk of crime victimisation for different groups in the population, information on the impact of the crime on the victim, the incidence of repeat victimisation, and related issues such as fear of crime.

Conversely, as with sample survey research generally, estimates derived from victim surveys are subject to a margin of error. This means that we can be confident, but not certain, that the "true" figures lie within a certain range of the numbers obtained from the sample. Moreover, and also similar to sample survey research, to the extent that not all of those selected actually respond to the survey, victim surveys may be subject to non-response bias.

Both police statistics and victimisation surveys are weak in terms of their coverage of white-collar crime. White-collar crime is rarely reported to the police (Maguire, 1994; McCullagh, 1996), and is often dealt with by other agencies such as the Revenue Commissioners or the Department of Social, Community and Family Affairs. Since much white-collar crime is targeted against businesses or other organisations (including Government organisations), it is not recorded in victimisation surveys, which are generally confined to private citizens.

Garda Síochána Annual Report

As noted above, the Garda Síochána Annual Reports are the primary source of regular crime statistics for Ireland. They have a number of strengths: the statistics are compiled centrally using consistent counting rules; the series is available as far back as 1947, and considerable detail is provided on the type of offence for indictable crimes (over 120 categories). However, the way the statistics are presented tends to reinforce the use of a single index in the form of the total number of indictable crimes, masking the diversity of the incidents involved in terms of their nature and seriousness.

A distinction is drawn between indictable and non-indictable offences, similar to the distinction in Britain between notifiable offences and summary offences. The distinction is based on the legal requirements for processing the offences. Non-indictable offences may be processed to a conclusion in the District Courts, while indictable offences may be tried by a judge and jury in the higher Courts. The bulk of the non-indictable offences involve breaches of regulations governing the use of motor vehicles: in 1998, 58 per cent were offences against the Road Traffic Acts, and a further 21 per cent were violations of Road Tax regulations. However, several types of non-indictable offence are similar in nature to — although they may be less serious than — their indictable counterparts. These include assault, "unauthorised taking" of vehicles, and "criminal damage". Non-indictable offences are reported in the Garda statistics only where proceedings are taken. This means that not all of the known offences will be included in the published total figure for non-indictable offences.

The extent of the undercount resulting from recording non-indictable incidents only where proceedings are taken can now be calculated for vehicle theft. Separate figures are provided (since 1992) for the total number of vehicles reported as stolen. In 1998, 15,293 vehicles were reported as stolen. Of these, 1,500 (10 per cent) were not recovered and were subsequently classified in the indictable statistics as larcenies. To be classified legally as a larceny, the intention must be present to permanently deprive the owner of the property. In the remaining 13,793 cases, the vehicle was recovered. However, proceedings were taken in only 2,506 of these cases, and these were recorded in the non-indictable crime statistics as "unauthorised takings". This means that, of the known cases of vehicle takings, 11,287, or 74 per cent of the total figure, are not counted in the published indictable or non-indictable crime figures.

Breakdowns of the indictable crime figures for the major cities and Garda Divisions are only provided at the level of the four major groups.

- Offences against the Person (murder, manslaughter, assault, sexual assault, rape);

- Offences against Property (including burglary, malicious injury to property, robbery);

- Larcenies (larceny from the person, larceny of motor vehicles, larceny from motor vehicles, other larcenies, fraud); and

- Other Offences (ranging from treason, to offences against the 1977 Misuse of Drugs Act,[3] to indecent exposure).

This classification system has a number of problems as a summary measure. The main one is the broad range of crimes included in the groups, particularly in the second and third groups. The second problem is that the groups do not clearly distinguish crimes involving violence or threat: a large number of these are found in the second and third groups. There were 3,703 recorded cases of armed robbery, robbery, armed aggravated burglary and other aggravated burglary in 1995, all included in Group 2 (Offences against Property). There were a further 2,520 recorded cases of "larceny from the person (muggings)", included in Group

---

[3] Most drugs offences, however, are *not* included in the indictable category. In 1997, for instance, a total of 7,927 individuals were prosecuted for drug offences, but only 276 were included in the total for indictable offences (under offences against the Misuse of Drugs Act, 1977).

3 (Larcenies, etc.). This compares with a total of 1,785 Offences against the Person recorded in Group 1.

Overall, then, the wealth of detail provided for the country as a whole, combined with the limited utility of the four-category classification provided by region, reinforces the use of a single index of crime in the form of the total number of indictable offences. This, in turn, reinforces the perception in popular and policy discourse of "crime" as a single phenomenon, masking the diversity of the incidents involved in terms of their targets, their settings and their impact on victims.

Reporting and Recording of Crime: the "Dark Figure" in Ireland

The first large-scale national crime victimisation survey in Ireland in over 15 years was conducted by the Central Statistics Office as a module of the Quarterly National Household Survey (QNHS) fielded in the fourth quarter of 1998. It collected information from 39,000 households and the adults living in them on victimisation and reporting of crime in the previous 12 months in eight categories: burglary with entry (including no-loss burglaries), theft of vehicle, theft from vehicle, theft of bicycles, vandalism, theft with violence, theft without violence, and assault (excluding domestic and sexual assault[4]). It also contained a set of questions on perceptions of crime (Central Statistics Office, 1999a). The results permit an assessment of the extent of unreported and unrecorded crime against individuals and private households in Ireland — information that is essential to the interpretation of the figures on recorded crime.

Table 1.1 compares the reporting rate for crimes in Ireland, based on the 1998 QNHS module (Central Statistics Office, 1999a), to those in England and Wales, based on the 1998 British Crime

---

[4] These types of incident were explicitly excluded in order not to put the respondent in an awkward position. Generally, questions on domestic and sexual assault require a different approach to that which is possible in a national survey such as the QNHS.

Survey (BCS) (Mirrlees-Black et al., 1998). The reference year for Ireland is late 1997 to late 1998, and for the BCS data it is 1997.

Table 1.1: Reporting Rates in 1997/98 from the Quarterly National Household Survey for the Republic of Ireland and the British Crime Survey for England and Wales

	Percentage Reported	
	A. QNHS Ireland, 1997–98	B. England and Wales, 1997
Theft of Vehicle	95	97
Theft from Vehicle	59	43
Burglary with entry	79	79
Vandalism	40	26
Bicycle Theft	58	64
Theft without violence (QNHS)	49	
Stealth Theft from Person		33
Other theft of personal property		33
Other household theft		33
Theft with violence (QNHS)	62	
Snatch Theft from person		50
Robbery		57
Assault (excluding domestic, sexual)	63	
Common assault		31
Wounding		45

Source: A: 1998 Quarterly National Household Survey (Central Statistics Office, 1999a); B: British Crime Survey, 1998 (Mirrlees-Black et al., 1998, Table A4.1).

The top rows of Table 1.1 show the reporting rates for crimes where the definition is comparable in the two surveys. Reporting rates are identical for burglary, slightly lower in Ireland for vehicle theft, six percentage points lower for bicycle theft, and considerably higher for theft from a vehicle and vandalism. The remaining three panels show the reporting rates for crimes where the definition differs somewhat between the two surveys, mainly because the categories used in the BCS are more detailed. It is clear, however, that reporting rates in Ireland are a good deal higher for theft without violence, theft with violence, and assault. The QNHS questions on assault specifically exclude domestic assault. Even if domestic assaults were excluded from the British figures, the reporting rate for assault would be higher in Ireland: reporting rates in England and Wales were 26 per cent for domestic assault, 45 per cent for assaults perpetrated by a stranger and 34 per cent for assaults perpetrated by an acquaintance (Mirrlees-Black et al., 1998).

Compared to the figures from Breen and Rottman (1985), which referred to incidents taking place in 1981/82, the 1998 figures for Ireland show a fall in the reporting rate for burglary (from 88 to 79 per cent), theft from vehicle (from 64 to 59 per cent) and vandalism (from 46 to 40 per cent), and a slight increase in the reporting rate for vehicle theft (from 92 to 95 per cent). There was also a fall in the reporting rate for theft from the person, but the magnitude of the fall is less clear since some incidents of theft from the person (64 per cent of which were reported) in Breen and Rottman's classification may have involved violence or threat (Breen and Rottman, 1985, Table 3.3).

The reporting rates found in the QNHS crime module are lower than those found in a number of recent smaller-scale surveys. Murphy and Whelan (1995) found an overall crime reporting rate of 91 per cent in the 1994 survey of public attitudes to the Gardaí, with a reporting rate of 98 per cent for burglaries. They asked respondents if they or any member of their household had been a victim of a crime within the previous three years and if they had reported it. This screening question probably resulted in the exclusion of minor incidents, which the respondents may be less likely to think of as "crimes", and which would also be less likely to be reported. In a survey of crime in Dublin by O'Connell and Whelan (1994), the overall reporting rate was 81 per cent. Since the proportions who had been victims of crime were small in these studies, the rates of reporting need to be treated with caution.

The overall pattern of reporting across type of incidents is similar to that found for 11 industrialised countries[5] in the 1996 International Crime Victim Survey (ICVS). The ICVS is conducted using a harmonised questionnaire, and employing telephone interviewing with samples of 1,000–2,000 households selected using some variant of random-digit dialling. Care is needed in comparing results from the ICVS to those from larger-scale surveys conducted using personal interviewing. The reporting rates found in the ICVS for England and Wales, for instance, tend to be considerably higher than those found in the 1996 and 1998 British Crime Survey for burglary, theft from a vehicle and bicycle theft, and somewhat lower for theft of a vehicle. Across all countries, 94 per cent of vehicle thefts were reported, as were 86 per cent of burglaries with entry (Mayhew and van Dijk, 1997, Appendix Table 9). About two-thirds of thefts from cars were reported. The reporting rates for assault and threat (38 per cent) and robbery (56 per cent) tended to be lower internationally than the QNHS figures for Ireland (Mayhew and van Dijk, 1997).

Recorded Crime

A second aspect of the "dark figure" of crime is the gap between the number of crimes reported to the police and the figures presented in the police statistics. This is often referred to as the gap between *reported* and *recorded* crime. However, it really has two components: the *definition* of the incident as a crime and the *counting* of incidents. The first component relates to whether the incident is accepted by the police as constituting a crime and the

---

[5] Austria, Canada, England and Wales, Finland, France, the Netherlands, Northern Ireland, Scotland, Sweden, Switzerland and the United States.

second concerns whether each reported crime is recorded as a separate incident in the police statistics.

There are a number of reasons why a crime may not be recorded initially: an incident may be deemed by the police not to be criminal in nature, to constitute a false or mistaken report, not serious enough to warrant the attention of the criminal justice system, fail to meet the requirements for reasonable evidence, or it may be recorded in a different category. Some incidents may not be recorded because of the victim's wish not to proceed with a complaint.

An incident which is accepted by the police as constituting a crime may still not be reflected in the published statistics. One of the main reasons for this in Ireland is that counts of non-indictable crimes, which include many cases of assault, vandalism and "unauthorised takings" of vehicles or bicycles, have not routinely been published in the Garda statistics unless proceedings are taken in the case — usually when the offender is apprehended.[6] Other differences may arise because of conventions adopted in the counting of incidents. For instance, a series of related incidents against the same victim attributable to a given offender — such as is often the case in domestic assault or sexual offences — may be counted by the police as a single incident.

Comparing Garda statistics on recorded crime with the results of victim surveys, such as the module contained in the QNHS, is not a straightforward exercise, then. The following summarises the main issues involved:

- It is difficult in the Irish published statistics to distinguish crimes targeted against individuals and private households, on the one hand, from those targeted against businesses or other organisations. The latter would not be covered in sur-

---

[6] Counts of the total number of vehicle thefts are now provided in the Garda Annual report, but in a separate table from the overall figures on non-indictable incidents.

veys of private households and individuals such as the QNHS crime module.

- Some crimes where the target is an organisation may be captured in surveys of individuals. For instance, the person (or several persons) present during an aggravated burglary of a shop may report being assaulted or threatened.[7] A shop owner living over the shop may report a burglary of the shop in a victim survey.

- Some crimes which occurred outside the target period may be captured in victim surveys, particularly if a victim remembers an incident as having occurred more recently than it actually did. This "telescoping" of incidents may be particularly likely with incidents that the victim regarded as more serious. The QNHS crime module endeavoured to avoid this kind of telescoping by asking the victim in which month the incident took place. Incidents taking place more than twelve months earlier were excluded.

- Victims may say that an incident was reported when it was not. There is little evidence on this issue, but some victims may be reluctant to admit in a survey context that they did not report a crime.

- Conversely, victims may "forget" having reported certain incidents, or even that it occurred. This is more likely to happen if the victim considered the incident to be less serious.

- The crime may be classified differently in the Garda records and in the victim survey. Differences in the meaning of crime categories were apparent in the results from the present survey, particularly with respect to whether the incident involved assault or threat. As we will see in Chapter 2, it emerged that

---

[7] The QNHS results indicate that 24 per cent of assaults captured in that survey took place when the person was at or near work or school/college (Central Statistics Office, 1999a, Table 11a).

30 per cent of those identified in the Garda records as victims of domestic aggravated burglary and aggravated theft from the person felt that the incident involved no assault or threat. On the other hand, 18 per cent of victims of theft from the person, and 22 per cent of institutional victims of other theft claimed that they were assaulted or threatened during the incident.

- Non-indictable crimes do not routinely appear in the Garda statistics unless proceedings are taken — typically when an offender is apprehended. This could result in different counts for assault, vandalism and bicycle theft. Figures on the total number of non-indictable vehicle takings (including cases where no proceedings are taken) are now provided in the Garda Síochána Annual Reports.

- Garda counting procedures may treat as one incident a series of incidents by the same offender against the same victim.[8] This is likely to primarily affect crimes which are, by their nature, "serial" — such as much domestic assault, sexual assault or fraud.

- The counting of complex incidents, such as a burglary where property is damaged and a car is stolen, may also differ. A complex incident is counted in the Garda statistics as one crime, and is classified according to its most serious aspect. While victim surveys endeavour to ensure that this would be treated as one incident, this may not always be the case, particularly in surveys where several household members are interviewed.

- The Garda figures include crimes against children, whereas the QNHS crime module covered only crimes against house-

---

[8] On the other hand, a series of crimes perpetrated by the same offender(s) against a number of different victims — such as theft from several vehicles parked at the same location — would be treated as separate incidents.

holds (such as burglary or vandalism) and against individual adults age 18 and over.

A further difficulty in comparing the 1998 QNHS figures with the Garda statistics is that the reference period is not identical. The QNHS gathered information on incidents taking place in the twelve months prior to the interview in the fourth quarter of 1998. As such, they refer to crimes which might have happened between late 1997 and late 1998, depending on the timing of the interview. The Garda statistics refer to crimes reported in the calendar year 1998. Since reporting would rarely be delayed, the figures refer, for the most part, to incidents taking place in 1998. If the crime rates were identical in the two periods this would not be a problem. However, between 1997 and 1998, there was a fall of about 9 per cent in the number of recorded incidents in categories covered by the QNHS survey. In order to make the comparison, then, the Garda figures on recorded crime should be "adjusted" by an amount which reflects the fact that some of the incidents would have taken place in the "higher crime year" of 1997.

An attempt has been made to "reconcile" the figures from the 1998 Quarterly National Household Survey with the published Garda Statistics on Crime, in order to get a picture of the extent of "unreported" and "unrecorded" crime in Ireland. It was not possible to include assault in the reconciliation. Assault in the Quarterly National Household Survey specifically excluded domestic assault. These cases would have been included in the recorded figures if the assault constituted an indictable crime, or if it was a non-indictable incident where proceedings were taken.[9]

In addition, caution is advisable in interpreting the results for non-violent theft. The question wording in the QNHS was: "In the

---

[9] Although the Garda Síochána Annual Reports do provide the total number of domestic violence incidents in a separate table, some of these would be non-indictable assaults where no proceedings were taken, and would not appear in the figures for indictable and non-indictable assaults.

last 12 months, have you been a victim of theft not involving force?" This wording may have led to the inclusion of incidents other than theft from the person, such as theft from the garden or of property from a locker, which would appear elsewhere in the Garda statistics as larcenies. The results of the reconciliation are shown in Table 1.2.

Table 1.2: Comparing Garda Statistics and Victim Survey Counts of Crimes in Ireland and England and Wales

	A	B	C	D	E	F	G
	QNHS Incidents	% Reported	N Reported	Est. N Recorded, Individual Target	% Recorded	Ratio A/D	1998 BCS Ratio (England & Wales)
Theft of Vehicle	16,500	94.9%	15,659	14,427	92%	1.14	1.19
Theft from Vehicle	47,200	58.9%	27,801	11,080	40%	4.26	3.92
Burglary (incl. aggravated)	52,900	78.6%	41,579	16,363	39%	3.23	3.16
Vandalism	99,000	39.6%	39,204	6,369	16%	15.54	6.58
Theft without violence	30,000	48.5%	14,550	3,315	23%	9.05	9.83*
Theft with violence	17,700	61.5%	10,886	3,847	35%	4.60	5.90**
Theft of bicycle	16,600	57.7%	9,578	339	4%	49.00	3.64
Total	279,900	56.9%	159,256	55,740	35%	5.02	4.08

Notes: * Includes snatch and stealth theft from the person. ** Robbery.
Sources: 1998 Quarterly National Household Survey (Central Statistics Office, 1999a); Garda Síochána Annual Reports, 1997 and 1998. British Crime Survey, 1998 (Mirrlees-Black et al., 1998, Table 4.1).

Column A shows the total number of incidents in the year from late 1997 to late 1998, derived from the QNHS estimates of the number of incidents in the target period. In the case of bicycle theft, households were asked only whether someone had a bicycle stolen, and not the number of times this happened. The figures in Table 1.2 for bicycle theft, therefore, show the number of victims:

this is the lower bound of the number of incidents, since more than one bicycle may have been stolen in the reference year.

The second column shows the percentage reported in each category, again using the QNHS figures. In cases where the victim experienced more than one crime of a given type, this percentage refers to the most recent incident. Column C shows the estimated total number of incidents reported, by multiplying column A by column B. Note that for victims experiencing more than one incident of a given type, this involves assuming that all incidents had the same reporting rate as the most recent one.

Column D shows the estimated total number of recorded incidents in the same one-year period, where the target was an individual or private household.[10] First, in order to adjust for the fact that the QNHS recording period spanned the last quarter of 1997 and the first three quarters of 1998, the one-year figure was estimated by adding three-quarters of the 1998 figure to one-quarter of the 1997 figure within each category. Since, as noted above, the number of recorded incidents in 1997 was higher than in 1998, this resulted in a figure for recorded crime that is somewhat higher than the 1998 figure. Next, figures from the present survey (Table 2.1, in Chapter 2 of this book) were used to estimate the number of recorded incidents in each category that affected domestic or individual targets (rather than businesses or other organisations). In the case of burglary (which includes aggravated burglary in the QNHS figures), the actual number of burglaries directed against dwellings is provided in the 1998 Garda Síochána Annual Report. The estimated number of aggravated burglaries directed against private individuals or households was added to this figure. In the absence of this information on bicycle thefts, it was assumed that all cases appearing in the Garda statistics involved individual victims.

---

[10] Table A.4 in Appendix A shows details of the estimation of the number of recorded incidents in the reference period.

The estimates of the proportion of incidents with individuals or private households as the target can only be approximate since they are subject to sampling error. Moreover, the balance between individual and institutional targets may have shifted between the target year of the *1996 Survey of Victims of Recorded Crime* (late 1994 to late 1995) and the target period of the QNHS crime module.

Note also that the Garda figures do not routinely include non-indictable incidents unless proceedings are taken. The total figure is available for vehicle theft, so that the figures in Column D represent all indictable and non-indictable incidents (even where no proceedings were taken). The figures for vandalism and bicycle theft include indictable crimes in the corresponding categories and only those non-indictable crimes where proceedings were taken. Figures are not published for reported cases of *non-indictable* vandalism or bicycle theft unless proceedings were taken.

Column E shows the estimated percentage of *reported* incidents that are *recorded* in the published Garda statistics — Column D expressed as a percentage of Column C. Apart from theft of vehicle, the number of incidents appearing in the Garda published statistics is considerably lower than the estimated number reported by individuals and private households in 1998. The published figures on vehicle theft are 92 per cent of the estimated number of reported incidents. For theft from a vehicle (40 per cent) and burglary (39 per cent) the published figures give a count that is less than half of the estimated number of reported incidents, while the published figures for theft with violence are 35 per cent of the victim survey count. Garda counts of non-violent theft (including only theft from the person) are 23 per cent of the victim survey estimate of the number of reported incidents. As noted above, it is possible that some non-violent thefts may be recorded in the Garda statistics as "other larceny" — a category which does not appear in the table. The very low percentages for vandalism (16 per cent) and theft of bicycles (4 per cent) is largely driven by the fact that figures for non-indictable incidents in these categories are only published where proceedings are taken.

Overall, then, taking account of non-reporting and of non-recording or counting differences, the victim survey count of incidents is about 5 times that in the recorded crime statistics across these seven categories (Column F in Table 1.2). The counts for vehicle theft are very similar, when the total count of all non-indictable vehicle thefts is taken into account. The victim survey count is three times the recorded figure for burglary, roughly four times for theft from a vehicle, nearly five times for theft with violence, nine times for theft without violence, 16 times for vandalism, and 49 times for bicycle theft. The biggest differences occur for those crime categories where the corresponding non-indictable crimes may not appear in the statistics if no proceedings are taken (vandalism and bicycle theft), or where it is possible that a different classification was used in the Garda statistics (theft without violence).

As noted earlier, these differences in counts of crime between police statistics and victim surveys are also found in other jurisdictions. The 1998 British Crime Survey, for instance, arrived at a count that was four times higher than the police statistics for notifiable offences in the categories where such a comparison was possible.[11] Column G in Table 1.2 shows the ratio of the 1998 British Crime Survey counts to the police counts for similar crimes for England and Wales (Mirrlees-Black et al., 1998, Table 4.1), for the reference year 1997.

Apart from vandalism and bicycle theft, the gap between the victim survey count and the police count is fairly close in the two jurisdictions. The gap between the two counts is slightly smaller

---

[11] These categories were vandalism, burglary, theft of vehicle, attempted vehicle theft, theft from vehicle, bicycle theft, theft from the person (snatch and stealth), wounding and robbery, excluding crimes targeted against businesses or other organisations.

in Ireland for vehicle theft, theft without violence and theft with violence, and is somewhat larger for burglary and theft from a vehicle. On the other hand, the gap between the numbers recorded in police statistics and the victim survey count is much greater in Ireland for vandalism and bicycle theft. Overall, apart from vandalism and bicycle theft, while the Garda figures for crime against individual and domestic targets would result in a considerably lower count than that from a victim survey, the gap between the two is broadly comparable to that in England and Wales. If bicycle theft and vandalism are excluded, the ratio of victim survey to police counts is almost identical in the two jurisdictions: 3.35 in Ireland compared to 3.39 in England and Wales. Given the generally higher reporting rates in Ireland (as seen in Table 1.1), this suggests that differences in recording and counting procedures work to depress the recorded crime figures in Ireland relative to England and Wales.

This does not mean that the police and Garda figures are "wrong" or that victim survey counts represent the "true" extent of crime. As Breen and Rottman (1985) note, victim surveys provide an alternative way of measuring the amount of crime, rather than a basis for improving police crime statistics. In particular, the crimes measured by victim surveys

> . . . are not screened by impartial observers as to whether they meet the criteria of criminal law. The victim is the policeman, judge and jury. Thus victimisation surveys are different rather than "better" measures of the amount of crime. (Breen and Rottman, 1985, p. 8)

The main strength of victimisation surveys is that they provide a count which is independent of victim reporting patterns or police recording procedures. Since methodologies can be standardised — or their differences clearly specified — across jurisdictions, they provide a means for comparing crime levels across different police jurisdictions. They can also prove crucial in the interpretation of police crime statistics, by revealing the impact of changes in reporting rates on police counts of crime.

The Current Research Design

This report analyses the results of the *Survey of Victims of Recorded Crime* carried out in 1996 by the Economic and Social Research Institute for the Garda Research Unit (GRU). The survey collected data on the experience of crime victimisation from a sample of those identified in the Garda records as having reported a crime in the year from November 1994 to October 1995. This means that the sample consists of those who (a) were victims of crime, (b) reported the incident to the Gardaí, and (c) had the incident recorded as a crime in the Garda records. The survey, which collected detailed information on the incident itself and on characteristics of the victims, provides a rich source of information on the nature of the events represented by the Garda crime statistics.

Since they are based on a survey with the sample drawn from the recorded crime figures, data used in this report share some of the strengths of official police statistics and of victimisation surveys, as well as some of the weaknesses of each.

The main strengths of the research design are:

1. The coverage of crimes against businesses or other organisations as well as those against individuals and private households;

2. The use of a stratified sample so that sufficient cases were included in the "rarer" crime categories to permit detailed analyses;

3. The collection of detailed information on the circumstances of the incident and the characteristics of victims;

4. Since information is available on the official classification of the incident in the Garda records and on the victim's understanding of the experience, it provides a unique opportunity

to explore the nature of some of the differences between police statistics and victim surveys in terms of how an incident is interpreted and classified.

The issue of crime directed against businesses and other organisations is one that has been — at least until recently — relatively neglected in the literature on criminal victimisation (Bowers, Hirschfield, and Johnson, 1998; Felson and Clarke, 1997). Felson and Clarke argue:

> Some people may be tempted to dismiss business and crime as a topic only relevant to business itself. This approach has two fallacies: (1) ignoring how business losses affect the larger community and society; (2) missing the extent to which business organises community life and, hence, sets the stage for a good deal of crime for which business is not itself the direct target. (1997, p. 2)

The detailed information provided in Chapter 2 on the location and timing of crime against business targets contains some important insights relevant to crime prevention.

In classic victimisation studies, the sampling frame is the national population and crime victims are identified by means of a screening question early in the interview. Since the risk of crime victimisation in a given year is relatively low, this means that a very large initial sample needs to be drawn, so that enough crime victims are identified to permit analysis by category of crime. For instance, the 1998 British Crime Survey involved interviews with nearly 15,000 individuals in England and Wales, while the US National Crime Victimisation Survey involves interviews with about 100,000 individuals in 50,000 households. Unless the initial sample is very large, it is likely that there will be very few identified cases of the more serious crimes — those involving violence — since these are not as frequent as non-violent theft and burglaries. The sampling frame in the present study — Garda records of recorded crimes — allowed us to stratify the sample so as to select a sufficiently large number of cases in the violent crime categories to permit some basic breakdowns. In particular, it allowed us to separate assault, aggravated burglary and aggravated theft from the person — the categories involving violence or threat — which, as we will see in Chapters 2 and 3, are very different in terms of the location, timing and other details of the incident, as well as in the characteristics of the victims.

The present research design differs from the classic crime victimisation surveys, where the goal is to estimate the prevalence of crime victimisation in the population, in that it collects no information from non-victims. Unlike the classic victimisation survey design, then, the present study lacks a built-in control group of non-victims. The section of the report dealing with characteristics of crime victims makes use of national data from other sources in order to compare victim characteristics to those of the general population. This has only been possible for victims who are individuals or private households, however.

The quality of Garda service to crime victims was the over-riding concern of the Garda Síochána Research Unit in commissioning the survey on which this report is based. The present design allows for a detailed analysis of victim satisfaction with Garda service, and of victim awareness of, and satisfaction with, the outcome of the case.

Typology of Crimes

Crimes were divided into ten categories for the purpose of sample selection and analysis. The crime categories were chosen so as to be as inclusive as possible, within the limits of what can be accomplished using survey methodology, and to distinguish between incidents along a number of dimensions:

- Whether the crime involved the theft of property;

- Whether the incident involved the use or threat of violence to the victim; and

- Within property crime, the broad context within which the incident occurred.

The third dimension results in a distinction between burglaries, vehicle theft, theft from a vehicle, theft from the person, fraud, and the residual category "other theft". This distinction was prompted by two considerations. First, the factors affecting the "opportunity structure" of these types of incident is likely to be very different. For instance, vehicle crime is likely to be related to the number of vehicles per head of the population, and the prevalence of anti-theft devices installed on them. The timing and distribution of domestic burglaries are likely to be affected by the reduced level of guardianship of residences as more women enter the labour force. The second consideration is that the psychological impact of a non-violent theft on the victim is likely to be greater where the theft involves either contact with the offender (theft from the person) or intrusion into the victim's home or workplace (Skogan, 1994).

The categories resulting from this typology are shown in Figure 1.1.

Figure 1.1: Typology of Crimes by whether Property was Stolen and whether the Victim suffered Violence or Threat

	Property Stolen	**No Property stolen**
Violence/Threat	Aggravated Burglary Aggravated Theft from the Person	Assault
No Violence/ Threat	Theft of Vehicle Theft from Vehicle Burglary Theft from the Person Fraud Other Theft	Vandalism

Aggravated burglary and aggravated theft from the person involve both the theft of property and the use of force or the threat of force. Assault involves the use of force without any theft taking place. Burglary, vehicle theft, theft from a vehicle, theft from the person, fraud, and "other theft" involve theft but no assault or threat. Finally, vandalism includes crimes where property is deliberately damaged, but not stolen, and where there is no assault or threat to the victim.

Details of the crimes included in each of the ten categories are provided below. Crimes in these categories accounted for 97 per cent of all indictable crime in Ireland in 1995. Certain types of serious crime were specifically excluded, such as those resulting in the death of the primary victim (murder, manslaughter, dangerous driving causing death or serious injury); crimes of a particularly sensitive nature (kidnapping, false imprisonment, and sexual crimes), which would have required a more in-depth approach than could be accomplished in a broadly based survey; crimes where, by definition, the victim was under age 18 (such as child neglect and cruelty); and crimes with no easily identifiable victim (possession of firearms with intent to endanger life, possession of articles with intent, handling stolen goods, offences against the Coinage Act and Debtors Act). Crimes against Gardaí in the course of their duties were not included since they fell outside the central focus of the research sponsors on the public's experience of crime and Garda service to victims.

While some of the more serious crimes, such as murder and indictable sexual offences, were excluded from the present study, the overall impact on the results would be small since they are few in number. The largest categories of excluded crimes with identifiable victims, numerically speaking, were assaults on a Garda on duty (56 indictable and 848 non-indictable incidents), and indictable sexual offences (191 rapes and 604 sexual assaults). There were 43 murders and 10 manslaughter incidents in 1995, and 10 traffic-related manslaughter or dangerous driving incidents resulting in death. All of these would have amounted to no more than 1.5 per cent of the crimes covered by all the categories included in the survey, and fewer than one in eight of the violent crimes covered in the survey (assault, aggravated burglary and aggravated theft from the person).

The bulk of crimes in the non-indictable category do not have an identifiable individual victim, which would place them beyond the scope of a survey of victims: four out of five involve violations of Road Traffic or Road Tax regulations. Non-indictable crimes in the categories of vehicle theft, assault and vandalism were included because, at least from the perspective of the victim, they are similar in nature, although less serious, than their indictable counterparts. Non-indictable offences are reported in the Garda statistics, only where they have been detected and where proceedings have been initiated. In the case of non-indictable assault and criminal damage, the sample was selected from those cases where proceedings were taken. As noted earlier, separate records are kept on stolen vehicles — including non-indictable "unauthorised takings" which were reported but where no proceedings were taken — so that it was possible to select the sample from all of those reporting a vehicle theft.

Crimes Included in Each Category

- *Theft of Vehicle* includes any theft of a motor-powered vehicle, most often cars, but also motorcycles, vans, and lorries. This category includes indictable vehicle thefts (where the intent is to permanently deprive the owner of the vehicle) and the non-indictable "unauthorised taking" of a vehicle, where there is no intention to permanently deprive the owner of the vehicle. A vehicle theft is normally classified as an "unauthorised taking" where the vehicle is found or returned within two months. Most (86 per cent) recorded incidents of vehicle theft in 1995 were in the non-indictable category.

- *Theft from Vehicle* includes any crime where property is stolen from an unattended vehicle. These may be vehicle accessories such as a car radio, personal property (such as a wallet or purse, tools, clothing and so on), or retail or manufacturing stock.

- *Fraud* includes a broad range of crimes where an individual or organisation is deprived of money or property by deception. It includes forging of cheques or banknotes, the use of stolen cheques and credit cards, or, more rarely, crimes such as embezzlement or blackmail. Although fraud is usually thought of as a "white-collar" crime, the bulk of the recorded incidents of fraud, as we will see in Chapter 2, show evidence of closer links to street crime than to "crime committed by a person of respectability in the course of his occupation" (Sutherland, 1949: 9). Much white-collar crime of the latter type goes undetected or unreported. It is worth noting that the figures do not include the numerous cases of tax and social welfare fraud known to agencies such as the Revenue Commissioners and the Department of Social, Community and Family Affairs, which deal with the vast majority of cases by using their administrative powers to impose financial penalties.

- *Assault* includes indictable "felony wounding" and "misdemeanour wounding", as well as the non-indictable "common assault".[12] Over 90 per cent of assaults in 1995 were in the non-indictable "common assault" category. The present sample does not include cases of assault against members of the Garda Síochána while on active duty, which fell outside the

---

[12] The distinction between felony and misdemeanour assaults was abolished by the Criminal Law Act, 1997 (s. 3). The non-indictable offence of "common assault" was abolished by the Non-Fatal Offences Against the Person Act, 1997, which introduced the offences of "assault", "assault causing harm" and "assault causing serious harm".

central concern of the research sponsors with Garda service to victims who were members of the general public.

- *Burglary* is the largest of our ten categories, accounting for over one-quarter of all crimes in the target sample. It involves theft from a building (a private house, garage or shed, or business or other premises) on the part of someone who does not have a right to be there.

- *Aggravated burglary* is a much smaller category in terms of the number of incidents in 1995. It differs from burglary in that violence or the threat of violence is used, and includes indictable crimes classified in the Garda statistics as "aggravated burglary" and "armed aggravated robbery".

- *Theft from the person* includes crimes classified in the Garda statistics as "larceny from person (pickpocket)". The individual might not be aware until later that property was stolen.

- *Aggravated theft from the person* includes indictable crimes in the categories "larceny from person (muggings)", "aggravated robbery (not in building)" and robbery without a weapon.

- *Other theft* is a very broad category that includes any theft other than burglary, theft of, or from, a vehicle, and theft from the person. About one-third of the cases involve "larceny from shops or stalls" (shoplifting).

- Finally, *vandalism* involves damage to property where nothing is stolen. Any property damage during the course of another, more serious, crime, such as burglary, would not be coded as vandalism. It includes crimes classified in the Garda statistics as "arson", "malicious damage to schools" (of which there were 861 incidents in 1995), and "other malicious injury to property", as well as non-indictable "criminal damage". Unlike the other categories that include non-indictable crimes, most (nearly 80 per cent) recorded incidents of vandalism fall into the indictable categories. This is largely a function of the small proportion of non-indictable incidents of vandalism where proceedings are taken, because of the difficulty in identifying an offender. As noted above, non-indictable incidents routinely appear in the Garda statistics only where proceedings are taken.

Sample Selection and Survey Methods

The initial sample for the 1996 *Survey of Victims of Recorded Crime* was selected by members of the Garda Research Unit, in consultation with the Survey Unit at the Economic and Social Research Institute, from Garda records of those who reported a crime in the reference period (November 1994 to October 1995). Most indictable crimes were included, as well as the associated non-indictable crimes in a number of categories — vehicle theft, assault, and vandalism. Crimes where the victim was a business or other institution were included as well as those where the victim was an individual or private household.

The sampling frame for the indictable crimes came from the central Garda records. The sampling frame for vehicle theft was the computer-based record of indictable thefts and unauthorised takings. No central records are kept of total reported non-indictable offences in the other two categories (assault and vandalism), however. The Garda Research Unit obtained lists of victims from the Garda Divisions and the sample was selected from these lists.

A disproportionate stratified random sample was employed. The sample was stratified by crime category, with disproportionate sampling to ensure an adequate number of cases to permit analysis of crimes of different types, particularly crimes involving violence, which tend to comprise a relatively small proportion of all reported crime.

In order to ensure the confidentiality of those reporting crime and to protect public confidence in reporting to the Gardaí, the

Garda Research Unit contacted all of those selected in the initial sample by letter, providing them with information on the proposed survey. Those who did not wish to participate in the survey, as well as those for whom An Post returned the initial letter as undeliverable,[13] were deleted from the sample at this stage. Details on the numbers excluded are shown in Table 1.3.

Letters were sent by the Garda Research Unit to an initial sample of over 2,500 victims. As shown in Table 1.3, 468 (19 per cent) were excluded from the sample at this stage: 258 (10 per cent) refused to participate; 191 (8 per cent) could not be contacted, either because they had moved away or because the name and address information was incorrect or incomplete. Smaller numbers were excluded because the person said they had not been a victim of a crime, had died, or had already been selected into the sample.[14] Cases where the person claimed not to have been a victim of crime mainly occurred in the category "vehicle theft". This can happen if the wrong person (perhaps a previous owner or someone with a similar vehicle registration number) is identified in the Garda records as the owner of a stolen vehicle. The percentage who declined to participate at this stage is shown in the final row of the table. Overall, 10 per cent of respondents refused, with figures ranging from 5 per cent for victims of vehicle theft to 15 per cent for victims of assault. No further information is available on the reasons for refusal.

---

[13] This might be because of an incorrect address, because the person had died or because they had moved and left no forwarding address. The distinction between cases identified as having "gone away" and those "not known at the address" is somewhat imprecise, as it depends on the information given to An Post when the letter was returned. In some cases — particularly where accommodation is rented — the current tenant may not know who the previous tenant of the accommodation was.

[14] This arose in two cases — both institutions — that reported a large number of criminal incidents in the target period.

Table 1.3: Cases Excluded Following Attempt to Contact Victims by Letter (number of cases)

	Crime Type (from Garda Records)										
	Theft of Veh-icle	*Theft from Veh-icle*	*Fraud etc.*	*Ass-ault*	*Burg-lary*	*Agg. Burg-lary*	*Theft from Person*	*Agg. Theft from Person*	*Other Theft*	*Van-dal-ism*	*Total*
Refusal	18	10	22	34	17	22	21	50	37	27	258
Not known at address	1	7	6	2	4	3	38	2	1	11	75
Gone away	15	5	8	12	10	10	12	25	9	10	116
Not a victim	11	1	0	0	0	0	0	1	1	2	16
Deceased	0	0	0	0	0	0	1	0	0	0	1
Already selected	0	0	1	0	1	0	0	0	0	0	2
Total excluded	45	23	37	48	32	35	72	78	48	50	468
Not Excluded	290	139	148	186	193	159	171	313	273	194	2,066
Total	335	162	185	234	225	194	243	391	321	244	2,534
Per cent Refusals	5%	6%	12%	15%	8%	11%	9%	13%	12%	11%	10%

To ensure that an adequate number of cases were available for analysis in each crime category, more names and addresses were selected from the Garda records than would be required in the survey phase. We anticipated that a certain proportion of the addresses would no longer be valid or that some respondents would decline to participate prior to being approached by an interviewer. The Garda Research Unit provided the ESRI with the names and addresses of the 2,066 victims who had not been excluded at the initial stage. From these, the survey sample was selected and the remaining cases from the initial sample were held in reserve (the "reserve" sample) for use if the response rate was lower than anticipated. It was not intended, therefore, that all of the 2,534 crime victims who were contacted by letter would be included in the survey sample.

Completion and Response Rates

The survey fieldwork and initial data preparation (coding, data entry, computation of sample weights) were conducted by the Economic and Social Research Institute. The questionnaire was piloted in June 1996, and the main survey went into the field in July 1996 following minor revisions to the questionnaire.

In order to achieve the target of 1,000 cases, we initially selected a sample of 1,340 cases from the Garda records provided to the ESRI from the Garda Research Unit. We anticipated that a response rate of 75 per cent from this sample would provide us with the required number of cases in each category. This response rate is typical of that achieved by other surveys of the general population conducted at the ESRI and allows for a certain amount of non-response due to non-contact (failure to contact the respondent despite repeated call-backs), refusals, or persons moving to a different location.

At the early stages of the fieldwork, however, it became evident that the response rate was lower than anticipated, notably in the theft of vehicle category. A relatively large number of addresses could not be located (or the named individual was unknown at that address), in part owing to the length of time that had elapsed between the reporting of the crime and the attempted interview. There were also a number of cases where respondents denied having reported a crime in the target period. In addition, a significant number of the victims who were contacted (7 per cent in all) claimed to have reported a crime that was different in nature from the crime category in the Garda records (Table 1.6). Again, this was a particular problem with the "theft of vehicle" category. In September and October 1996, additional quotas were assigned to the interviewers from the reserve sample to make up the shortfall in certain crime categories (principally theft of vehicle, fraud, other theft, and assault), bringing the total survey sample size up to 1,560 cases.

Table 1.4: Target and Completed Sample Size by Crime Category

Crime category	Target number of cases	Number completed this crime category	Per cent of target
Theft of Vehicle	100	83	83%
Theft from Vehicle	83	95	114%
Fraud	83	79	95%
Assault	100	96	96%
Burglary	100	126	126%
Aggravated Burglary	83	87	105%
Theft from Person	100	85	85%
Aggravated Theft from Person	100	98	98%
Other Theft	150	125	83%
Vandalism	100	85	85%
Total	1,000	959	96%

The target completed sample (Table 1.4) was 1,000 cases, with numbers in each crime category ranging from 83 to 150. The completed sample size was 959 cases. The completed sample was at least 80 per cent of the target in all crime categories. The completed sample size exceeded the target sample size for theft from vehicle, burglaries and aggravated burglaries.

Table 1.5 shows the survey response rate by crime category at the fieldwork stage. The survey response rate was 61 per cent, ranging from a low of 42 per cent for theft of vehicle to a high of 74 per cent for aggravated burglary. The main reasons for non-response were persons moving with no forwarding address available (8 per cent), non-contact (8 per cent), a failure to locate the address or a house demolished or vacant (6 per cent), refusals (6 per cent), and the respondent claiming not to have reported a crime in the relevant period (5 per cent). The refusal rate (6 per cent) was higher than expected, given that the Garda Research

Unit had already contacted the crime victims. However, the refusals appeared not to be due to the trauma associated with the incident: the interviewers were asked to note whether a refusal was
related to the trauma associated with the incident, and only 5 of
the 91 refusals appeared to be of this nature.

Table 1.5: Survey Outcome by Crime Type (column percentages)

	Crime Type (from Garda Records)										
	Theft of Veh-icle	Theft from Veh-icle	Fraud etc.	Ass-ault	Burg-lary	Agg. Burg-lary	Theft from Person	Agg. Theft from Person	Other Theft	Van-dal-ism	Total
Completed	42	69	67	56	71	74	60	69	59	63	61
Completed by Proxy	0	0	0	1	1	0	0	0	0	1	0
Deceased	0	0	1	1	0	0	1	0	0	0	0
Moved away	8	9	2	9	10	6	9	8	6	7	8
Temp. absent	1	1	2	2	2	1	3	1	1	3	2
Could not locate / not known	7	8	3	3	2	4	7	11	8	5	6
Refusal	4	4	7	13	4	7	5	4	6	5	6
Non-contact	10	8	5	8	6	4	9	5	9	8	8
Did not report crime	19	0	3	2	1	0	4	0	4	4	5
Other reason	7	2	10	4	3	4	3	1	7	4	5
Total N cases	230	118	135	160	146	114	147	145	218	147	1,560

Almost one in five of the victims of vehicle theft claimed not to
have reported a crime in the relevant period, but the figure was
below one in 20 for the other categories. This could happen if the
vehicle had been mistakenly reported as stolen. Alternatively, it
may arise due to erroneous reporting or recording of the vehicle
registration number or reporting of the incident by someone other
than the owner (especially where the owner was an organisation).
It can also occur if a stolen vehicle had recently changed ownership and the change of ownership had not yet been carried

through to the National Vehicle File. In this circumstance, the name and address of the previous owner may be recorded as the victim of the crime.

Among the "other reasons" for non-response were a substantial number of victims of fraud (which tended to be institutions) who either could not identify the incident in question or where the person who had dealt with it no longer worked there.

In 71 of the 959 completed interviews, the crime the victim claimed to have reported in the target period differed from that in the Garda records (see Table 1.6).[15] This appears to have arisen partly because of differences between Garda recording procedures and the way the respondent understands the incident. For instance, if a vehicle is stolen, and later recovered with property or vehicle accessories missing from it, it may be recorded in the Garda records as theft from a vehicle (an indictable crime) rather than as an "unauthorised taking" (the non-indictable crime category used where a vehicle is recovered within three months). Alternatively, if the vehicle is recovered with substantial damage, it may be recorded as an indictable "malicious injury to property".

Other discrepancies can arise because of Garda recording procedures for complex incidents, where the incident would normally be recorded according to the more serious violation. In addition, where an offender is identified and brought to court, the classification of the crime may be "updated" in the light of court proceedings. The victim, for instance, may report that a vehicle was taken during the course of a burglary. If the Gardaí judge that the evidence of illegal entry is not strong enough, the incident may be "updated" (and the case pursued in court) as a vehicle taking rather than a burglary.

---

[15] This does not include cases where the victim's interpretation of whether or not the crime involved violence or threat differed from the Garda classification (see Table 2.12 in Chapter 2).

Table 1.6: Crime on Garda Records by Crime Type According to Respondent (column percentages)

	Crime Type (from Garda Records)										
	Theft of Veh-icle	*Theft from Veh-icle*	*Fraud etc.*	*Ass-ault*	*Burg-lary*	*Agg. Burg-lary*	*Theft from Person*	*Agg. Theft from Person*	*Other Theft*	*Van-dal-ism*	*Total N Cases*
Crime Type (Respondent)											
Theft of Vehicle	75	6	0	0	0	0	0	0	2	3	83
Theft from Vehicle	11	94	0	0	0	0	2	1	2	2	95
Fraud	0	0	87	0	0	0	0	0	1	0	79
Assault	3	0	0	99	0	0	0	0	1	1	96
Burglary	5	0	9	0	99	0	0	1	4	3	126
Agg. Burglary	1	0	1	0	0	100	0	0	0	1	87
Theft from Person	0	0	0	0	0	0	97	0	0	0	85
Theft from Person (aggravated)	0	0	0	0	0	0	0	98	0	0	98
Other Theft	2	0	3	0	1	0	1	0	91	1	125
Vandalism	2	0	0	1	0	0	0	0	0	88	85
Total N cases	97	81	90	92	105	84	88	100	129	93	959

Another type of discrepancy arises where the victim is unaware of the attempted use of stolen cheques or credit cards. A person who has a wallet stolen during a burglary or a mugging, for instance, may be unaware that the thief (or someone else) subsequently tried to use cheques or credit cards. This would be recorded as a separate crime (forgery and uttering) by the Gardaí in addition to the original burglary or theft from person.

The survey was conducted by personal interview with the respondents. The named victim was interviewed, where possible.[16] In cases of crimes such as burglary that affect a whole household, this would normally be the household member who reported the crime (usually the male in couple households). In crimes where

---

[16] In a small proportion of cases — fewer than 1 per cent overall — someone else in the household or organisation provided the information by proxy.

the target was an organisation, the person reporting the crime was approached. This was most often the owner or manager, and occasionally another staff member or security person. If this person had left the organisation, an interview was obtained with someone who had been present at the time and could provide details of the incident.

Those participating in the survey were invited to answer questions regarding the crime itself; any injuries, losses or other impact of the crime on their lives; their satisfaction with the service they received from the Gardaí; their view of crime generally; and whether they had been victims of any other crime in recent years. The questionnaire for the survey was designed by the Garda Research Unit, in consultation with the Economic and Social Research Institute. A copy of the questionnaire is included as Appendix B.

Sample Weights

The unit of analysis in police crime statistics is the incident — a burglary, mugging, car theft and so on. This is different from the classic victimisation survey, where the unit of analysis is the victim. To the extent that some individuals or organisations are targeted several times in a given year, the figures produced from the two sources will differ. For instance, if someone has a wallet or handbag snatched several times in a given year, we have one victim but several incidents. Multiple victimisation of this type happens much more frequently in the case of shops, which may experience several shoplifting incidents in a given period. In the present study, we begin with a sample drawn on the basis of incidents, and devise two sets of sample weights (the incident weight and the victim weight) so that either the incident or the victim can be the unit of analysis, depending on the requirements of the discussion.[17]

---

[17] Fuller details on the construction of sample weights are shown in Appendix A.

Both sets of weights adjust for sampling or response deviations associated with type of victim (individual/private household versus organisation), category of crime and type of area where the crime was reported (Dublin or elsewhere). The "incident weight" grosses the sample up to the total number of incidents recorded in 1995. The "victim weight" grosses the sample up to the total number of victims in 1995, by adding an adjustment to take account of the fact that some victims are likely to have reported several different crimes in the target period. This is the appropriate weight to use in analyses comparing the characteristics of crime victims to those of the general population. It approximates the kinds of totals that would be achieved in the classic victimisation survey results, where the victim is the unit of analysis.

The figures in Table 1.7 illustrate the implications of the two types of weight.

Table 1.7: Number of Incidents and Estimated Number of Victims by Crime Category in 1995

	Numbers of Incidents and Victims in 1995		
	Total Incidents of this type recorded	*Estimated Number of Victims*	*Mean N. reported per victim*
Theft of Vehicle	13,898	13,301	1.04
Theft from Vehicle	18,838	17,142	1.10
Fraud etc.	3,578	2,785	1.28
Assault	7,046	6,590	1.07
Burglary (not aggravated)	30,993	24,739	1.25
Aggravated burglary	1,489	1,222	1.22
Theft from person	3,083	3,032	1.02
Theft from person, aggravated	6,650	6,489	1.02
Other theft	23,720	16,655	1.42
Vandalism	10,199	8,821	1.16
Total	*119,494*	*74,564**	*1.60*

Note: * this figure is based on the separate "total victim weight" described in Appendix A.

The first column of the table shows that, of the crimes covered in the survey, the most common type in 1995 was burglary, with over 30,000 recorded incidents, followed by other theft (23,700 incidents), theft from a vehicle (almost 19,000 incidents) and vehicle theft (14,000 incidents). Crimes involving violence or threat were less common: there were 7,000 assaults, about the same number of aggravated thefts from the person, and about 1,500 aggravated burglaries.

The second column in Table 1.7 shows the number of victims of each type of crime. The number of victims differs from the number of incidents to the extent that some victims are likely to have experienced multiple incidents. "Other theft" — a category that includes shoplifting — is the crime category with the greatest discrepancy between the number of victims (estimated at 16,600) and the number of incidents (23,700). The smallest discrepancy is found for theft from the person, where each victim reported an average of 1.02 incidents of that type. The total row — which takes account of multiple victimisation across *all* of the ten types of incident — indicates that there were about 75,000 different victims of the 120,000 separate incidents that occurred in 1995, representing an average of 1.6 incidents per victim. The total number of victims is less than the sum of the victims across categories, because some of the victims appear in more than one row of the table. For instance, some of the victims of car theft were also counted as victims of burglary in the target year.

The estimated number of victims of recorded crime needs to be interpreted with caution. A number of assumptions were made in calculating these weights, as detailed in Appendix A. In particular, we assumed that variations in the number of crimes the victims claim to have reported accurately reflect variations in the number of crimes recorded in the Garda records for the victims. A second assumption made was that taking one-third of the incidents that respondents claim to have reported in a three-year period would accurately reflect variations in reporting over one year. Finally, where information was missing or incomplete, the values were imputed[18] so that victim weights could be calculated for all cases.

Other Sources of Data

In a number of tables throughout the report, we compare the profile of the individual crime victims to a national sample, using micro-data from the 1995 Labour Force Survey or from the *Living in Ireland Survey*. The latter is a large-scale national panel survey of households and individuals. The data from the 1995 wave of the survey is used here. This data is based on a sample of 3,584 households and the 8,534 individuals age 16 or over living in them. The survey collected detailed information on household composition, labour force status and sources of income of all adult household members. Further details on the selection of the initial sample in 1994 and on the sample weights are available in Callan et al. (1996 and 1999).

Trends in Different Types of Recorded Crime Since 1982

In this section, we examine trends since 1982 in the number of recorded crimes in the categories adopted in this report. This is intended to provide background to the detailed discussion of the incidents and victims affected in the 1994–95 period, and also to highlight the need to avoid treating crime as a unitary phenomenon. As Rottman (1980) noted, a single index of crime would obscure more than it reveals if some offences are changing over time more rapidly than others are.

The 17-year period from 1982 to 1998 is used, since total numbers of vehicle thefts (including non-indictable "unauthorised taking" cases where no proceedings were taken) are available in the published statistics[19] for this period. The figures for "theft

---

[18] See Appendix A for details.

[19] The retrospective figures are shown in the 1996 Garda Síochána Annual Report.

from person" and "aggravated theft from person" are combined in the chart, since no distinction between these two was made in the published statistics before 1993.

In the context of longer-term trends in indictable crime, the early 1980s represented a peak in the recorded figures. The level of indictable crime rose markedly in the mid-1960s, from fewer than 20,000 cases in 1965 to over 100,000 cases in 1983 (Brewer et al., 1997). After 1983, there was a sharp decline in the overall level of recorded indictable crime. The period covered in the figures presented in the following charts, then, begins at the point where levels of indictable crime were at their highest in Ireland.

Figure 1.2 shows the trends between 1982 and 1998 in the number of crimes in the four largest categories: burglary, other theft, vehicle theft and theft from a vehicle. These four categories account for over 70 per cent of all crimes covered in this report. The overall crime figure will be dominated by the number of incidents of these types.

Apart from a drop following the high figures in the early 1980s, these four types of crime show no definite trend since that time. The number of recorded burglaries reached a peak in 1983 (nearly 36,000 cases), dropping back to fluctuate between 26,000 and 33,000 from 1986 to 1998. The most recent three years have all shown an annual decline in the numbers. The number of cases of theft from a vehicle peaked at just over 20,000 cases in 1982, fluctuated between 15,000 and 20,000 cases from 1984 to 1996, and fell to about 12,400 cases in 1998. The number of stolen vehicles fell from nearly 22,000 cases in 1982 to fluctuate between 12,000 and 16,000 from 1987 to 1998. The lowest figures for vehicle theft were in the late 1980s. Cases of other theft showed a similar fluctuating pattern, with figures ranging from 20,000 to 25,000, and the lowest figure occurring in 1989.

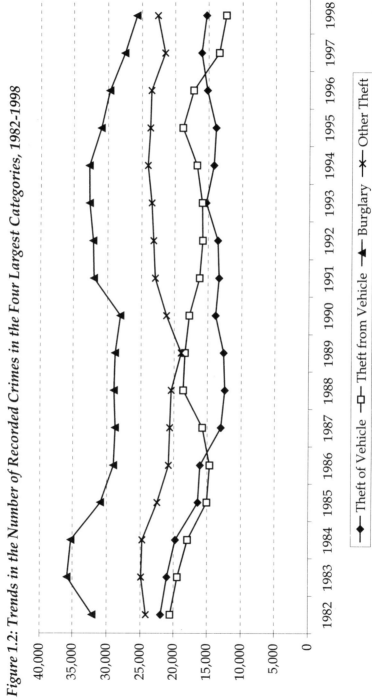

Figure 1.2: Trends in the Number of Recorded Crimes in the Four Largest Categories, 1982-1998

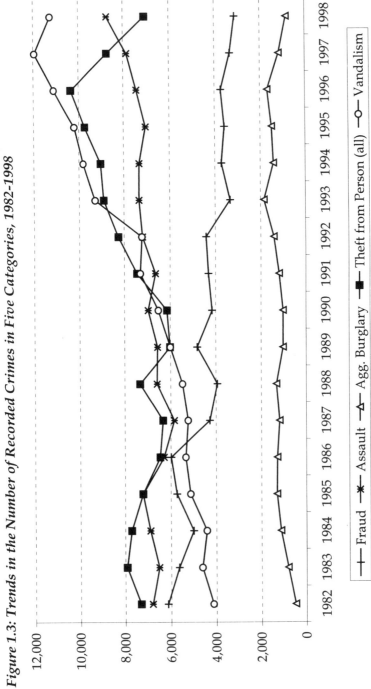

Figure 1.3: Trends in the Number of Recorded Crimes in Five Categories, 1982-1998

The other five categories occur less frequently than the "top four", and are shown in Figure 1.3. Recorded fraud cases have tended to decline from around 6,000 cases in 1982, to under 4,000 cases from 1993 onwards, with the sharpest drop between 1986 and 1987. The number of incidents of theft from the person (which includes aggravated theft from the person in the chart) fluctuated between about 6,000 and 8,000 until 1992, rose steadily to over 10,000 cases in 1996, and dropped sharply to about 7,000 incidents in 1998. The general trend is upward over time, but with a decline in the last two years.

Vandalism is the only category that showed an increase almost every year, with a particularly sharp rise in 1993. By 1998, there were over 11,000 recorded incidents, compared to 4,100 in 1982. The number of recorded assault cases has ranged between 5,800 and 8,700 in the 17-year period, with sizeable annual fluctuations, and some tendency to increase over time. Aggravated burglary is the smallest of the ten categories. The number of cases increased annually in the early 1980s — from fewer than 500 in 1982 to 1,300 in 1985, remained at a plateau of around 1,000–1,300 cases for the next six years, peaked at about 1,800 cases in 1993 before dropping back again under 1,000 cases by 1998.

Overall, the trends for different types of crime do not follow a common pattern, so that an overall index that included all indictable crimes would tend to obscure some important differences in trends. The profiles for a number of the larger categories — burglary, vehicle theft, theft from a vehicle, other theft — have remained relatively flat after falling from their highest figures in the early 1980s period, although with some notable peaks and valleys, and a tendency to decline in recent years. Vandalism is the one category where there was a clear upward trend throughout the period, but assault and aggravated burglary have also tended to increase over time. This suggests that violent crime may have increased over the period, but it may also be due to an increased propensity to report violent crime. Recorded cases of fraud have tended to decline since the early 1980s.

Moreover, there is no immediate link between trends in property crime and important social changes such as the high unemployment rates in 1980s and their fall in the 1990s. While recorded crime grew rapidly during the period of economic expansion in the 1960s, no such escalation is apparent with the economic expansion of the 1990s. This suggests that an understanding of crime levels and trends requires an attention to the specificity and immediate setting of the incidents in question, and points to the inadequacy of treating crime as a single phenomenon. This is not to say that broader social phenomena such as unemployment, economic growth and relative deprivation do not have an impact on the level and nature of crime. Rather, it points to the need for a more sophisticated understanding of the opportunity structure in which crime takes place. The economic and social context is an important component of that opportunity structure. Other components depend on the more specific features of crimes that can only be understood by means of a detailed analysis of what happens during a criminal incident, who it happens to, where it takes place and who the offender is. The analysis in this report is intended to contribute towards such an understanding.

Outline of the Chapters

The next chapter examines the details of the incident itself: whether the target was an individual or private household on the one hand, or a business or organisation on the other; where the incident took place; the timing of the incident in terms of daylight/night or weekend/weekday; in the case of assault, the type of assault that occurred; in the case of theft, the nature of the property stolen. It is clear throughout this chapter that an approach to crime which locates it in the context of everyday routines and activities is most productive in terms of understanding the patterning of crime and in suggesting strategies for prevention.

Chapter 3 turns to the victims of crime, and the analysis uses the victim weights described above. The first section provides an overview of the characteristics of the crime victims in terms of whether they are individuals or institutions; characteristics of individual victims such as age group, sex, social class; and household characteristics. Where the victim is an institution, the type and size of organisation involved is examined. In the case of private households or individuals, we will compare the profile of crime victims to that of a national sample, using data from other sources, to ask whether crime victims are a representative cross-section of the Irish population generally, or whether particular groups are more at risk. The second part of the chapter draws on information regarding other crimes faced by members of our sample in a three-year period in order to explore the extent of repeat victimisation and broad variations in reporting rates.

In Chapter 4, we begin by examining characteristics of the offender, where these are known to the victim, in terms of age group, sex, the number of offenders, and whether the offender was known to the victim. Then we turn to the interaction between the crime victims and the Gardaí: how the crime was reported, the victim's level of satisfaction with various aspects of the Garda service, whether the victims belong to a Neighbourhood Watch or Community Alert Scheme, and the victim's perception of the effectiveness of these schemes. We also examine the outcome of the case: whether the offender was apprehended, the victim's perception of whether the crime was alcohol-related or drug-related; whether the victim experienced intimidation from the offender; and the victim's level of satisfaction with the outcome of the case.

Chapter 5 focuses on the impact of the crime on the victim in terms of physical injury, financial loss, or psychological distress. Then, in the second part of the chapter, we turn to an examination of the respondent's perception of crime generally: the perceived likelihood of future victimisation, and whether they feel safe in their neighbourhood and in their homes. The victims' assessment of the amount of crime in the areas where they live can be compared to a corresponding question put to a national sample in the *Living in Ireland Survey*. The third part of Chapter 5 uses a multivariate analysis to examine the effects of aspects of the crime itself, characteristics of the victim, the outcome of the case and Garda service on the level of psychological distress experienced by the individual victims. The "incident" weights are used in the first part of this chapter, since the focus is on the impact of a particular incident. In the second part of the chapter, the focus is on the victims of crime as a group, and the "victim" weights are used. The analysis in the third part of the chapter uses the unweighted data for individual victims.

The final chapter draws together the results in order to highlight the new insights it provides into recorded crime in Ireland. It then examines the policy implications of the results in three main areas:

- **How can the service to crime victims be improved?**

- **What conclusions can be drawn regarding strategies for crime prevention?**

- **What are the implications for the production and interpretation of statistics on crime in Ireland?**

Chapter 2

The Facts of the Case: Details of the Reported Incident

This chapter represents the first step in "going behind" the crime statistics. We examine the details of the incident reported by the survey respondent for each of the ten crime categories described in Chapter 1. This allows us to address issues such as where the crime took place, whether there were witnesses, the timing of the incident in terms of daylight/night or weekend/weekday. We examine whether the victim was assaulted and, if so, the nature of the assault or threat. In Chapter 5, we will look in more detail at the impact of the crime on the victim, including the extent of any injury or financial loss incurred.

The data are weighted by the "incident weight": the sample cases are weighted so as to represent all of the reported incidents in the target categories in 1995. The numbers in this chapter refer to numbers of incidents. In the next chapter we will change the emphasis from incidents to victims and a slightly different weighting scheme will be used to take account of the fact that one victim may have reported several incidents of a given type in the target year.

Who Was the Target?

As noted in Chapter 1, classic victimisation surveys such as the QNHS crime module, the British Crime Survey and the National

Survey of Criminal Victimization in the United States collect no systematic information on crimes against institutions. This is because they are based on samples of individuals living in private households. However, the present survey collected information on reported crimes against both types of target. We are in a position, therefore, to identify whether the target of the crime was a business or other organisation, on the one hand, or an individual or private household, on the other. This, as we will see, has an impact on aspects of the incident such as its timing and the type of property stolen. Table 2.1 shows the breakdown of recorded crimes in terms of whether the target was an individual or an institution.

Table 2.1: Whether Target of the Incident is an Individual/Private Household or Institution by Crime Type (column percentages)

	Theft of Vehicle	Theft from Vehicle	Fraud etc.	Assault	Burglary	Agg. Burglary	Theft from Person	Agg. Theft from Person	Other Theft	Vandalism	Total
Individual	89	88	5	97	54	23	100	91	45	52	65
Institution	7	12	93	2	44	74	0	8	55	44	33
Both	4	0	2	0	2	3	0	1	0	4	1
Total	*13,898*	*18,838*	*3,578*	*7,046*	*30,993*	*1,489*	*3,058*	*6,650*	*23,720*	*10,199*	*119,469*
Row %	*12%*	*16%*	*3%*	*6%*	*26%*	*1%*	*3%*	*6%*	*20%*	*9%*	*100%*

Cases weighted to total crimes in 1995.

In this context, "individual" refers either to an individual or private household[1] — in crimes such as burglary or vandalism, the property of several members of a household may be stolen or damaged in the same incident. "Institutions" include public and private sector businesses, hospitals, schools, clubs and so on. The third row in Table 2.1, labelled "both", includes cases where it is

---

[1] A household consists of an individual living alone or a group of people living together who share some form of budgeting arrangement. Individuals living together are usually related, but this is not necessarily the case.

difficult to classify the target, such as burglaries of businesses run from home, or shops where the owner lives overhead, or theft of a vehicle used for both business and domestic purposes.

Two-thirds of the incidents were targeted against individuals or private households, while the remaining third were directed at businesses or other organisations. Vehicle crimes, assault and theft from the person mainly have individuals or private households as the target, whereas fraud and aggravated burglary were directed mainly at institutions. Other theft, non-aggravated burglary and vandalism were more evenly divided in terms of whether the victim was an individual or an institution. Since we have very few sample cases of fraud against individual victims, and few or no cases of vehicle theft, assault and personal theft where the victim was an institution, these categories will be excluded in tables showing the breakdown by crime type and victim type.

The greater number of domestic than of institutional burglaries differs from the pattern reported in Rottman (1980):

> In all 25 years [from 1951 to 1975], the number of shopbreakings exceeds that of recorded housebreakings, with particularly marked differentials in the 1960s. . . . by the early 1970s the differential has narrowed. (Rottman, 1980, p. 53)[2]

The present results suggest that, since the mid-1970s, the number of domestic burglaries has risen more rapidly than the number of burglaries targeted against institutions. This trend has continued in recent years. The Garda Annual Report for 1998 provides a breakdown of burglaries according to whether the target was a dwelling or some other type of premises for the period from 1994

---

[2] Up until the mid-1970s housebreaking and shopbreaking were violations of different laws, and the Garda Síochána Annual Reports provided separate figures for each. The distinction was eliminated by the Criminal Law (Jurisdiction) Act, 1976, which also created a new offence of aggravated burglary (in which a real or imitation firearm or explosives are used).

to 1998. The proportion of burglaries targeted against dwellings had increased from 57 per cent in 1994 to 62 per cent in 1998 (Garda Síochána, 1999, p. 73).

Where the Crime Took Place

Previous research has consistently found that crime rates are higher in urban than in rural areas. Most people living in cities are strangers to each other, so that informal social control is weakened. In addition, strangers from other areas come to cities for business or entertainment purposes. The reduced "guardianship" which ensues, combined with increased opportunity arising from the concentration of people and goods (particularly in the retail areas), as well as the concentration of potential offenders, makes crime more likely (Felson, 1998).

Earlier research noted the strong concentration of Irish crime in the Dublin area. Evidence from the 1982/83 Crime Victimisation Survey in Ireland, compared to victimisation surveys in Britain, suggests that the "Dublin concentration" of crime in Ireland is exceptional.

> The extent to which that risk is concentrated in Dublin can be illustrated by a simple comparison to London's share in English crime. A family living in Dublin's inner city has 12 times the risk of becoming a burglary victim than someone living in rural Ireland; the typical family in inner London has a fivefold greater risk than their rural counterpart. (Rottman, 1989, p. 98)

However, Brewer et al. (1997) note that the "Dublin concentration" in the Republic of Ireland is comparable to the "Belfast concentration" of crime in Northern Ireland. The greater "Dublin concentration" of Irish crime compared to the "London concentration" of English crime is probably due to the fact that Ireland has fewer other large cities outside the capital.

The recently published figures from the QNHS crime and victimisation module confirm the greater incidence of criminal incidents in the Dublin region compared to other parts of the country. For all of the types of crime covered in that study,[3] the number of incidents per 10,000 households or individuals was greater in Dublin than elsewhere (Central Statistics Office, 1999a).

Table 2.2 shows the broad region of the country where the incident took place. Overall, the results support the research finding and popular image of cities as more "dangerous" places in terms of crime. Well over half of all crimes in our ten categories took place in Dublin city or county, a figure considerably higher than the 30 per cent of the adult population living in this area.[4] The concentration in Dublin is more noticeable for crime targeted against individuals (63 per cent of the total) than for crime targeted against institutions (46 per cent of the total), and is particularly marked in the case of theft from the person, both aggravated and non-aggravated, where almost nine out of ten incidents were in the Dublin area. Over two-thirds of vehicle crime (theft of or from a vehicle) also occurred in the Dublin area.

The concentration of aggravated thefts from the person in urban areas itself is not unusual, although its extent is particularly marked. According to the Uniform Crime Reports in the United States, 41 per cent of all reported robberies in 1992 were reported in the 20 largest cities, which made up 11.5 per cent of the US population (cited in Zimring and Hawkins, 1997, p. 225).

There are three crime categories where the proportion of recorded incidents in the Dublin area is not substantially greater than the region's population: vandalism, fraud and assault. Recorded vandalism and fraud show a greater concentration in the South-West/Mid-West, an area that includes two other large cities, Cork and Limerick. This does not appear to be due to reporting differences between Dublin and other areas in terms of these

---

[3] Burglary, vandalism, theft of vehicle, theft from vehicle, bicycle theft, theft with violence, assault and non-violent theft.

[4] *Labour Force Survey, 1995*, microdata.

crime types. The QNHS results show a reporting rate by house-holds in Dublin that is slightly higher for vandalism (39.8 per cent) and only slightly lower for assault (61.3 per cent) than for the country as a whole (39.6 and 62.7 per cent, respectively) (Central Statistics Office, 1999a, Tables 7 and 11a). The results in Chapter 3 of the present survey find no overall difference between Dublin and other parts of Ireland in the reporting of crime by institutions.

Table 2.2: Region Where Crime Occurred by Crime and Victim Type (column percentages)

	Theft of Vehicle	Theft from Vehicle	Fraud etc.	Assault	Burglary	Agg. Burglary	Theft from Person	Agg. Theft from Person	Other Theft	Vandalism	Total
Individual											
Dublin City & County	70	72	*	35	57	59	88	90	64	38	63
Rest of East & South	13	5	*	12	14	12	1	3	12	13	10
South-West & Mid-West	7	15	*	28	17	17	9	6	8	38	15
North-East, North-West	1	6	*	10	9	9	1	1	7	5	6
Midlands and West	9	2	*	15	4	3	2	0	9	6	6
Weighted N cases	12,953	16,510	240	6,875	17,445	391	3,058	6,123	10,726	5,680	80,002
Institution											
Dublin City & County	*	66	26	*	47	84	*	*	48	23	46
Rest of East & South	*	13	16	*	16	6	*	*	9	12	12
South-West & Mid-West	*	11	32	*	20	5	*	*	24	25	22
North-East, North-West	*	6	10	*	8	2	*	*	4	12	7
Midlands and West	*	4	16	*	9	3	*	*	15	29	14
Weighted N cases	945	2,328	3,338	171	13,548	1,098	0	527	12,994	4,519	39,467

Note: Sample weighted to total crimes. * indicates too few sample cases to provide breakdown.

As noted above, however, the QNHS results find a higher incidence of all types of crime, including vandalism and assault, in the Dublin area than elsewhere. The QNHS results indicate that the Dublin incidence of assault (104 cases per 10,000 adults) and vandalism (1,316 per 10,000 households) are considerably higher than in the country as a whole (64 and 800 per 10,000, respectively for assault and vandalism). The pattern in the Garda statistics is probably due to recording difference by region. Cases of non-indictable vandalism and assault do not appear in the Garda statistics unless proceedings are taken. Proceedings may be taken less often in Dublin because the offender is less likely to be identified. This points to the danger involved in drawing conclusions from the recorded statistics when they do not include all reported incidents of crimes in certain categories.

In the case of fraud, the regional pattern may reflect recording differences or real difference in the incidence of such crimes, possibly due to more stringent checking and security measures taken by Dublin businesses or residents.

Table 2.3 provides a location breakdown from the perspective of the respondent. Respondents were asked whether the crime took place "here, in this area" or "elsewhere". The concepts of "here" and "elsewhere" are interpreted fairly narrowly, typically as the area or part of a town/city where the respondent lived or had the place of business.[5]

---

[5] The proportion of cases where the crime took place in a different county from the victim's address (only 7 per cent) was much lower than the 28 per cent of incidents individual which victims defined as taking place "elsewhere" in Table 2.3.

Victims of Recorded Crime in Ireland

Table 2.3: Whether Incident Took Place "Here" or "Elsewhere" by Crime and Victim Type (column percentages)

	Theft of Veh- icle	Theft from Veh- icle	Fraud etc.	Ass- ault	Burg- lary	Agg. Burg- lary	Theft from Per- son	Agg. Theft from Per- son	Other Theft	Van- dal- ism	Total
Individual											
Here	75	60	*	68	92	94	39	50	70	82	72
Elsewhere	25	40	*	32	8	6	61	50	30	18	28
Weighted N cases	12,953	16,315	240	6,875	17,445	391	3,083	6,058	10,726	5,680	79,767
Institution											
Here	*	33	98	*	95	98	*	*	93	97	91
Elsewhere	*	67	2	*	5	2	*	*	7	3	9
Weighted N cases	945	2,328	3,262	171	13,548	1,098	0	527	12,994	4,352	39,224

Note: Sample weighted to total incidents. * indicates too few cases to provide breakdown.

In just under three-quarters of incidents targeted against individuals and over 90 per cent of those directed at institutions, the incident occurred "here, in this area". Theft from the person (such as having a pocket picked), aggravated theft from the person, and theft from a business vehicle were crime types where one half or more of the incidents took place "elsewhere". Forty per cent of thefts from individually owned vehicles and nearly one-third of assaults took place elsewhere. If we interpret the risks in the light of where people are likely to spend their time, areas at some remove from the home would seem to be associated with a relatively higher risk of personal crimes such as theft from the person, aggravated theft from the person and assault, and also for theft from a vehicle.

Table 2.4 examines the location in terms of the different kinds of places people are likely to spend time: the home, workplace, or other, usually more public, places. For individual victims, over half of the incidents took place in the home, its vicinity (the garden, garage, shed, outbuildings and so on) or in the area near the home. This is very similar to the international figure for 1988: of the offences measured in the International Crime Victimisation Survey, nearly half had taken place near the victim's own home (van Dijk et al., 1991).

Table 2.4: Location Where Crime Occurred by Crime and Victim Type (column percentages)

	Theft of Vehicle	Theft from Vehicle	Assault	Burglary	Agg. Burglary	Theft from person	Agg. Theft from person	Other Theft	Vandalism	Total
Individual										
Home	0	0	12	84	82	1	1	17	45	26
Vicinity of Home	33	25	8	9	0	0	1	29	14	18
Near Home	28	20	12	0	0	11	30	8	4	14
Business/ organisation premises/ workplace	0	0	9	4	12	1	4	1	17	4
Elsewhere	39	55	59	4	6	87	63	44	20	39
Weighted N cases	11,421	15,159	6,670	17,166	391	3,043	6,123	10,402	5,212	75,588
Institution										
Home	*	0	*	0	0	*	*	0	1	0
Vicinity of Home	*	0	*	5	0	*	*	2	0	3
Near Home	*	26	*	0	0	*	*	0	0	2
Business/ organisation premises/ workplace	*	0	*	88	100	*	*	88	89	82
Elsewhere	*	74	*	6	0	*	*	10	9	14
Weighted N cases	611	2,106	171	13,333	1,098	0	527	12,696	4,391	34,933

Note: Sample weighted to total incidents. * indicates too few cases to provide breakdown. Fraud is not included in this table.

Apart from burglary, which was almost always to the home or its vicinity (Table 2.5), 59 per cent of vandalism incidents with individual targets were directed against the home or its vicinity. The relatively large percentage of vandalism incidents against individuals taking place in "other" areas reflects the substantial proportion of such incidents that involve damage to a car rather than to premises (see Table 2.16, later).

Table 2.5: Detailed Location Where Crime Occurred for Burglary, Aggravated Burglary and Vandalism by Victim Type

	Burglary	Agg. Burglary	Vandalism	Total
Individual				
Home	84	82	45	75
Vicinity of home	9	0	14	10
Farm	0	0	1	0
Business	2	12	9	4
Non-business premises	2	0	8	3
Other	4	6	24	8
Weighted N Cases	*17,166*	*391*	*5,212*	*22,769*
Institution				
Home	0	0	1	0
Vicinity of home	5	0	0	4
Business	81	100	58	76
Non-business premises	8	0	31	13
Other	6	0	9	7
Weighted N Cases	*13,333*	*1,098*	*4,391*	*18,822*

Cases weighted to Total Crimes in 1995.

Table 2.6 provides a more detailed breakdown of the locations for vehicle crimes. While stolen vehicles were most likely to have been taken from the person's driveway or street outside the home (59 per cent), a further quarter were stolen from private car parks — such as those at apartment complexes, workplaces, shopping centres, cinemas and so on. Similarly, over two-fifths of thefts from a vehicle happen near the home, but one half took place at other public places where the vehicle might be parked, such as car parks, public streets or roads.

Table 2.6: Detailed Location Where Crime Occurred for Vehicle Crime by Victim Type (column percentages)

	Theft of Vehicle	Theft from Vehicle	Total
Individual			
Garage	2	0	1
Driveway	31	25	27
Street near home	28	20	24
Public Car Park	6	6	6
Private Car Park	23	16	18
Street elsewhere	9	28	20
Other	0	6	4
Weighted N cases	*11,421*	*15,159*	*27,486*
Institution			
Driveway	*	0	3
Street near home	*	26	21
Public Car Park	*	7	5
Private Car Park	*	14	21
Street elsewhere	*	46	35
Other	*	7	15
Weighted N cases	*611*	*2,106*	*2,718*

Note: Sample weighted to total incidents. * indicates too few cases to provide breakdown. Individual total includes small number of cases of vandalism involving a vehicle.

The risk should be assessed in the light of the length of time cars are parked in each of these types of location, however. Felson draws on work by Clarke and Mayhew[6] to give estimates for the number of car thefts per million hours parked in different locations (Felson, 1998, p. 32). For a car parked in a residential garage, we would expect less than one theft per million hours parked. This rises to about two and a half for a car parked on the street near home or near the workplace, and to nearly ten incidents per million hours parked in a public parking lot.

Table 2.7 shows that about one assault in eight took place in the person's home. A further one-fifth took place in the vicinity of the home or near home. Most incidents take place outside either of these locations. Further breakdowns, shown in Table 2.7, show that one-third occurred at or near a public house or night-club, and one-fifth happened in another public place.

The 1998 QNHS module on crime explicitly excluded domestic assaults, whereas if the incident constituted an indictable offence or was a non-indictable offence where proceedings were taken, it would be included in the present sample. As a result, the proportion of assaults that took place in the home is higher (12 per cent) for the victims of recorded crime in the present study than is true in the QNHS data (6 per cent). On the other hand, the QNHS showed a higher proportion of assaults taking place in the vicinity of the home (18 per cent, compared to 8 per cent in the present study; Central Statistics Office, 1999a). Assaults taking place near home are probably more likely to be perpetrated by people known to the victim, such as relatives, neighbours or other acquaintances. Research findings elsewhere point to a lower reporting rate for acquaintance assault than for stranger assault (see, for example, Mirrlees-Black et al, 1998). This would account for

---

[6] R.V. Clarke and P. Mayhew (1998) "Preventing Crime in Parking Lots: What We Need to Know" in R.B. Peiser (ed.) *Reducing Crime Through Real Estate Development and Management*, Washington, DC: Urban Land Institute.

the higher proportion of QNHS assaults taking place near home than the proportion found in the present study, which includes only reported and recorded incidents.

Table 2.7: Detailed Location Where Crime Occurred for Assault, Theft from the Person and Other Theft (individual victims, column percentages)

	Assault	Theft from person	Aggravated Theft from Person	Other Theft	Total
Individual					
Home	12	1	1	17	10
Vicinity of home	8	0	1	29	14
Near home	12	11	30	8	15
Work	9	1	4	1	4
Near Work	0	3	6	2	3
At/near pub/ night-club	36	11	8	9	16
Other public place	20	65	43	23	32
Other	2	8	6	10	7
Weighted N cases	6,670	3,043	6,123	10,402	26,238

Cases weighted to Total Crimes in 1995.

Nearly one-quarter of the QNHS assault victims reported an assault taking place at or near work or school/college, compared to 11 per cent[7] of victims of recorded assault. Again, this may partly reflect a reluctance to report assaults where the offender is an acquaintance, such as a work colleague. It also suggests, however, that surveys of individuals may capture some incidents that are targeted against businesses or other organisations. For instance, a shop employee assaulted during a robbery of the shop may report the incident in a victim survey as an assault.

---

[7] Nine per cent take place at work — the other 2 per cent taking place at or near school or college are included in the "Other" category in Table 2.7.

Theft from the person is the crime most likely to occur away from home or the workplace. Public places generally (other than those near home or near the workplace) were the site of two-thirds of the incidents of theft from the person. Over two-fifths of the aggravated thefts from the person took place in public areas, but these incidents are more likely than non-aggravated thefts from the person to occur in the area near the home (32 per cent compared to 11 per cent).

The bulk of crime against institutional targets occurs at the place of business or the premises of the organisation (Table 2.4). Theft from a vehicle directed against institutions is the only category where most (two-thirds) of the incidents take place elsewhere. In all other cases of institutional victims, as expected, more than nine out of ten incidents occur at the business or organisation premises.

Timing of Incident

Common sense might lead us to expect crimes to happen more often at night than during the daytime, since darkness and the presence of fewer people out of doors is likely to reduce the risk of the incident being witnessed. Table 2.8 shows when the crime occurred in terms of day or night and weekday or weekend.[8] "Night" is defined here as between the hours of 8.00 p.m. and 8.00 a.m., regardless of seasonal differences in hours of daylight. The "weekend" begins on Friday night, and ends at 8.00 on Monday morning.

Overall, for incidents targeted against individuals, 57 per cent took place by night and 43 per cent by day — a more even distribution than we might expect. Some crimes were clearly more likely to take place in the evening or at night. About 80 per cent of vandalism incidents occurred between 8.00 p.m. and 8.00 a.m., with vandalism directed at institutions skewed towards the

---

[8] These questions were not asked in the case of fraud.

weekend nights. Over three-quarters of assaults happened at night and they, too, tended to be concentrated in weekend nights.

Table 2.8: Day and Time Crime Occurred by Crime and Victim Type (column percentages)

	Theft of Vehicle	Theft from Vehicle	Assault	Burglary	Agg. Burglary	Theft from person	Agg. Theft from person	Other Theft	Vandalism	Total
Individual										
Weekday Daytime	25	33	15	43	35	57	56	40	7	34
Weekday Night	34	33	20	26	26	10	15	28	40	28
Weekend, day	2	8	7	6	9	22	16	7	8	8
Weekend, night	38	22	55	20	27	8	11	24	41	27
Daytime, day unknown	0	0	1	2	0	3	1	0	0	1
Night-time, day unknown	1	4	2	3	3	0	1	0	4	2
Weighted N Cases	11,752	15,966	6,625	16,952	391	3,043	5,993	9,275	5,581	75,577
Institution										
Weekday Daytime	*	55	*	14	57	*	*	64	7	38
Weekday Night	*	32	*	34	17	*	*	9	10	20
Weekend, day	*	0	*	10	12	*	*	10	10	9
Weekend, night	*	13	*	40	11	*	*	10	69	29
Daytime, day unknown	*	0	*	0	2	*	*	8	0	3
Night-time, day unknown	*	0	*	3	2	*	*	0	4	2
Weighted N Cases	945	2,328	171	13,333	1,086	0	462	12,435	4,034	34,794

Note: Sample weighted to total crimes. Fraud is not included in this table.

Roughly two-thirds of vehicle thefts took place at night, and were slightly more likely to occur on a weekend night than on a weeknight. While three-quarters of burglaries of institutions occurred at night, only about half of the residential burglaries happened between 8.00 p.m. and 8.00 a.m. In contrast, aggravated burglaries of institutions were much more likely to happen during the day (71 per cent), with over half occurring on a weekday; while fewer than half of those directed against private residences took place by day.

There is an interesting contrast when we compare weekday and weekend crimes, however. For incidents targeted against individuals or private households, weekday crimes are more likely to take place during the day (34 per cent compared to 28 per cent at night), whereas the crimes occurring on weekends are much more likely to take place at night (28 per cent at night compared to 8 per cent by day). This is a pattern driven by a combination of increased opportunity and reduced risk from the perspective of the offender. The role of opportunity is evident in the timing of thefts from the person: both kinds (aggravated and non-aggravated) are more likely to take place during the day when people are more likely to be out in public places. Shopping areas are likely to be particularly attractive for these kinds of thefts, since people will be carrying cash, credit cards or cheques. Only about one in five thefts from the person and one in four aggravated thefts from the person take place at night.

The role of reduced risk from the point of view of the offender is evident in the pattern for burglaries: weekday domestic burglaries are more likely to occur by day (43 per cent take place on a day during the week compared to 26 per cent on a week night) when homes are empty while people are at work or school. In contrast, weekend domestic burglaries take place more often at night: people are more likely to be at home during the day on Saturdays and Sundays. Aggravated burglaries against individual victims follow a very similar pattern, except that fewer take place during a weekday, and more take place on a weekend night. The similarity in the timing suggests that in many aggravated burglaries, the threat or violence is unplanned: the burglar is "caught" by the resident in a house which appears to be empty or where the residents are assumed to be asleep.

Almost by definition, most aggravated burglaries of businesses or other organisations take place during business hours. The timing of aggravated burglaries against institutions is very similar to that of aggravated theft from the person, with about 70 per cent taking place by day, and over half on a weekday. Again, this is likely to be related to opportunity — in the absence of "shop-breaking skills", it is probably easier to obtain cash (the favoured target in this type of crime) when businesses are open, than when cash is locked away in a safe.

Table 2.9 sheds some further light on the times at which homes or premises might be most vulnerable to burglary. A premises is considered "normally" empty for two or more hours a day if it is empty for this period on four or more days of the week. Premises are considered "normally" empty on weekends if they are empty most weekends. Comparing individual and institutional victims of burglary, it is clear that domestic premises are more likely (52 per cent) to be empty for two or more hours during the daytime than institutional premises (36 percent); and that institutional premises are more likely to be empty on the weekends (61 per cent, compared to 22 per cent for individual premises). The two types of premises are similar in terms of the predictability of their empty periods during the day: 42–43 per cent are empty at the same time from one day to the next. However, institutional premises are more predictably empty at night: three-quarters are empty at the same time each night, compared to only 15 per cent of individual victims.

The premises of domestic aggravated burglary victims are less likely to be empty on a regular or predictable basis. They are only half as likely to be empty by day as their non-aggravated burglary victim counterparts, and are very rarely (3 per cent) empty at weekends or at predictable times by night. This suggests that the victims of aggravated residential burglary are out of their homes less frequently than victims of other residential burglaries. This contrast between burglary and aggravated burglary for individual victims holds in part for institutional victims. Institutions which have suffered aggravated burglary are less likely to be empty by day or on weekends, than those that suffered non-aggravated burglary, but they are more likely to be empty by night (85 per cent).

Table 2.9: Whether Premises Empty at Certain Times for Burglary Incidents by Victim Type (column percentages)

	Burglary	Agg. Burglary	Total
Individual			
Empty two hours a day	52	26	51
Empty on weekends	22	3	22
Empty at same time each day	42	33	42
Empty at same time each night	15	0	15
Weighted N cases	*16,421*	*345*	*16,766*
Institution			
Empty two hours a day	36	22	35
Empty on weekends	61	32	59
Empty at same time each day	43	19	41
Empty at same time each night	75	85	75
Weighted N cases	*11,398*	*955*	*12,353*

Note: Sample weighted to total crimes.

Table 2.10 explores another aspect of the timing of an incident: whether it is associated with a special event that drew large numbers of people to the area, such as a match, concert or festival. The risk of crime may increase at such times for several reasons: an increased number of potential victims carrying cash in the area; special events are typically associated with the consumption of alcohol, which may increase the risk of assault and vandalism; homes and vehicles are likely to be left unattended.

Table 2.10: Whether Crime Associated with Special Event by Crime Type (column percentages)

	Theft of Vehicle	Theft from Vehicle	Assault	Burglary	Agg. Burglary	Theft from person	Agg. Theft from person	Other Theft	Vandalism	Total
Individual										
Yes	5	11	20	3	3	9	4	2	5	7
No	95	89	80	97	97	91	96	98	95	93
Weighted N Cases	12,805	16,510	6,875	17,445	391	3,083	6,058	10,726	5,680	79,574
Institution										
Yes	*	13	*	1	9	*	*	2	7	3
No	*	87	*	99	91	*	*	98	93	97
Weighted N Cases	945	2,328	171	13,548	1,098	0	527	12,815	4,519	35,949

Note: Sample weighted to total crimes. Fraud is not included in this table.

It is not possible, of course, to say on the basis of these figures to what extent the risk of crime increases during special events: we do not have information on the number and duration of special events in an area in a year-long period. However, it is clear that some crimes are associated with special events to a greater degree than others, and that crimes against individuals are more likely to increase at such times than are crimes against institutions. One-fifth of assaults, and about one tenth of thefts from a vehicle and thefts from the person (without aggravation) occur during special events, compared to about one in twenty of crimes generally. Aggravated burglary of institutions also seems to be somewhat higher at such times. The greater Garda presence which often accompanies special events may contribute to higher reporting levels. Moreover, it could well be that assaults taking place during a special event are more likely to be by a stranger, and to be witnessed by bystanders, both of which may increase the likelihood of reporting.

Who Was Present

As Table 2.11 shows, crimes vary a great deal in terms of whether someone (other than the offender) was present at the time. The victim was more often present (46 per cent) in cases of crimes against individuals than those involving institutional victims (34 per cent). In most vehicle crimes, vandalism incidents, and burglaries the victim was not present.[9] By their nature, on the other hand, the victim is always present in cases of assault, aggravated burglary, and theft from the person.

The popular perception of assault is of a lone and vulnerable victim confronted by one or more offenders with no bystanders present. This is not the case for recorded assaults, however: the victim was alone with the offender in only one in six cases of assault. In half of the assault cases, friends, acquaintances or work colleagues accompanied the victim; and in a further third of cases, there were bystanders present. This may partly be an artefact of the reporting and recording process: witnessed assaults are probably more likely to be reported, and they may be more likely to be recorded, once reported, since there is corroborating evidence that the incident was criminal in nature. The presence of others also fits with the arguments of previous researchers on the

---

[9] In the case of burglary, the victims are considered present if they are in the house or on the premises, even if they do not actually witness the crime.

importance of the role played by an audience, as well as the assailants themselves, in contributing to an escalation from disagreement to violence. Felson (1998, p. 66), in a review of research on the antecedents of violence, points out that a fight "is most likely to occur if these combatants also converge with an audience and troublemakers in the absence of peacemakers".

Table 2.11: Who Was Present at Time by Crime and Victim Type (column percentages)

	Theft of Vehicle	Theft from Vehicle	Assault	Burglary	Agg. Burglary	Theft from person	Agg. Theft from person	Other Theft	Vandalism	Total
Individual										
Victim Alone	1	12	17	9	65	32	50	18	9	15
Victim & bystanders	1	1	34	0	6	40	15	11	0	8
Victim accompanied	20	14	50	23	29	28	34	24	18	24
Victim not present	78	72	0	68	0	0	0	47	73	54
Weighted N cases	12,805	16,510	6,875	17,445	391	3,083	6,123	10,726	5,680	79,639
Institution										
Victim Alone	*	9	*	3	25	*	*	12	4	9
Victim & bystanders	*	0	*	0	21	*	*	24	0	11
Victim accompanied	*	0	*	12	54	*	*	22	2	15
Victim not present	*	91	*	85	0	*	*	42	93	66
Weighted N Cases	945	2,328	171	13,548	1,098	0	527	12,598	4,519	35,733

Cases weighted to Total Crimes in 1995. Fraud is not included in this table.

The victim was alone in a more substantial proportion of thefts from the person (about one-third), aggravated thefts from the person (half) and, especially, aggravated burglaries (about two-thirds of those directed against individual targets). In these cases, it is probably the vulnerability of a lone target that makes him or her attractive to the offender. Results presented in the next chapter, which looks at characteristics of the victims, confirm that the presumed vulnerability of the victim is more of a factor in aggravated theft and aggravated burglary of domestic targets than in assaults.

Crimes of Violence

Table 2.12 shows the victim's assessment of whether someone was assaulted or threatened during the incident. Vehicle crimes, burglary, theft from the person and vandalism rarely involve violence or the threat of violence, while assault invariably does; and aggravated burglary of institutions almost invariably does, from the perspective of the victim.

It is interesting to note that more than half the incidents of assault involved violence or threat to someone else[10] as well as the respondent victim. An anomaly revealed in this table is that in 30 per cent of aggravated burglaries and aggravated theft, the individual victim did not feel that threat or violence had been used. On the other hand, 18 per cent of cases of theft from the person, 22 per cent of institutional incidents of other theft, and 10 per cent of non-residential burglaries were perceived to have involved assault or threats. These differences between respondent perception and official classification may be due to a number of factors. These include the classifying of a crime as "aggravated" if the offender was carrying a weapon, even though it was not used or explicitly threatened during the incident; and differences between the respondent and Garda interpretation of what constitutes "threat" or assault. In this respect, "snatch thefts" such as a handbag snatch appear to be classified as "larceny from the person (muggings)". In addition, the amount of detail provided by the respondent to

---

[10] This does not count any defensive measures taken by the victim against the assailant.

the Garda, or elicited by the Garda, at the time of reporting the crime, could affect whether a crime is classified as aggravated or not. Moreover, the time-lag between the survey interview and the incident may have led the respondent to "forget" some of the details if the threat or assault itself was not perceived as severe by the victim.

Table 2.12: Whether Someone Was Assaulted or Threatened by Crime and Victim Type (column percentages)

	Theft of Vehicle	Theft from Vehicle	Ass-ault	Burg-lary	Agg. Burg-lary	Theft from person	Agg. Theft from person	Other Theft	Van-dalism	Total
Individual										
Respondent only	0	1	46	3	50	16	53	5	1	11
R and other	0	0	54	0	21	1	12	0	3	6
Other only	0	2	0	0	0	1	5	0	0	1
No assault/ threat	100	97	0	97	30	82	30	95	97	83
Weighted N cases	12,656	16,217	6,875	17,445	391	3,083	6,058	10,317	5,680	78,723
Institution										
Respondent only	*	0	*	0	33	*	*	7	0	5
R and other	*	0	*	3	49	*	*	5	0	5
Other only	*	0	*	8	13	*	*	10	0	7
No assault/ threat	*	100	*	90	4	*	*	78	100	83
Weighted N Cases	945	2,328	171	13,548	1,098	0	527	12,815	4,519	35,949

Cases weighted to Total Crimes in 1995. Fraud is not included in this table.

Table 2.13 shows the kind of assault or threat that was involved. Since up to three types of assault were coded, the percentages do not necessarily add to 100. Assault generally took the form of being pushed or dragged, punched, kicked, or being threatened with a weapon.

Table 2.13: Nature of Assault or Threat by Crime Type (column percentages)

	Theft of Veh-icle	Theft from Veh-icle	Ass-ault	Burg-lary	Agg. Burg-lary	Theft from per-son	Agg. Theft from per-son	Other Theft	Van-dal-ism	Total
Not assaulted	98	98	0	94	12	82	30	86	98	83
Verbal threat	0	0	1	0	0	1	1	3	0	1
Pushed/ dragged	0	0	51	2	17	13	25	7	0	7
Punched	0	1	77	0	6	2	14	1	0	6
Kicked	0	1	52	0	5	0	7	4	0	5
Bitten	0	0	9	0	0	1	1	0	0	1
Threatened (weapon)	2	0	9	1	73	3	31	6	0	5
Hit with blunt object	0	0	23	1	8	1	2	2	0	2
Stabbed	0	0	5	0	5	0	3	0	0	1
Other	0	2	14	3	12	1	8	1	1	3
Weighted N cases	*13,601*	*18,545*	*7,046*	*30,993*	*1,489*	*3,083*	*6,585*	*23,131*	*10,199*	*114,672*

Cases weighted to total crimes in 1995. Fraud is not included in this table.

There are only two crime categories where a substantial proportion of incidents involved threat with a weapon: aggravated burglary (almost three-quarters) and aggravated theft from the person (nearly one-third). Where something was used or threatened as a weapon, it was most often a blunt object, such as a stick, a tool such as a hammer, or a hurley stick or golf club (Table 2.14). Nearly one-quarter of the assault cases involved something of this nature being used as a weapon.

Knives and guns were used or threatened with about equal frequency in aggravated burglaries (28–29 per cent of cases), with blunt objects showing up in only 13 per cent of cases. Knives were also involved in about one in seven of the aggravated thefts from the person. Apart from these two crimes, knives and guns were rarely used or threatened. Only 4 per cent of the assault cases involved a knife and 1 per cent involved a gun.

The use of a syringe as a weapon is generally accepted as indicative of a relationship between crime and drug use. A syringe was used as a weapon in 12 per cent of aggravated burglaries and in 11 per cent of aggravated thefts from the person.

Table 2.14: Nature of Weapon Used or Threatened by Crime Type (column percentages)

	Theft of Vehicle	Theft from Vehicle	Ass-ault	Burg-lary	Agg. Burg-lary	Theft from person	Agg. Theft from person	Other Theft	Van-dalism	Total
Knife	2	0	4	1	29	3	14	2	0	2
Club/Blunt object	0	0	23	1	13	1	7	2	0	3
Gun	0	0	1	0	28	0	3	1	0	1
Syringe	0	0	0	0	12	0	11	0	0	1
Other	0	0	5	1	5	0	0	3	0	1
No weapon	98	100	69	98	20	96	68	94	100	93
Weighted N cases	13,601	18,545	7,046	30,993	1,489	3,083	6,585	23,336	10,199	114,877

Cases weighted to total crimes in 1995. Fraud is not included in this table.

Tables 2.13 and 2.14 throw some light on the discrepancy between the Garda and victim classification of the incident as involving violence or threat. In general, the type of assault involved in those cases not classified as "aggravated" by the Gardaí (theft from the person, other theft, burglary) tended not to be of the kind that would cause serious injury to the victim. For instance, in 13 per cent of the incidents classified as "theft from the person" the victim was "pushed or dragged" during the incident.

Stolen Property

Some property is stolen in 83 per cent of all crime in the ten categories covered in this study. Assault and vandalism are the only two categories where most incidents did not involve theft. Those cases of assault and vandalism where something was stolen were presumably not classified by the Gardaí as larcenies because the assault or damage to property, respectively, was more serious than the theft. The "theft" categories where nothing was stolen (over one in ten burglaries and aggravated burglaries) represent failed attempts.

By far the favourite target in theft crimes, to judge from Table 2.15, is cash. The reasons are understandable: as Felson notes, stealing cash "avoids the extra baggage of trading, unloading, stashing, or selling stolen goods" (1998, p. 61). Cash is stolen in 28 per cent of incidents overall, with the proportion being slightly higher (at 31 per cent) in the case of institutional victims. The proportion is highest, over 80 per cent, for aggravated burglaries targeted at institutions and for theft from the person.

Furthermore, three-quarters of aggravated thefts from the person and 62 per cent of domestic aggravated burglaries involve cash, and it is also the most frequently stolen item in cases of burglary against institutions (49 per cent) and other theft directed at individuals, and is second only to jewellery in domestic burglaries (36 per cent).

The theft of credit cards and cheques involves some additional risk for the thief, compared to cash, since the cards or cheques have to be used or sold on in order to realise their value. Credit cards are stolen in 13 percent of incidents directed against individuals, much more frequently than cheques which are taken in only 6 per cent of incidents. Credit cards are taken in over one third of aggravated thefts from the person and over one half of non-aggravated thefts from the person.

Table 2.15: Nature of Property Stolen by Crime and Victim Type (column percentages)

	Theft of Vehicle	Theft from Vehicle	Ass-ault	Burg-lary	Agg. Burg-lary	Theft from person	Agg. Theft from person	Other Theft	Van-dal-ism	Total
Individual										
Nothing Stolen	0	4	98	14	21	4	4	1	88	19
Cash	7	13	2	36	62	83	77	42	4	27
Cheques	2	6	0	0	0	29	20	10	2	6
Credit cards	5	11	0	8	0	53	38	22	2	13
Jewellery	3	1	0	37	15	5	15	11	1	12
Handbag/ wallet	0	13	0	12	15	75	59	35	4	18
Other personal accessories	25	28	2	29	6	23	33	17	5	22
(Video) Camera	3	4	0	17	0	3	0	2	0	6
Television/VCR	3	0	0	18	0	0	0	0	3	5
Sound system	2	6	0	16	0	0	0	1	1	5
Computer/ mobile phone	1	6	0	2	0	3	0	0	0	2
Furniture	0	0	0	1	0	0	0	4	0	1
Other House-hold Item	2	9	2	18	3	0	1	9	1	7
Tools/ Equipment	8	17	0	11	0	0	0	17	7	10
Vehicle accessory	8	40	0	0	0	0	0	6	0	10
Vehicle	100	4	0	0	0	0	0	0	2	17
Cigarettes/ tobacco	0	0	0	3	3	0	1	0	0	1
Documents	2	1	0	4	6	7	5	9	0	3
Savings/social welfare book	0	0	0	0	6	5	2	1	0	1
Ticket/voucher	0	2	0	2	3	7	2	3	0	2
Keys	0	2	0	3	0	7	11	4	0	3
Other	2	5	1	5	3	0	4	12	2	4
Weighted N cases	12,953	16,510	6,875	17,445	391	3,083	6,123	10,726	5,680	79,787

Table 2.15 (continued)

	Theft of Vehicle	Theft from Vehicle	Ass-ault	Burg-lary	Agg. Burg-lary	Theft from person	Agg. Theft from person	Other Theft	Van-dal-ism	Total
Institution										
Nothing Stolen	0	0	*	7	9	*	*	2	78	14
Cash	28	11	*	49	87	*	*	18	7	31
Cheques	0	0	*	3	11	*	*	4	2	3
Credit cards	0	6	*	0	4	*	*	2	0	1
Jewellery	0	0	*	3	1	*	*	0	0	1
Handbag/wallet	0	10	*	0	4	*	*	3	0	2
Other personal accessories	11	6	*	4	5	*	*	0	0	2
(Video) Camera	0	0	*	3	0	*	*	0	2	1
Television/VCR	0	0	*	3	0	*	*	0	6	2
Sound system	0	13	*	1	0	*	*	0	4	2
Computer/ mobile phone	0	6	*	3	4	*	*	2	0	2
Furniture	0	0	*	0	5	*	*	0	0	0
Other Household Item	0	0	*	0	0	*	*	0	4	0
Tools/Equipment	16	34	*	27	4	*	*	5	13	16
Vehicle accessory	16	28	*	0	0	*	*	0	2	3
Vehicle	100	0	*	2	3	*	*	0	0	3
Cigarettes/ tobacco	0	0	*	21	8	*	*	5	0	10
Retail/manuf. stock	0	16	*	28	11	*	*	71	11	39
Ticket/voucher	0	0	*	1	3	*	*	5	0	2
Keys	28	4	*	0	0	*	*	1	0	1
Safe/Cash register	0	0	*	9	12	*	*	2	2	5
Other	0	0	*	6	3	*	*	2	4	4
Weighted N cases	945	2,328	171	13,548	1,098	0	527	12,994	4,519	36,129

Cases weighted to total crimes in 1995. * indicates too few cases to provide breakdown. Fraud is not included in this table. Columns need not add to 100 per cent since all types of property stolen in an incident are included in the table.

There is some difference between the aggravated and non-aggravated theft from the person in terms of what is stolen. Aggravated theft is more likely to involve personal accessories such as watches, personal electronic equipment or clothing (33 per cent compared to 23 per cent) and jewellery (15 per cent compared to 5 per cent) — items which would be difficult to take from someone without an element of aggravation.

Overall, jewellery is not one of the most frequently targeted types of property, but it is stolen about as often as cash in residential burglary (37 per cent). From the thief's perspective, it has a high value-to-weight ratio, although its profitable disposal would require a reasonably sophisticated network of contacts.

In many cases of vehicle theft, something else is stolen as well as the vehicle. These items are most often personal accessories, vehicle accessories and tools or equipment. Cash is stolen in 7 per cent of vehicle thefts. It is most likely that these are incidental to the main motivation for the theft — they just happened to be in the car or van at the time it was stolen.

In the case of theft from a vehicle, where the victim is an individual, vehicle accessories, such as a car radio or stereo, are stolen most frequently (40 per cent); while personal accessories are stolen in over one-quarter of the instances, and tools or equipment are taken in 17 per cent. Where the victim is an institution, the most common items stolen from a vehicle are tools or equipment (34 per cent), vehicle accessories (28 per cent), and retail or manufacturing stock (16 per cent).

Personal accessories also emerge as items that are stolen in a significant number of residential burglaries (29 per cent), while tools or equipment are taken in 27 per cent of institutional burglaries. Cigarettes or tobacco are stolen in one-fifth of institutional burglaries, and other retail or manufacturing stock is stolen in 28 per cent.

According to Felson (1998, pp. 36–37):

> . . . much can be learned by asking not only what gets stolen but also where it ends up. A property offender who takes possession of something besides cash can keep it, trade it, or sell it. If the offender keeps it, the range of goods is very limited (for example, clothes that fit). If he or she trades with friends or acquaintances, there are still few customers. Often the best choice is to find someone to receive the stolen goods and resell them. In the meantime, the criminal has to stash the stolen goods somewhere to avoid getting caught.

It is easy to see, then, why cash is the most frequently stolen type of property since it avoids the additional risk of storing and re-selling that accompany other types of goods.

If the goods are to be resold, second-hand shops, pawn shops, or selling through newspaper "small ads" or, in the Irish context, "Car Boot Sales" or the growing number of trade magazines are possible options. As Felson puts it: "Knowingly, unknowingly, or half-knowingly, these establishments provide an easy outlet for the sale of stolen goods, even if mixed in with many goods that are totally legitimate" (1998, pp. 36–37). The theft of property other than cash, then, has a "ripple effect" that extends well beyond the incident itself. Outlets where second-hand goods can be resold, and a public willing to buy them, are important elements of the opportunity structure of theft.

Damage to Property

Apart from vandalism, where damage to premises or other property defines the nature of the crime, incidental damage may also occur in the case of other crimes, particularly burglary. Table 2.16 shows whether any property was damaged, apart from any property stolen during an incident. All types of damage are counted in the table, so the percentages do not add to 100. In just under half of the crimes, exclusive of fraud, some property damage occurred.

Table 2.16: Whether Property Damaged (other than property stolen) by Crime Type (column percentages)

	Theft from Vehicle	Bur- glary	Aggravated Burglary	Vandal- ism	Others	Total
Vehicle damaged	89	1	0	43	3	20
Premises damaged	0	58	25	53	4	22
Pers. Accessories	0	2	1	0	3	2
Furniture/ equipment	0	7	2	2	0	2
Other property	1	7	9	12	3	5
Nothing damaged	11	38	65	0	88	53
Weighted N cases	*18,838*	*30,435*	*1,477*	*10,199*	*52,859*	*113,808*

Cases weighted to total crimes in 1995. Fraud is not included in this table. Since more than one type of damage may have occurred, percentages need not sum to 100.

Table 2.17: Nature of Damage to Premises by Crime Type (column percentages)

	Burglary	Aggravated Burglary	Vandalism	Others	Total
Ransacked	26	32	10	0	20
Graffiti	0	0	13	0	3
Broken windows/doors	83	80	75	85	81
Damaged fences	4	0	6	0	4
Damaged garden furniture etc.	2	0	8	0	3
Other	27	8	20	15	24
Weighted N cases	*14,476*	*263*	*5,322*	*1,481*	*21,541*

Cases weighted to total crimes in 1995. Since more than one type of damage may have occurred, percentages need not sum to 100.

In the case of theft from a vehicle, it is most often the vehicle that is damaged in some way — usually broken door locks or windows. Some damage — usually to the doors and windows of premises or ransacking the premises (see Table 2.17) — is a feature of over three-fifths of the burglaries, but is less common in the case of aggravated burglary. In cases of vandalism, the damage is to premises in about half of the cases and to a vehicle in 43 per cent of cases. As with burglary, the premises damage most often takes the form of broken windows or doors (Table 2.17).

Security Measures and Premises Crime

Where the crime took place at a particular premises (burglary, vandalism to premises, or other theft from the vicinity of premises) we asked the respondents what type of security measures had been in place at the time of the incident, and whether any security measures had been added since that time. While the measures clearly did not prevent the crime in this instance, we cannot comment on the effectiveness of these security measures without knowing their distribution in the non-victim population. However, it is instructive to look at how the security measures differed by type of crime, and at the changes, if any, made by the victims since the incident.

Table 2.18 shows that over 90 per cent of institutional victims of such "premises crime" had some form of special security measure designed to prevent crime, while nearly three-quarters of individual victims had some such measures in place. The most common security measures taken by individuals prior to the incident were reinforced door locks (44 per cent) and window locks (50 per cent). A further 23 per cent had a security chain on the door. Thirteen per cent had an "ordinary" alarm — one that was not monitored or linked to the Gardaí, while one in 20 had a monitored alarm or one linked to the Gardaí. Generally, victims of vandalism tended to be more likely than victims of burglary or aggravated burglary to have an alarm, reinforced door locks, window locks, or a wall or fence around the property. Victims of aggravated burglary were slightly less likely to have had reinforced door locks or window locks than the other victims of premises crimes, but a higher proportion (about one-fifth) had window grilles and shutters.

Table 2.18: Type of Security on Premises at Time of Incident, and Added or Improved Since the Incident by Crime and Victim Type (column percentages within victim type)

	At Time of Incident				Added/Improved Since Incident			
	Burg-lary	Agg. Burg-lary	Van-dalism	Total	Burg-lary	Agg. Burg-lary	Van-dalism	Total
Individual								
Alarm linked to Gardaí	0	3	7	1	3	3	3	3
Monitored alarm	3	3	0	4	5	9	8	5
Other alarm	10	21	23	13	26	9	11	22
Reinforced door locks	40	37	57	44	37	3	25	34
Window locks	51	34	58	50	26	0	3	23
Window grilles/shutters	3	21	16	4	0	12	11	1
Security chain on door	24	16	15	23	5	13	11	6
Automatic lights	1	0	7	2	8	0	11	8
Dog	0	3	0	0	6	3	0	6
Wall or fence	6	12	20	10	0	9	19	2
Caretaker/guard	0	0	7	1	0	0	0	0
Security camera	1	0	0	1	0	0	0	0
Other	2	9	0	2	0	0	0	0
None of these	28	31	18	28	31	63	41	36
Weighted N Cases	16,564	368	1,729	20,658	16,564	368	1,729	20,658

Table 2.18 (continued)

	At Time of Incident				Added/Improved Since Incident			
	Burg-lary	*Agg. Burg-lary*	*Van-dalism*	*Total*	*Burg-lary*	*Agg. Burg-lary*	*Van-dalism*	*Total*
Institution								
Alarm linked to Gardaí	10	61	36	18	11	16	9	11
Monitored alarm	20	25	18	20	3	5	8	4
Other alarm	20	34	22	21	8	10	6	8
Reinforced door locks	47	64	67	52	30	13	8	24
Window locks	40	51	53	43	15	7	20	15
Window grilles/shutters	40	71	20	38	7	4	15	8
Security chain on door	11	10	0	9	2	0	8	3
Automatic lights	0	15	27	6	16	4	12	14
Dog	0	3	0	0	0	1	0	0
Wall or fence	16	3	12	15	7	1	5	7
Caretaker/guard	13	16	38	18	3	6	4	4
Security camera	0	1	0	0	2	7	0	2
Other	1	3	0	1	0	0	0	0
None of these	7	3	14	8	38	56	43	40
Weighted N Cases	*13,362*	*1,098*	*3,450*	*18,108*	*13,362*	*1,098*	*3,450*	*18,108*

Note: Cases weighted to total crimes in 1995. Includes only cases where crime took place in or around premises. Total figure includes Other Theft from vicinity of premises. Since more than one type of security measure could have been present (or added), percentages need not sum to 100.

Reinforced door locks (52 per cent) and window locks (43 per cent) were also the most common precautions taken prior to the incident by institutions. They were much more likely than the individual victims to be protected by window grilles or shutters (38 per cent), and by alarms: 47 percent had at least one type of alarm,

18 per cent had an alarm linked to the Gardaí, 20 per cent had another monitored alarm (such as Telecom Éireann's "Phonewatch"), and 21 per cent had a non-monitored alarm. Nearly one in five were protected by a caretaker or security guard.

Generally, the institutions that had been targeted in an aggravated burglary had already been protected to a greater extent than the other institutional victims of premises crime: 61 per cent had an alarm linked to the Gardaí, 64 per cent had reinforced door locks, and 71 per cent had window grilles or shutters. Since most aggravated burglaries of institutions took place during the day when the business or organisation was open, however, the door locks and window shutters would not have been in place.

More than three-fifths of the victims of premises crime had added some form of security or improved their security measures following the incident (Table 2.18). The individual victims were most likely to add or improve reinforced door locks (34 per cent), window locks (23 percent) or an ordinary alarm (22 per cent). Individual victims of aggravated burglary were more likely than other victims to add window grilles or shutters (12 per cent), a security chain on the door (13 per cent) or a monitored alarm (9 per cent).

Institutional victims of premises crime who increased their level of protection were also likely to add or improve reinforced door locks (24 per cent) or window locks (15 per cent). They were more likely to add an alarm linked to the Gardaí (11 per cent) than an ordinary alarm (8 per cent). Fourteen per cent of the institutional victims added automatic lighting as a deterrent.

The QNHS crime module contained a question to all households, whether crime victims or not, on the forms of extra security measures they had in place. Among the victims of crimes, it was not possible to say whether these had been in place at the time of the crime or had been added since the incident. As such, the figures provide an indication of the distribution of various forms of protection across households in 1997/98. In general, households in 1998 were slightly more likely to have devices such as alarms and sensor lights than the sample of victims of recorded crime in 1994/95. About one-quarter of the households were protected by an alarm in the 1998 survey, and 29 per cent had a sensor light (Central Statistics Office, 1999a, Table 2). Given the high level of consciousness of crime in recent years, and the marketing and availability of alarms and other security measures, however, it is likely that at least part of the difference is explained by the difference in the reference period.

Table 2.19: Type of Security on Premises at Time of Burglary, Aggravated Burglary or Vandalism Incident by Region and Victim Type (column percentages within victim type)

	Dublin	Elsewhere	Total
Individual			
Alarm	26	2	15
Door/window locks/shutters	83	56	71
Other security measures	14	11	13
None of these	17	41	28
Weighted N Cases	*11,356*	*9,302*	*20,658*
Institution			
Alarm	55	40	47
Door/window locks/shutters	90	65	76
Other security measures	26	32	29
None of these	0	14	8
Weighted N Cases	*8,098*	*10,009*	*18,108*

Note: Includes only cases where crime took place in or around premises. Since more than one type of security measure could have been added, percentages need not sum to 100.

Table 2.19 examines the broad categories of security measure taken at the time of the incident by victims of premises crimes in

Dublin and elsewhere in the country. Individual victims living in the Dublin area clearly had more protective measures in place at the time of the crime than those living elsewhere. For instance, 83 per cent had some form of entry protection (reinforced door locks, window locks, or window grilles/shutters) compared to 56 per cent of the victims living elsewhere, and 26 per cent had some type of alarm installed, compared to 2 per cent elsewhere. The difference is also apparent for institutional victims: those in Dublin were much more likely to have some form of special entry-protection (90 per cent compared to 65 per cent), and also more likely to have an alarm (55 per cent compared to 40 per cent).

Table 2.20 looks at vehicle protection for individual victims of vehicle crimes. Two-thirds of the vehicles had some form of protection (most often a steering lock) at the time of the incident. Stolen vehicles were less likely (59 per cent) to have some form of protection than vehicles from which property was taken (74 per cent). Twenty-nine percent of the latter were protected by an alarm at the time of the incident, compared to only 11 per cent of the stolen vehicles.

Table 2.20: Type of Vehicle Protection at Time of Incident, and Added/Improved Since Then for Individual Victims of Vehicle Crime (column percentages)

	At Time of Incident			Added/Improved Since Incident		
	Theft of Vehicle	*Theft from Vehicle*	*Total*	*Theft of Vehicle*	*Theft from Vehicle*	*Total*
Alarm	11	29	21	28	16	21
Steering Lock	55	61	59	28	7	16
Reg. Etched on Window	9	17	14	5	2	3
Other	10	12	11	23	4	12
None of these	41	26	32	37	66	53
Weighted N cases	12,329	16,510	28,838	11,040	15,274	26,314

Note: Since more than one type of security measure could have been present or added, percentages need not sum to 100.

The second panel of the table shows the percentage of cases where individual victims of vehicle crime added or improved the vehicle protection since the crime. Improvements in protection appear to have been made to a greater extent where they were initially lacking: more security measures were adopted or improved in the case of stolen vehicles than in the case of theft from a vehicle. Nearly two-thirds of vehicle thefts led to added or improved security measures, compared to one-third of thefts from a vehicle. Alarms were the device most often added or improved, although incidents of vehicle theft resulted just as often in the addition (or improvement) of a steering lock.

The presence of security measures at the time of the incident may reflect earlier experiences of victimisation. In the course of the survey we asked respondents whether they had experienced any other incidents, apart from the one which formed the basis of the bulk of the interview, during a three-year period from mid-1993 to mid-1996. Since we cannot be sure that these other incidents pre-dated the target incident (which took place between November 1994 and October 1995), the figures in Table 2.21 are suggestive only. We can at least identify those who had not been victims of another burglary or vehicle theft in the three-year period, and repeat victimisation may be an indicator of location in a high-crime area.

Table 2.21 shows that those individual victims experiencing another burglary in the three-year period were more likely to be protected by some form of entry security, or other security measures, but that they were not more likely to be protected by an alarm at the time of the target incident. Those institutions which experienced another burglary were more likely to have both types of alarm system (monitored and non-monitored) and more likely to have entry security than institutions which had not been burgled on another occasion.

Table 2.21: Type of Security on Premises by Whether Victim Experienced Another Burglary in the Three-year Period and Victim Type (column percentages within victim type)

	Whether Another Burglary		
	No other burglary	*Another burglary*	*Total*
Individual			
Garda/other monitored alarm	5	3	5
Other alarm	14	7	13
Door/window locks/shutters	69	79	71
Other security measures	8	30	13
None of these	31	15	28
Weighted N Cases	*16,377*	*4,281*	*20,658*
Institution			
Garda/other monitored alarm	23	33	31
Other alarm	12	24	21
Door/window locks/shutters	64	80	76
Other security measures	28	30	29
None of these	25	2	8
Weighted N Cases	*4,407*	*13,701*	*18,108*

Note: Includes only cases where crime took place in or around premises. Since more than one type of security measure could have been added, percentages need not sum to 100.

Table 2.22 looks at the presence of vehicle security at the time of the target incident according to whether the individual victim had a vehicle stolen or something stolen from a vehicle on another occasion in the three-year period. The table includes those who were victims of theft of vehicle and theft from a vehicle in the target period.

Table 2.22: Type of Vehicle Protection at Time of Target Incident by Whether Individual Experienced Another Vehicle Crime in the Three-year Period (individual victims only, column percentages)

	Experienced Another Theft of Vehicle		Experienced Another Theft From Vehicle		Total
	No	*Yes*	*No*	*Yes*	
Alarm	20	34	18	36	21
Steering Lock	57	75	56	68	59
Reg. Etched on Window	15	0	14	14	14
Other	10	18	9	17	11
None of these	34	14	36	16	32
Weighted N cases	*25,588*	*3,251*	*23,219*	*5,619*	*28,838*

Note: Since more than one type of security measure could have been added, percentages need not sum to 100.

Those victims of vehicle crime in the target period who had experienced another incident of this type in the three-year period were twice as likely to have vehicle security measures in place at the time of the target incident. Overall, taken together with the results in Tables 2.18 and 2.20 on security measures added since the incident, the findings in Tables 2.21 and 2.22 suggest that a good deal of the variation in security measures taken are likely to be a response to previous criminal victimisation.

Fraud

Most of the tables in this chapter have not included fraud. This crime differs from the others in being less tied to time and place, in being almost invariably directed against businesses, and in involving cash (or the use of cheques or credit cards to obtain cash) rather than other types of property. In addition, many cases of fraud are handled by regulatory agencies — such as the Revenue Commissioners or the Department of Social, Community and Family Affairs — without being reported to the Gardaí. Moreover, as we will see in the next chapter, fraud is a category of crime with a particularly low reporting rate: businesses often prefer to handle the problem themselves rather than involve the Gardaí.

Table 2.23: Nature of Recorded Fraud

	Column per cent
Cashed cheque made out to someone else	21
Lodged cash/cheques in own account	6
Forged accounts	2
Obtained cash under false pretences	18
Used stolen cheque/credit cards	38
Used forged bank notes	14
Absconded without paying bills	3
Made false claim	6
Other fraud	10
Weighted N cases	*3,758*

Cases weighted to total crimes in 1995. Since up to three types of fraud were coded, percentages need not add to 100.

Table 2.23 provides a breakdown of recorded incidents of fraud in terms of the type of incident that occurred. High-profile cases involving embezzlement of large sums of money are not the stuff of the fraud making up the bulk of the crime statistics in that category. Most instances of fraud involve the use of stolen cheques or credit cards (38 per cent) or cashing a cheque made out to someone else (21 per cent). This suggests that the perpetrators have close links to (if they are not the same person as) those involved in theft of these items. Obtaining cash under false pretences, the next most common category, suggests a different type of criminal activity, involving deception in order to obtain cash or property.

The use of forged bank notes account for one in seven cases of fraud. This activity is indicative of contacts in an extremely specialist field of crime.

Summary

We have seen in this chapter that about one-third of recorded crime is directed at businesses or other institutions, while the remaining two-thirds target private individuals or households. Crime tends to be more concentrated in urban areas, particularly in the Dublin region. The "Dublin concentration" was particularly marked for certain categories of violent crime involving theft: over 80 per cent of aggravated burglary against institutions and of aggravated theft from the person took place in Dublin city or county. Theft from the person and theft from a vehicle were also particularly concentrated in Dublin.

On the other hand, recorded cases of assault and vandalism did not seem to be over-represented in Dublin relative to the population of this region. This finding contrasted with the higher risk of crime generally, including assault and vandalism, identified in the QNHS crime module for individuals and households. The difference between the QNHS results and those for recorded crime is probably due to the fact that non-indictable incidents in these two categories do not appear in the Garda records unless proceedings are taken. Proceedings may be taken less often in Dublin if, for instance, the offender is less likely to be identified.

Crime is not generally something that happens to people when they are "away from home": almost three-quarters of incidents occur in what individual victims consider to be their "own area", with more than half occurring at, or near, the home. Nearly nine out of ten of all crimes against institutional targets, apart from theft from a vehicle, take place on the premises of the organisation.

The distribution of criminal incidents between day and night was fairly uniform. Overall, for incidents targeted against individuals, nearly three-fifths took place by night and about two-fifths by day, while the division between day and night was about even for those targeted at institutions. Some crimes are clearly daytime incidents, particularly those associated with businesses and their customers: this accounts for a sizeable proportion of other theft, aggravated burglary, aggravated and non-aggravated theft from the person, and, to a lesser extent, theft from a vehicle. On the other hand, assault, vandalism, non-domestic burglary and vehicle thefts are more likely to take place at night. About half of domestic burglaries take place during the day, particularly on weekdays when the home is most likely to be empty.

Half of the incidents against individuals and two-thirds of the incidents against institutions occurred when the victim was not present. The proportions are highest for vehicle crime, burglary, and vandalism.

The image of assault as involving a lone victim in a situation with nobody else around apart from the offender is not supported by the evidence. Only 17 per cent of assault victims were alone with the offender, and half of the assault victims were accompanied by someone they knew (apart from the offender) at the time. As noted earlier, this may be an artefact of the reporting and recording process: witnessed assaults may be more likely to be reported to the police, and, once reported, to be accepted as constituting a criminal incident. Aggravated burglary against individual targets and aggravated theft from the person are more likely to involve a lone victim, however.

From the victim's perspective, one incident in six involves some element of assault or threat, with the proportion being similar for crimes against individuals and against institutions. This most often takes the form of being pushed, dragged, kicked or punched. The threat or use of a weapon is most common in aggravated burglary (nearly three-quarters of the cases) and occurs in nearly one-third of the incidents of aggravated theft from the person, and nearly a quarter of assault cases. The weapon is usually a "blunt instrument" in assault cases, and either a knife or a gun in aggravated burglaries. The use of a syringe to assault or threaten the victim occurs in about one in eight cases of aggravated theft from the person and aggravated burglary.

Property is stolen in over four-fifths of recorded criminal incidents across the categories covered in this study. Cash is the most frequently stolen type of property. Over one-quarter of incidents directed against individuals and nearly one-third of those directed against institutions involve the theft of cash. The figure is over three-quarters for personal theft, and aggravated burglary of institutions; nearly two-thirds in the case of domestic aggravated burglary; almost half for burglary of institutions; and over one-third for domestic burglary. Personal accessories, vehicles, tools or equipment, and retail or manufacturing stock are among the kinds of property taken in over ten per cent of all criminal incidents. Jewellery is stolen in over one-third of domestic burglaries, although it is taken much less frequently in other forms of theft. The most common forms of fraud — the use of stolen cheques or credit cards and cashing a cheque made out to someone else — are indicative of links to the theft where these items were originally stolen. Obtaining cash under false pretences and the use of forged banknotes, each accounting for over one in seven incidents of fraud, would seem to suggest criminal activity of a different, and perhaps more "specialist" nature.

Nearly nine out of ten institutional victims and nearly three-quarters of the individual victims of premises crimes (burglary, aggravated burglary, vandalism of premises, and theft from the vicinity of the premises) had some form of security measure in place at the time of the incident. These were usually reinforced door locks, window locks, and — in the case of institutions — alarms. The Dublin crime victims, in response to the greater risks they face, had already been taking greater security precautions at the time of the incident. Over half of the victims of premises crime had added or improved their security measures following the incident. In the case of vehicle crime directed against individuals, two-thirds of the vehicles had some form of protection (most often a steering lock) at the time of the incident. Stolen vehicles were less likely to have some form of protection than vehicles from which property was taken. We cannot comment on the effectiveness of security measures without knowing how they are distributed in the non-victim population. In addition, security measures are most likely to be put in place where the risk is highest: the proportion of victims with some security measure in place was higher in Dublin, and among those who had experienced another burglary in the three-year period from mid-1993 to mid-1996.

In this chapter, we have focused on criminal incidents and the unit of analysis was the incident itself. In the next chapter, we shift the focus to victims of crime. When the unit of analysis is the victim, we adopt a slightly different weighting system to take account of the fact that a given victim may have reported several incidents of crime in a year. As we shall see early in the chapter, because some businesses or organisations are targeted frequently, the proportion of *victims* of crime that are institutions is smaller than the proportion of *incidents* of crime directed at institutions.

Chapter 3

Characteristics of Crime Victims and Repeat Victimisation

In this chapter we shift the focus from the crime itself to the crime victim. The term "crime victim" typically brings to mind an individual who has been robbed or assaulted. Because of the connotations of the word "victim", it also conjures up images of those generally regarded as the more physically vulnerable members of society: particularly women, the elderly or those living in "dangerous areas". However, as we shall see in this chapter, a significant proportion of all recorded crime is committed against businesses or other organisations. And when it comes to recorded cases of assault, young men rather than women or the elderly are more likely to be the victims.

The chapter has two main parts. The first part of the chapter examines the characteristics of crime victims. We begin by asking what proportion of crime victims are businesses or other organisations rather than individuals or private households. We examine the age group, sex, economic status, social class and household type of individual victims; and the type and size of organisation where the victim is a business/institution. In the case of private households or individuals, we will compare the profile of crime victims to that of a national sample from the *Living in Ireland Survey* (Callan et al., 1996) or the microdata from the 1995 Labour Force Survey to ask whether crime victims are a representative cross-section of the Irish population generally, or whether particular groups are more at risk.

The second part of the chapter examines the victims' experiences of other criminal incidents — apart from the target incident on the basis of which they were selected into the sample — over the three-year period from mid-1993 to mid-1996. These incidents may have happened to the victim himself or herself, or to another member of their household. This allows us to explore the issue of repeat victimisation: the extent to which those reporting crime to the Gardaí, or members of their households, have been victims of other crimes in a given period. We are also able to examine the reporting rates for any other crimes they experienced.

In order to provide details on the victims of crime, the tables in this chapter are weighted by the "victim weights" described in Chapter 1. This means that an individual or institution is not double-counted in the totals, even though they may have been the victims of more than one incident in the target period. In addition, since victims may have reported crimes in more than one category, the number of cases in the total column in the tables is less than the sum of totals of the other columns.

It is worth noting that in comparing the *relative risk* of certain groups in the population, the *absolute risk* of victimisation must also be kept in mind. Some crime categories, such as aggravated burglary and aggravated theft from the person, as we shall see, disproportionately affect certain groups. However, the absolute risk of being a victim of violent crime is low overall, since the total number of incidents is low.

Individual and Institutional Victims of Crime

In the previous chapter we saw that one-third of the criminal incidents were directed against businesses or other organisations. Since institutions are more likely than individuals to be victimised several times in a given period — particularly when it comes to crimes such as shoplifting — they will account for less than one-third of all of those victimised in that period. This can be seen in Table 3.1, which shows the proportion of victims of each crime type who are individuals or private households, on the one hand, or institutions, on the other. In a small number of cases, it can be difficult to draw the distinction, such as where the individual is self-employed and the premises or vehicle is used for business and domestic purposes. These cases are shown in the third row of Table 3.1.

Table 3.1: Whether Victim is Individual/Private Household or Institution by Crime Type (column percentages)

	Theft of Vehicle	Theft from Vehicle	Fraud etc.	Ass-ault	Burg-lary	Agg. Burg-lary	Theft from Person	Agg. Theft from Person	Other Theft	Van-dal-ism	Total
Individual	89	90	6	98	65	27	100	91	62	56	79
Institution	7	10	91	2	34	70	0	8	38	39	20
Both	4	0	2	0	2	3	0	1	0	5	1
Total (N cases)	13,301	17,142	2,785	6,590	24,739	1,222	3,032	6,489	16,655	8,821	74,564

Overall, roughly one-fifth of victims of recorded crime are institutions, while the remaining four-fifths are individuals or households. In the case of crimes involving vehicles (theft of a vehicle or of property from a vehicle), as well as assault, and theft from the person (both aggravated and non-aggravated) the victims are usually individuals or private households. Fraud is predominantly a crime against businesses or other organisations, and victims of aggravated burglary are over twice as likely to be institutions as individuals or private households. Other theft, burglary (without violence) and vandalism are crimes where most victims are individuals or households, but over one-third of the victims are institutions.

Characteristics of Victims: Individual or Private Households

At this point we examine the characteristics of the non-institutional victims of crime. In the following tables, the characteristics of crime victims are compared to the characteristics of the national population of adults age 15 and over, using microdata from the *Labour Force Survey 1995* (LFS) or the *Living in Ireland Survey 1995*. Since the number of cases in several of the crime categories is very small (notably aggravated burglary of domestic targets), statistical tests are conducted to check whether the distribution of crime victims differs significantly from the overall population distribution in terms of characteristics such as age group and social class. Whether a difference is statistically significant depends partly on the size of the observed difference, and partly on the sample size.

It is worth noting that any conclusions about the distribution of "risk" that are drawn here are based on *recorded* crime only. If there are differences by age group, sex or social class in the propensity to report crime, or if Garda recording of reported crime varies by these characteristics of the victims, then the "true" distribution of risk of victimisation is likely to be distorted. For instance, the QNHS crime and victimisation module found that those under age 25 are less likely than older adults to report crime to the Gardaí. This means that the recorded crime statistics will tend to understate the victimisation risk of younger adults.

Age and Sex of Individual Victims

Table 3.2 shows the sex and age distribution of the person reporting the crime. Note that in the case of crimes like burglary or vehicle theft, other members of that person's household may be equally affected, and the sex of the victim is the sex of the person reporting the crime. In couple households, this is more likely to be the husband or male partner: in 73 percent of burglaries or aggravated burglaries involving couple households, the crime was reported by the male.

Table 3.2: Sex and Age Group of Individual Crime Victim by Crime Type (column percentages)

	Theft of Vehicle	Theft from Vehicle	Assault	Burglary	Agg. Burglary	Theft from person	Agg. Theft from person	Other Theft	Vandalism	Total	% of Pop Age 15+
Male											
Under 35	9*	22	49*	15	3*	6*	26	17	29	20	21%
35–49	26*	28*	28*	25*	6	3*	3*	18	32*	23*	13%
50–64	21*	16	3*	9	8	1*	1*	11	6	12*	9%
65 and over	7	4	0*	11	21*	1	1*	5	0	6	6%
All Males	64*	71*	81*	59	39*	12*	30*	52	67*	61*	49%
Female											
Under 35	8*	12*	11*	12*	13	42*	22	20	11*	13*	21%
35–49	18	15	7*	13	11	26*	21	18	19	16*	13%
50–64	10	2*	1*	8	9	10	20*	5	2	7	8%
65 and over	0*	0*	0*	8	28*	10	6	5	1	3*	8%
All Females	36*	29*	19*	41	61	88*	70*	48	33*	39*	51%
All											
Under 35	17*	34	60*	27*	16*	49	48	37	40	33*	42%
35–49	44*	44*	35	38*	17	29	25	36	51*	39*	26%
50-64	32*	18	5*	16	17	11	21	16	8	19	17%
65 and over	7*	5*	0*	19	50*	11	7	11	1*	9*	14%
Unweighted N	76	82	89	71	22	84	91	59	49	629	108,830
Weighted N Cases	12,373	15,247	6,326	16,205	366	2,993	5,994	10,301	5,377	58,964	100%

Notes: Number of sample cases is too small for breakdowns for individual victims of Fraud. Estimates in final column from Labour Force Survey, 1995, microdata. * indicates proportion for sample of crime victims differs significantly (p<.05, two tailed, using large sample z test, or where sample too small, Chi-Square test) from the population distribution.

The final column of Table 3.2 shows the percentage of individuals age 15 and over in each age group by sex, estimated from the microdata of the 1995 Labour Force Survey. These figures allow us to assess the distribution of crime victims by age and sex relative to the representation of each group in the population. If the risk of being a victim of a specific crime were equally distributed across the population, we would see the same distribution in the column for that crime as in the final column of the table.

Overall, three-fifths of the victims of recorded crime are male, while two-fifths are female. In several categories — vehicle crimes, assault, burglary and vandalism — the person reporting the crime is more likely to be male than female. The predominance of male victims is particularly marked in the case of assault, where 81 per cent of the victims are male. On the other hand, there are more female than male victims of recorded theft from the person (both aggravated and non-aggravated), and aggravated burglary. Victims of other theft are more evenly divided between males and females.

The general finding of higher victimisation risk for men than for women, and the pattern within crime category, conforms to the international pattern (e.g. van Dijk et al., 1991). Van Dijk et al. found that risks among women were more similar to those of men in countries such as the United States, which had higher female employment levels.

The QNHS crime and victimisation module, which included unreported and unrecorded crimes, found a similar pattern of risk by gender (Central Statistics Office, 1999a, Table 8). The risk of assault was 2.3 times greater for males than for females. Females faced a slightly higher (1.2 times) risk than males of theft with violence, and the female risk of theft without violence was a good deal higher (1.7 times) than that faced by males (Central Statistics Office, 1999a). In general, the gap between male and female victimisation rates was smaller in the QNHS survey, however, suggesting that some of the observed differences by gender in the recorded statistics may be driven by differences in reporting patterns, or in the recording or classification of crimes based on the gender of the victim.

A higher level of risk for women from personal theft was also found in the Dublin Crime Survey (O'Connell and Whelan, 1994). The authors found that Dublin women had a higher risk of victimisation for personal crime (theft from the person, assault and mugging) than men. O'Connell and Whelan explain the higher risk faced by women in terms of their greater "street vulnerability": they are generally physically weaker than men, and more often carry cash and other valuables in handbags which are more easily stolen than a wallet in an inside pocket (1994, p. 100). It is clear from the present data and from the QNHS results, however, that the pattern is very different for assault, on the one hand, and contact theft (aggravated and non-aggravated theft from the person), on the other.

There are clear differences in the age profiles of victims according to crime type. Victims of vehicle crime and non-aggravated burglary are concentrated in the 35 to 64 age group. This undoubtedly reflects rates of vehicle ownership and household headship among these groups, in contrast to those under age 35. The QNHS crime victimisation results, which controlled for vehicle ownership, found a higher risk of both vehicle theft and theft from a vehicle in households where the reference person was under age 25 (Central Statistics Office 1999, Table 1). The QNHS figures also showed a higher risk of household burglary for young adult households, however,[1] suggesting that the recorded figures may partly reflect differences by age in the reporting rates or recording of crime.

Recorded assault is more likely to affect the younger age groups, with 60 per cent of the assault victims under age 35. We saw in Chapter 2 that most incidents of assault occur in public places or in the vicinity of pubs and night-clubs, where younger adults probably spend more time than older adults. The QNHS

---

[1] In households where the reference person was under 25, 4.8 per cent were burgled, compared to 3.4 per cent overall.

results confirm the higher risk of assault faced by young adults (Central Statistics Office, 1999a, Table 8).

At the other end of the age distribution, those over age 65 are at a higher risk of aggravated burglary. Note that the number of cases of domestic aggravated burglary in the sample is small. This means that there is a wide margin of error (in the region of ±20 per cent) around the 50 per cent figure in Table 3.2 for the percentage of aggravated burglaries against individuals over age 65. Moreover, since the number of aggravated burglaries is low, accounting for only about 0.5 per cent of crimes against individual targets, the overall risk of crime victimisation for the elderly remains lower than for other age groups. The lower risk of criminal victimisation overall for those over age 65 conforms to general international findings (van Dijk et al. 1991), as well as to other research results for Ireland (Murphy and Whelan, 1995; Breen and Rottman, 1985; Central Statistics Office, 1999a) and for Dublin (O'Connell and Whelan, 1994).

Household Type and Size

Table 3.3 shows the household type distribution of recorded crime. The figures in the final column show the estimated (from the 1995 *Living in Ireland Survey*) national distribution of adults age 15 and over by household type. For most of the crime categories, the distribution of victims follows fairly closely the distribution of the household types for members of the adult population: the predominant household type among victims is "couple and children", reflecting the fact that most of the population lives in this household type. Adults living alone, however, are at a higher risk of burglary and aggravated burglary. The greater risk of burglary may well be due to the reduced level of guardianship of these residences: the dwelling may be empty for a greater proportion of the time. The association between living alone and increased risk of burglary was also noted by Breen and Rottman (1985, Table 5.3), and in the QNHS crime victimisation survey.

The increased risk of burglary associated with living alone in the QNHS results was fairly small, however: 3.5 per cent of one-person households were burgled, compared to 3.4 per cent overall (Central Statistics Office, 1999a).

Table 3.3: Household Type for Individual Victims by Crime Type (column percentages)

	Theft of Veh-icle	Theft from Veh-icle	Ass-ault	Burg-lary	Agg. Burg-lary	Theft from per-son	Agg. Theft from per-son	Other Theft	Van-dal-ism	Total	% Pop age 15+
Live alone	9	10	3*	30*	49*	10	14	12	7	14*	10%
Couple, no children	12	14	8	15	13	12	7*	10	15	12	14%
Couple & dep. children	57	51	44	38	17*	47	40	44	57	47	46%
Couple & adult children	18	12	20	7	13	17	21	15	11	14	15%
Other	3*	13	25*	10	9	15	18	19	10	13	14%
Unweighted N	*73*	*81*	*89*	*70*	*22*	*83*	*90*	*58*	*48*	*620*	*3,584*
Total (Weighted N Cases)	*12,091*	*14,968*	*6,326*	*15,926*	*366*	*2,962*	*5,930*	*10,121*	*5,235*	*57,989*	*100%*

Note: Number of sample cases is too small for breakdowns for individual victims of Fraud. Estimates in final column from *Living in Ireland Survey, 1995*. * indicates proportion for sample of crime victims differs significantly (p<.05, two tailed, using large sample z test, or where sample too small, Chi-Square test) from the population distribution.

Those living alone are under-represented as victims of assault in the recorded crime figures, while those in the "other" household type category (which includes unrelated adults sharing accom-modation) are over-represented relative to their share of the population.

The figures in Table 3.4, which shows the breakdown by household size, suggest that the risk of vehicle theft and assault are greater for individuals living in larger households, perhaps reflecting the fact that these households are more likely to own a vehicle, or more than one vehicle,[2] and to have young adults (the high-risk group for assault) living in them. The QNHS results also showed a higher risk of vehicle-related crime and vandalism among households with three or more persons (Central Statistics Office, 1999a).

Table 3.4: Household Size for Individual Victims by Crime Type (column percentages)

	Theft of Veh-icle	Theft from Veh-icle	Ass-ault	Burg-lary	Agg. Burg-lary	Theft from per-son	Agg. Theft from person	Other Theft	Van-dal-ism	Total	% Pop age 15+
1 person	9	10	3*	30*	49*	10	14	12	7	14*	10%
2 people	12	20	17	17	21	17	16	19	19	17	19%
3 people	12	20	14	12	6	14	16	17	11	16	17%
4 people	18	24	14	14	16	18	25	27	22	21	21%
5 people	11	16	26*	14	0	20	16	13	15	16	16%
6 or more	36*	12	26	12	8	21	12	12	26	18	17%
Unweighted N	*73*	*83*	*86*	*70*	*22*	*82*	*90*	*57*	*48*	*617*	*108,830*
Weighted N Cases	*12,002*	*15,441*	*6,142*	*15,998*	*366*	*2,930*	*5,941*	*10,152*	*5,235*	*58,057*	*100%*

Note: Number of sample cases is too small for breakdowns for individual victims of Fraud. Estimates in final column from Labour Force Survey, 1995, microdata. * indicates proportion for sample of crime victims differs significantly (p<.05, two tailed, using large sample z test, or where sample too small, Chi-Square test) from the population distribution.

Work Status of Individual Victims

Table 3.5 examines the work situation of the individual victim of crime. Employees are over-represented in most categories, especially theft from a vehicle, other theft, assault and vandalism. The self-employed are over-represented as victims of burglary. In

---

[2] Figures from the 1995 *Living in Ireland Survey* suggest that 42 per cent of individuals living alone have use of a car, compared to 77 per cent of households with six or more persons.

many cases, if the business is run from home, it can be difficult to separate whether the target was the self-employed person as an individual, or the business. The retired are, as we might expect from the age distribution figures discussed earlier, at higher risk than other groups of aggravated burglary. The risk of assault is higher for employees and the unemployed, and lower for the retired and those engaged on home duties. The unemployed face a lower risk of theft from the person.

Table 3.5: Work Situation of Individual Victims by Crime Type (column percentages)

	Theft of Vehicle	Theft from Vehicle	Assault	Burglary	Agg. Burglary	Theft from person	Agg. Theft from person	Other Theft	Vandalism	Total	% Pop age 15+
Employee	56*	65*	60*	39	38	56*	42	61*	60*	55*	36%
Self-employed	16	17	7	20*	18	4	6	5	15	13*	10%
Unemployed	5	2	17*	6	3	1*	12	9	5	7	7%
Education/ training	0*	0*	11	5*	0	11	17	6	2*	5*	14%
Home duties	10*	6*	4*	16	9	24	11*	5*	16	9*	23%
Retired	13	9	0*	12	28*	4	9	10	3	10	8%
Other	1	0	1	1	3	0	4	2	0	1*	3%
Unweighted N	76	83	90	72	22	85	91	59	49	633	108,830
Weighted N Cases	12,373	15,441	6,406	16,419	366	3,032	5,994	10,301	5,377	59,282	100%

Note: Number of sample cases is too small for breakdowns for individual victims of Fraud. Estimates in final column from Labour Force Survey, 1995, microdata. * indicates proportion for sample of crime victims differs significantly (p<.05, two tailed, using large sample z test, or where sample too small, Chi-Square test) from the population distribution.

Housing Tenure of Individual Victims

Table 3.6 shows the housing tenure of individual crime victims by crime type. Those who own their homes outright are at a higher risk of aggravated burglary. This reflects the relationship between age and housing tenure: older people are more likely to have paid off any mortgage on their homes. Local Authority Tenant Purchasers have a greater risk of being victims of vehicle theft or assault. Those purchasing on a private mortgage face a lower risk of assault and aggravated burglary, but an above-average risk of theft from a vehicle. Renters — both those renting from the Local Authorities and in the private sector — face a slightly lower risk of victimisation overall.

Table 3.6: Housing Tenure of Individual Victims by Crime Type (column percentages)

	Theft of Veh-icle	Theft from Veh-icle	Ass-ault	Burg-lary	Agg. Burg-lary	Theft from per-son	Agg. theft from person	Other theft	Van-dal-ism	Total	% Pop age 15+
Owner outright	39	33	35	44	70*	40	41	43	33	40	40%
L.A. Tenant purchaser	11*	8	17*	3	0	4	3	5	10	7*	5%
Mortgage Purchaser	39	50*	22*	41	9*	44	34	35	45	39	38%
Rented – L.A.	6	2	13	4	16	5	11	5	1	5*	7%
Rented other	3	2*	10	9	5	6	8	11	6	6*	8%
Rent free	1	5	2	0	0	0	2	2	5	2	1%
Other	1	0	0	0	0	1	1	0	0	0	0%
Unweighted N	74	83	86	70	22	82	90	58	49	614	108,830
Weighted N Cases	11,824	15,441	5,940	15,926	366	2,912	5,940	10,096	5,377	57,789	100%

Note: Number of sample cases is too small for breakdowns for individual victims of Fraud. Estimates in final column from Labour Force Survey, 1995, microdata. * indicates proportion for sample of crime victims differs significantly (p<.05, two tailed, using large sample z test, or where sample too small, Chi-Square test) from the population distribution.

Largest Source of Household Income for Individual Victims

In Table 3.7, we examine the largest source of household income. This differs from the results on work situation reported in Table

3.5, in that the income might be received by someone other than the person reporting the crime. Note also that households mainly dependent on social welfare could be receiving income from unemployment, old age, lone parent, or disability payments. Apart from burglary and aggravated burglary, wages are the main source of household income for half or more of all individual crime victims, mainly reflecting the fact that half of the adult population lives in households where wages are the most important income source. However, even taking account of the large number of households depending on wage income, adults in wage-dependent households are over-represented among victims of theft from a vehicle, other theft, theft from the person (including aggravated theft from the person) and vandalism.

Table 3.7: Largest Source of Household Income of Individual Victims by Crime Type (column percentages)

	Theft of Veh-icle	Theft from Veh-icle	Ass-ault	Burg-lary	Agg. Burg-lary	Theft from per-son	Agg. theft from person	Other theft	Van-dal-ism	Total	% Pop age 15+
Wages	59	62*	59	48	29*	78*	64*	64*	66*	60*	51%
Self-employment	23*	26*	14	21*	22	7	9	12	17	17*	8%
Agriculture	2	0	4	2	6	2	1	2	3	2*	6%
Private pensions	5	4	0	6	6	3	6	2	0	4	4%
Social Welfare	10*	7*	22	22	34	10*	17*	15*	11*	15*	30%
Other	1	1	1	1	3	0	3	4	3	2	1%
Unweighted N	75	83	87	70	22	84	86	57	47	617	3,584
Weighted N cases	12,305	15,441	6,213	15,926	366	3,002	5,714	10,029	5,190	58,100	100%

Note: Number of sample cases is too small for breakdowns for individual victims of Fraud. Estimates in final column from Living in Ireland Survey, 1995. * indicates proportion for sample of crime victims differs significantly (p<.05, two tailed, using large sample z test, or where sample too small, Chi-Square test) from the population distribution.

Individuals in households where the main source of income is from self-employment are at a higher risk of vehicle crime and burglary. The risk of being a crime victim for those in households where the main source of income is agriculture is somewhat lower than average, while that of households depending on private pensions is about average. It is interesting that the risk for those in households where the main source of income is social welfare (which includes social welfare pensions) is low, except in the case of aggravated burglary, where the risk is at about the average.

Table 3.8 shows the Irish Social Class category of the crime victim. Social class is based on the occupation of the individual reporting the crime if that person is at work or ever worked, or else on the occupation of the main earner in the household.[3] In general, and in common with other findings for Ireland (Murphy and Whelan, 1995; O'Connell and Whelan, 1994; Breen and Rottman, 1985) and internationally (van Dijk et al., 1991), the risk of crime is greatest for those in the higher social classes.

There is an interesting contrast between the higher and lower professional/managerial groups, however. Those in the lower professional/managerial social class are at a greater risk of burglary, vehicle theft and vandalism than their population proportions would indicate, but this is not true for the higher professional/managerial social class. We saw in Chapter 2 that burglary, vandalism and vehicle theft are most likely to take place in the person's home, or its surroundings — such as a car parked on the street near home. It may well be that residential patterns within cities are such that those in the lower professional/managerial social class live closer to potential offenders than those in the higher professional/managerial social class.

---

[3] Cases where social class is unknown — usually because the person has never worked and there is nobody else who ever worked in the household, or because the information is missing — are excluded from the table to provide figures that are comparable to those in the final column from the *Living in Ireland Survey*, 1995.

Table 3.8: Social Class of Individual Victims by Crime Type (column percentages)

	Theft of Vehicle	Theft from Vehicle	Assault	Burglary	Agg. Burglary	Theft from person	Agg. theft from person	Other theft	Vandalism	Total	% Pop age 15+
High prof./ managerial	10	19*	9	13	6	8	16*	20*	13	15*	8%
Low prof./ managerial	31*	33*	15	31*	22	23	13	25	33*	27*	15%
Other non-manual	26	14*	16	15	29	42*	26	25	20	21	23%
Skilled manual	27*	22	29*	13	19	6*	15	13	18	19	16%
Semi-skilled manual	5*	8*	14*	16	18	15	22	12*	13*	12*	23%
Unskilled manual	1*	4*	16	11	6	5*	7*	4*	3*	6*	15%
Unweighted N	67	80	80	64	22	78	85	55	45	581	3,584
Weighted N Cases	11,081	14,926	5,951	14,754	366	2,752	5,602	9,740	4,931	54,659	100%

Note: Number of sample cases is too small for breakdowns for individual victims of Fraud. Estimates in final column from Living in Ireland Survey, 1995. * indicates proportion for sample of crime victims differs significantly (p<.05, two tailed, using large sample z test, or where sample too small, Chi-Square test) from the population distribution.

The risk of assault, however, is highest for those in the skilled manual social class. The risk of being a crime victim tends to be lower for those in the semi-skilled and unskilled manual social classes, and is significantly lower for vehicle crime (perhaps reflecting rates of vehicle ownership), other theft and vandalism. Some of the observed risk pattern by social class for recorded crime may be driven by reporting differences. Later in this chapter, we will see that other incidents experienced by these victims were more frequently reported by those in the non-manual social classes.

The findings with respect to risk and social class generally conform to the international pattern. Van Dijk et al. (1991), examining criminal victimisation risk in 1988 using survey data from 14 countries, found an increased risk of victimisation among those in higher-income categories than lower-income groups. The findings differ from results reported for Britain, however, where the British Crime Survey has tended to show an increased risk of property crime for those in lower socio-economic groups (Hough and Mayhew, 1983; Mayhew, Maung and Mirrlees-Black, 1993; see also Maguire, 1982). Community-based studies of crime in Britain also point to the extent to which residents of working-class communities restrict their activities in order to avoid becoming victims (e.g. Jones et al., 1986). Again, the explanation for differences between Ireland and Britain may lie in differences by social class in the residential patterns in large towns and cities. The long-standing policy of enabling local authority tenants in Ireland to purchase their houses (Fahey and Watson, 1995) may have resulted in residential patterns in cities that are less segregated by social class in Ireland than in Britain. This could well mean that potential burglars (who tend to be drawn from the manual social classes; see review by McCullagh, 1996) in Ireland do not have as far to travel to the more lucrative middle-class residential areas.

Institutional Victims of Recorded Crime

So far in this chapter, we have focused on the characteristics of victims of reported crime who were individuals or private households. We saw at the beginning, however, that about one-fifth of the victims of reported crime were businesses or other organisations. In this section, we examine the characteristics of these institutions and look at whether they vary by the type of crime.

Since the nature of crime committed against institutions is different from that committed against individuals, we have too few cases in a number of the categories to provide separate breakdowns. There are very few cases in our sample of theft of vehicle, assault, and theft from the person where the victim is an institution. These categories are not analysed separately in the following tables, but they are included in the totals.

As in the previous section of this chapter, the weights used are the "victim weights". This means that, for instance, a particular shop is counted only once even if it experienced several incidents of shoplifting in the target reporting period. Moreover, since victims may have reported crimes in more than one category, the number of cases in the total column in the tables is less than the sum of totals of the other columns.

Table 3.9: Nature of Institution by Crime Type (column percentages)

	Theft from Vehicle	Fraud etc.	Bur- glary	Aggravated Burglary	Other Theft	Vandal- ism	Total
Manufacturing	15	2	4	0	3	6	6
Pub/Restaurant	0	13	16	5	3	14	9
Bank/Post Office	0	8	0	9	2	7	3
Shop	17	66	35	69	62	19	38
School	0	0	7	0	0	18	7
Other private sector/ business	64	8	26	13	23	22	27
Other	4	2	11	3	7	13	10
Total (Weighted N Cases)	*1,701*	*2,507*	*8,320*	*844*	*6,354*	*3,445*	*15,162*

Note: Too few cases to provide breakdown for Theft of Vehicle, Assault, and Theft from Person, but cases are included in total.

Shops are the most common of the institutional victims overall, and dominate in a number of crime categories. They account for 60 to 70 per cent of the institutional victims of fraud, other theft (which includes shoplifting) and aggravated burglary, as well as for over one-third of the victims of burglary. Private sector institutions outside the manufacturing sector are the main (64 per cent) victims of theft from a vehicle and account for 20–26 per cent of institutional victims of burglary, other theft and vandalism. Nearly one-fifth of the victims of recorded vandalism are schools.

Public houses and restaurants account for 13–16 per cent of the victims of fraud, burglary and vandalism; while manufacturing businesses constitute about one-sixth of the victims of theft from a vehicle. While hold-ups at banks and post offices are likely to be given prominent position in the news headlines, these organisations account for only one in ten of the institutional victims of reported aggravated burglary.

Table 3.10 shows the size of the institution in terms of the numbers employed in the local branch or outlet. With the exception of theft from a vehicle, the dominant size category for organisations that are victims of crime is between one and five employees. Firms or organisations of this size account for one-third or more of the institutional victims in all categories except theft from a vehicle, and even in this latter category they account for one-quarter of victims.

Table 3.10: Size of Institution by Crime Type (column percentages)

	Theft from Vehicle	Fraud etc.	Burglary	Aggravated Burglary	Other Theft	Vandal-ism	Total
Self only	13	11	14	6	3	2	10
1–5 employees	25	35	39	50	33	44	41
6-10 employees	14	20	12	18	14	17	14
11-30 employees	15	15	18	22	30	14	19
31-50 employees	0	8	4	0	4	14	5
Over 50 employees	32	12	13	4	16	9	12
Total (Weighted N Cases)	*1,701*	*2,475*	*8,320*	*832*	*6,173*	*3,445*	*14,979*

Note: Too few cases to provide breakdown for Theft of Vehicle, Assault, and Theft from Person, but cases are included in total.

It is the larger institutions, with over 50 employees, that constitute the biggest group of victims of theft from a vehicle. Organisations with 11 to 30 employees also appear to be frequent targets in a number of categories: accounting for 30 per cent of victims of other theft and for roughly one in five institutional victims of burglary. Individuals working on their own account with no employees constitute just over one in eight victims of theft from a vehicle, and one in seven victims of non-aggravated burglary.

As noted at the beginning of this section, the figures from our sample are based on recorded crime. If businesses and organisations of different types, or different sizes, differ in their propensity to report crime, then the figures for recorded crime would not provide an accurate picture of the true distribution of criminal victimisation across organisations.

Other Incidents Experienced by the Crime Victims in a Three-year Period

So far, we have focused on one incident per crime victim: the "target" incident reported between November 1994 and October 1995, on the basis of which the victim was selected into the sample. In this section, we turn to the issue of repeat victimisation: to what extent have the victims in our sample, or members of their households, experienced other criminal incidents (apart from the target crime) in a three-year period. We also use information on these other incidents to look at variations in reporting rates by type of crime.

The literature on criminal victimisation has consistently pointed to the fact that an individual's past crime victimisation is a good predictor of his or her subsequent victimisation, often inflicted by the same offender (Farrell and Pease, 1993; Pease and Laycock, 1996; Pease, 1994, 1998). Those who have been victimised once are at greater risk of being victimised again. Pease (1994) notes that for some kinds of crimes, repeat victimisation is almost an inherent part of the nature of the incident itself — domestic violence, embezzlement (where the employer–employee relationship is a necessary condition of the offence), and many kinds of fraud, including computer and cheque fraud. Repeat victimisation is less obviously an inherent part of the crime, but very prevalent for commercial burglaries, domestic burglaries, racial attacks, and serious property crimes against schools (Pease, 1994).

The reasons for repeat victimisation comprise a combination of factors such as "target attractiveness", vulnerability, an absence of guardians, and — particularly in the case of burglary — proximity to potential offenders. The pattern of repeat victimisation in the case of burglary is distinctive, with the greatest risk in the week or so following the initial offence, and declining exponentially thereafter — a pattern which has been found to hold true for domestic (Johnson et al., 1997; Ratcliffe and McCullagh, 1998; Robinson, 1998) and for commercial burglaries (Bowers et al., 1998). This pattern is strongly suggestive of offences committed by the same offender or close associates of the original offender: we would not expect the strong exponential pattern of decline over time if different offenders were involved.

The 1998 British Crime Survey of individuals and private households found that repeat victimisation, defined as the risk of experiencing more than one incident of a particular crime in 1997, was most common for victims of domestic violence, with more than half of victims experiencing two or more incidents. The repeat victimisation rate was also high for vandalism (33 per cent) and assault by an acquaintance (28 per cent). The repeat victimisation rate was 14 per cent for burglary with entry, 6 per cent for vehicle theft, 20 per cent for theft from a vehicle, 15 per cent for bicycle theft, 12 per cent for mugging (robbery and snatch theft from the person) and 15 per cent for assault by a stranger (Mirrlees-Black, 1998, Table A5.17).

The QNHS crime and victimisation module collected information on the number of incidents in seven categories[4] experienced in a one-year period by individuals and private households in Ireland (Central Statistics Office, 1999a). Initial indications from

---

[4] The number of incidents was not asked in the case of bicycle theft.

the QNHS suggest that repeat victimisation rates in the 1997/98 reference period may be slightly higher in this country than in England and Wales for burglary with entry (17 per cent) and vehicle theft (10 per cent), and somewhat higher for theft with violence (14 per cent). The repeat victimisation rate is similar for vandalism (34 per cent), and theft from a vehicle (20 per cent). Directly comparable figures are not available for assault, since the QNHS excluded domestic assault, or for theft without violence. The QNHS found a repeat victimisation rate of 17 per cent for assault and 13 per cent for theft without violence (Central Statistics Office, 1999a).

The present survey provided an opportunity to investigate whether repeat victimisation had a similar profile among victims of recorded crime. The QNHS crime and victimisation module provides a better source of data on repeat victimisation for crimes targeting individuals and private households, because it has a larger sample size and is based on a survey of all households and individuals (not just victims of recorded crime). However, the present survey is unique in that it allows us to assess the extent of repeat victimisation of businesses and other organisations. Information was collected on other criminal incidents experienced by the respondents themselves or members of their household or organisation in the three years from mid-1993 to mid-1996. The set of questions were prefaced as follows:

> Individuals: "Now I'd like to ask you some questions about *other incidents* (apart from the crime we discussed earlier) that may have happened to you or other members of your household over the last three years in the Republic of Ireland."

> Institutions: "Now I'd like to ask you some questions about *other incidents* (apart from the crime we discussed earlier) that may have happened within this establishment (that is, on the premises, or to someone working here while on duty) over the

last three years. Please only tell us about crimes that occurred
in the Republic of Ireland."

Interviewers were briefed to exclude the target incident (the
criminal incident on the basis of which the individual or institution was selected into the sample), and to ensure that each incident was counted only once (according to its most serious aspect),
even if it had a number of elements. For example, if there was a
break-in during which property was stolen from the house, the
home was vandalised, and a bicycle was stolen from outside the
house, this was to be counted only once as a burglary with theft.
The three-year period extended from June 1993 to May 1996.

A number of points should be noted regarding this set of
questions. The first is that they include incidents directed against
other members of the household or against someone other than
the proprietor/manager of the organisation. In the case of individual victims, crimes against the person (such as assault, theft
from the person and aggravated theft from the person) as well as
crimes where the household may be considered the victim (burglary, aggravated burglary, vandalism, vehicle theft, theft from
vehicle) are recorded where they happen to *any* member of the
household, not just to the individual being interviewed. Similarly,
for institutions, a crime against an individual staff member would
be recorded once the staff member was on duty at the time. To the
extent that the respondent was not aware of crimes affecting other
members of the household, or organisation, there may be some
undercounting of incidents.

The second point to note concerns the use of a three-year recall
period. The advantage of using a three-year period, rather than a
shorter period such as a year or six months, is that it allows us to
"capture" a larger number of events when we are dealing with a
relatively rare phenomenon such as criminal victimisation. The
International Crime Victim Survey, for instance, used both a five-
year and a one-year recall period in recording criminal incidents

(Mayhew and van Dijk, 1997; van Dijk et al., 1991). However, the longer period means that the incidents recorded on the questionnaire may suffer from problems of respondent recall. These can take a number of forms. One is the issue of "telescoping", where the timing of events that occurred in the past is distorted. In the present case, this would mean that events that happened more than three years ago are remembered as having occurred more recently. The second type of recall problem is that of a "tapering off" effect in respondent recall of offences. In a review of evidence on this issue, Breen and Rottman note that recent incidents are more likely to be recalled than more distant events, and that the probability of recall appears to decline in a fairly linear fashion over time (Breen and Rottman, 1985, pp. 31–32). However, in the 1982/83 Survey, Rottman and Breen, using information on the month in which the incident occurred, did not find evidence of a "tapering off" of recall over a one-year period. Nevertheless, the three-year period used here is longer and may be more prone to respondent recall problems. On balance, respondents are probably likely to forget relatively minor incidents, and to "telescope" the more serious ones.

The third point to note concerns the counting of criminal incidents. This is particularly important in comparing the results from victim surveys to police crime statistics. Counting and classification procedures used by most police forces would count a complex incident (such as a break-in where property is stolen from the house, the window is broken, furniture damaged, and the car stolen) as one criminal event classified according to its most serious aspect (Breen and Rottman, 1985; Maguire, 1994). There is a potential in victimisation surveys to double-count or triple-count such events as burglary, vandalism and vehicle theft, for instance. This is true of surveys that present respondents with a set of items and asks whether each occurred in a given period. In the present survey, we sought to eliminate this kind of double-counting through the question wording used, and through the instructions to interviewers. The interviewers were briefed to count each incident only once and additional checks on interviewer notes were used at the coding stage to ensure that events were not double-counted.

Perhaps a more serious source of discrepancy between Garda and victimisation survey counting procedures concerns the Garda treatment of a "series" of incidents. If a person's house or car is repeatedly vandalised by the same offender(s), this may be counted as one incident. If one shoplifter steals several times from the same store in a given period, this may be counted as a single shoplifting "spree". A pattern of repeated assault on a victim by the same offender (as often happens in cases of domestic assault) is likely to be counted as one incident.

A final point concerning the present results on repeat victimisation and reporting rates concerns the nature of the sample. These are individuals who have suffered at least one criminal incident in the target period, and that incident was serious enough to them to be reported to the Gardaí. This means that they are likely to differ from the general population in at least two respects: they have experienced criminal victimisation in a one-year period, a relatively rare occurrence; and they have reported that to the Gardaí and it has been recorded in the Garda statistics on crime. Moreover, we are only able to examine reporting rates for incidents other than the target incident on which the sample was selected. The estimates of reporting rates, then, are based on a sample of individuals who are, by definition, repeat victims — although not necessarily repeat victims of the same type of crime.

The crime victim weights are used to weight the sample in the following analysis. These weights take account of the fact that victims reporting a large number of crimes in the target year were more likely to be selected into the sample (see Chapter 1 and Appendix A for details). Using these weights means that victims reporting one crime are given "equal representation" to victims reporting several crimes, and make the unit of analysis (the individual victim) more comparable to that in crime victimisation surveys.

For analysis purposes, the incidents were grouped into the categories we have used so far. The items and the corresponding categories are shown in Figure 3.1. Information was also collected on "any other criminal incident" that the individual (or their household/organisation) may have experienced, and a description of the incident was obtained. Where possible, the incident was "coded-up" into one of the ten categories. For instance, malicious damage to a car was included in the "vandalism" category. The remaining cases are too diverse (ranging from obscene telephone calls to violation of a barring order) and too small in number to analyse separately.

Figure 3.1: Classifying "Other Incidents" into Ten Categories

Individual	Category	Institution
A. Were you or any member of your household assaulted — that is, punched, kicked or pushed to the ground etc., or injured or threatened with a weapon? A1.Did this assault [any of these assaults] occur as part of a [tick one] burglary/robbery or mugging/theft from person?	*Assault, if no theft* *Aggravated Burglary, if theft and "robbery/burglary"* *Aggravated Theft from Person, if theft, and "mugging/ theft from person"*	A. Was anyone within this establishment assaulted — that is, punched, kicked or pushed to the ground etc., or injured or threatened with a weapon? A1. Did this [any of these] assault(s) occur as part of a [tick one] burglary/robbery or mugging/theft from someone in the establishment?
B. Did anyone illegally enter your home, that is, by breaking in or gain entry without your permission? B1.Was anything stolen during this [any one of these] illegal entry [entries] that occurred during the last 3 years?	*Burglary (even if nothing stolen)*	B. Did anyone illegally enter the premises, that is, by breaking in or gaining entry without permission? B2. Was anything stolen during this [any one of these] illegal entry [entries] that occurred during the last 3 years?
C. Was there evidence [e.g. broken window, door locks etc.] that someone attempted to illegally enter your home?	*Burglary*	C. Was there evidence (e.g. broken windows, door locks) that someone attempted to illegally enter the premises?
D. Was anything stolen by someone who had a right to be in your home? (e.g. salesperson, acquaintance, repairman)	*Other Theft*	D. Was anything stolen by someone who had a right to be on the premises? (e.g. employee, customer, repairman)

Figure 3.1 (continued)

Individual	Category	Institution
F. Did anyone steal (or use without permission) a car, truck, van or motorbike belonging to you or to someone in your household?	*Theft of Vehicle*	F. Did anyone steal (or use without permission) a car, truck, van or motorbike belonging to this establishment?
G. Was anything stolen from inside a car, van or truck belonging to you or someone in this household?	*Theft from Vehicle*	G. Was anything stolen from inside a car, van or truck belonging to this establishment?
H. Was any item that is kept outside — like a bicycle, garden furniture, tools, farm machinery or equipment etc. — stolen? [Exclude if already entered above]	*Other Theft*	H. Was any item that is kept outside — like tools, machinery or equipment etc. — stolen? [Exclude motor vehicles which should be entered under G]
J. Was there any other occasion when a valuable item was stolen from you or someone who lives in your household, such as in the street, a shop, on holidays in Ireland etc. [e.g. handbag snatch / pocket picked. Exclude if entered above].*	*Theft from Person, individual victims* *Other Theft, Institutional victims*	J. Was there any other occasion when a valuable item was stolen from you or someone within this establishment? [e.g. shoplifting / handbag snatched / pocket picked etc. Exclude if already entered above].
K. Was the outside of your home or any property attached to the home (such as the garden, outbuildings or a car parked outside) damaged or vandalised?	*Vandalism (also includes vandalism to vehicle which took place away from home/ premises)*	K. Was the outside of the premises or any property attached to the premises (such as outbuildings or a car parked outside) damaged or vandalised?
L. Has anyone absconded without paying money owed, or defrauded or embezzled money from you or anyone in your household?	*Fraud*	L. Has anyone absconded without paying money owed or defrauded or embezzled money from this establishment?

* Note that "snatch thefts" (such as a handbag snatch) that did not involve assault or threat are included with "Theft from the Person" rather than with aggravated theft from the person.

In many of the tables in this section, the "target incident" — the one on the basis of which the individual was selected into the sample — is included in the figures, so all of the victims will have experienced at least one incident in the three-year period. In the section on reporting rates, the target incident (which was, by definition, reported) is excluded.

Table 3.11 examines the total number of incidents of different types — including the "target incident" — experienced by the victims in the three-year period. Note that the rows in this table are based on all victims, not just those selected into the sample on the basis of the type of incident referred to in that row. Thus, 76 per cent of the individual victims (selected into the sample in any crime category) experienced no vehicle theft in the three-year period, 20 per cent had a vehicle stolen once, 4 per cent had a vehicle stolen on more than one occasion. Of the victims (again, selected into the sample in any category) who did have a vehicle stolen, 17 per cent experienced this incident more than once.

"Repeat victimisation", taking account of incidents of all types over the three-year period, is quite extensive, particularly for institutions. Overall, as can be seen in the last row of the table, just over half of the individual victims (53 per cent) and four-fifths of the institutions (81 per cent) had experienced at least one other crime, apart from the target incident, in the three-year period.

In looking at the distribution of repeat victimisation across types of incident, we can ask what types of incident are most likely to have occurred to the same person or organisation more than once.[5] Among individual victims, this distribution tends to follow the overall frequency distribution of types of incident: crimes that are most likely to occur once are more likely to occur more than once to the same person or household. Thus, burglary (attempted or actual) is among the types of incident where repeat victimisation is most common for individual victims: 24 per cent of the individual burglary victims had experienced more than one burglary in the three-year period. This is followed by theft from a

---

[5] There were too few sample cases in a number of categories to provide reliable estimates of repeat victimisation rates: aggravated burglary and fraud against individual victims; vehicle theft, assault and theft from the person against institutions.

vehicle: 21 per cent of victims of this crime, or someone else in the household, had something stolen from a vehicle on more than one occasion. The repeat victimisation rate for vandalism is 20 per cent.

Table 3.11: Number of Incidents in Last Three Years (including Target Incident) and Percentage of Victims Experiencing Two or More of Each Type by Victim Type (row percentages)

	All Individual Victims						All Institutional Victims					
	Per cent experiencing . . .						Per cent experiencing . . .					
	None	1	2-5	6-10	11 or more	% 2+*	None	1	2-5	6-10	11 or more	% 2+*
Vehicle Theft	76	20	4	0	0	17	90	8	2	0	0	—
Theft from Vehicle	70	24	6	0	0	21	77	10	12	0	1	55
Fraud	94	5	1	1	0	—	66	11	18	2	3	69
Assault	86	12	2	0	0	17	93	4	2	0	0	—
Burglary	62	28	9	0	0	24	31	18	40	8	4	74
Aggravated Burglary	98	1	1	0	0	—	91	6	2	0	0	28
Theft from Person	89	10	1	0	0	9	100	0	0	0	0	—
Agg. Theft from Person	87	12	1	0	0	10	97	2	1	0	0	—
Other Theft	69	26	4	0	0	14	39	22	24	6	8	64
Vandalism	83	13	3	0	0	20	64	15	15	4	2	58
Any of these	0	47	43	7	3	53	0	19	31	17	32	81

Notes: Weighted by Total victim weight. Note that the rows in this table are based on all victims, not just those selected into the sample on the basis of the type of incident referred to in that row. * The percentage of victims of this crime who experienced more than one incident of this type. "−" indicates too few cases to provide breakdown.

Among institutions, repeat victimisation rates are highest for burglary (74 per cent of burglary victims experienced two or more incidents), fraud (69 per cent) and other theft (64 per cent). The repeat victimisation rate for burglary is particularly marked: more of the institutions in the sample experienced two or more burglaries or attempted burglaries in the three-year period than experienced one such incident.

As noted earlier, the QNHS crime survey provided estimates of repeat victimisation rates over a one-year period for individuals and private households. In that survey, the repeat victimisation rate was highest for vandalism (34 per cent), followed by theft from a vehicle (20 per cent), burglary and assault (both 17 per cent). The difference in pattern between the victims of recorded crime in the present study and the victims of all incidents (whether reported and recorded or not) in the QNHS survey may be due to the difference in the length of the reference period (one year in the QNHS compared to three years in the present survey), differences in timing (the QNHS reference period was 1997/98, while that in the present survey was 1994/95), differences in the question wording, or the nature of the sample. The higher repeat victimisation rates for vehicle theft and burglary in the present sample, for instance, are probably due to the longer reference period or to the fact that the QNHS does not include attempted burglaries. On the other hand, an explanation of the higher repeat victimisation rate for vandalism found in the QNHS may well lie in the reporting pattern for these kinds of incidents. It suggests that many households are subject to multiple instances of vandalism, *none* of which are reported.

A second question we can ask about repeat victimisation concerns the pattern of incidents experienced by victims. To what extent are victims of burglary, for example, also victims of other types of crime? Table 3.12 looks at the percentage of victims selected in each "target crime" category who experienced *other* incidents of each type in a three-year period.

Table 3.12: Per Cent of Victims Experiencing Other Incidents in Last Three Years by Target Crime Type and Victim Type (column percentages within victim type)

	Target Crime Category										
	Theft of Veh-icle	*Theft from Veh-icle*	*Fraud*	*Ass-ault*	*Burg-lary*	*Agg. Burg-lary*	*Theft from person*	*Agg. Theft from person*	*Other Theft*	*Van-dal-ism*	*Total*
Other Incidents: Individual Victims											
No other incidents	34	36	*	44	48	50	42	37	48	44	48
Same type only	1	2	*	4	1	5	4	2	4	7	3
Different type only	54	43	*	41	39	34	45	53	35	35	38
Same and other type	11	19	*	11	12	11	9	8	14	13	11
Weighted N cases	12,373	15,441	240	6,469	16,419	366	3,032	5,994	10,301	5,377	59,360
Other Incidents: Institutions											
No other incidents	*	9	19	*	13	16	*	*	14	18	19
Same type only	*	4	12	*	9	7	*	*	5	7	9
Different type only	*	22	26	*	21	43	*	*	27	36	23
Same and other type	*	66	43	*	57	34	*	*	54	40	48
Weighted N cases	928	1,701	2,545	122	8,320	856	0	495	6,354	3,445	15,204

Weighted by Victim Weight (Final column uses "Total" Victim Weight). Note that the columns in this table include only victims selected into the sample in that crime category. As such, the figures will differ from those in the rows of Table 3.11, which include victims selected in any crime category. * indicates too few cases to provide breakdown.

The figures in each column in Table 3.12 refer to victims selected into the sample on the basis of the crime in that column. They differ from the rows in Table 3.11, which include victims selected into the sample in any crime category. Thus, in Table 3.12, one per cent of individual victims who were selected on the basis of a re-porting a vehicle theft in the target period, experienced a second vehicle theft in the three-year period and no other crime, 54 per cent experienced some other type of crime, but no other vehicle theft, and 11 per cent experienced another vehicle theft and some other crime in one of the ten categories.

What is most striking in the table is the absence of specificity in terms of the pattern of repeat victimisation. Where individual victims suffered another criminal incident in the three-year pe-riod, it was most likely to be of a different type than the target in-cident. Even institutional victims were more likely to have experienced both another incident of the same type *and* an inci-dent of a different type than to have experienced another incident of the same type only. This generality holds true even for victims of the more common categories of crime, such as burglary, vehicle theft, theft from a vehicle and other theft. The second point of note is that at least half of the individual victims and at least four-fifths of the institutional victims selected in *each category* had experi-enced at least one other criminal incident of any type in the three-year period.

Among individuals and private households, victims selected on the basis of vehicle crime and aggravated theft from the person were most likely to have experienced another criminal incident of any type in the three-year period, while victims of burglary and aggravated burglary were least likely to have done so. Institu-tional victims of theft from a vehicle were most likely to have ex-perienced another criminal incident of any type, while those selected into the sample as victims of fraud or of vandalism were least likely to have done so.

Since the other criminal incidents may have happened to someone else in the victim's household or organisation, we cannot assume that all characteristics of the victim of the "target" inci-dent are shared by those of the victim of the "other" incidents. Two exceptions to this are region and, for individual victims, social class. While the social class of household members may differ, they are usually correlated, especially when aggregated into manual and non-manual categories. Social class, as used here, is based on the person's current or former occupation, or on the occupation of the main breadwinner if the individual never worked. A check using the *Living in Ireland Survey* data for 1995 indicates that taking the manual/non-manual classification of any adult household member would lead to the "correct" classification of 86 per cent of individuals.

Table 3.13 shows the extent of repeat victimisation in the last three years (including the target crime) by region and, for individual victims, by social class. It is important to keep in mind that we are looking at a sample of victims of recorded crime: all of them have experienced and reported at least one criminal incident in the target period. The figures cannot, therefore, be taken as population "risk" figures. However, the figures can be used to compare repeat victimisation rates between individuals and institutions, and across groups in the population by variables such as region and social class.

The regional breakdown shows that the percentage of victims who experienced more than one incident in the three-year period is higher in Dublin. Overall, 59 per cent of the Dublin individuals and households experienced more than one incident in the three-year period, compared to 42 per cent of those living outside Dublin city and county. The breakdown by social class for the individual victims shows that 56 per cent of those in the non-manual social class were victimised more than once, compared to 48 per cent of those in the manual or "unknown" social class.[6]

---

[6] In many cases where the social class is unknown, the individual has never worked for pay.

Table 3.13: Repeat Victimisation in Last Three Years by Region and Victim Type and by Social Class for Individual Victims (row percentages)

	Number of Incidents		Total	
	One	*2 or more*	*Per cent*	*Weighted Cases*
Individual				
Region:				
Dublin	41	59	100	36,874
Elsewhere in Ireland	58	42	100	22,487
Social Class of Victim:				
Non-Manual	44	56	100	34,255
Manual	52	48	100	25,105
Institution				
Region:				
Dublin	9	91	100	5,352
Elsewhere in Ireland	25	75	100	9,852

Weighted by "Total" Victim Weight.

The risk of multiple victimisation is also greater in the Dublin area for institutions. Among institutional victims of recorded crime, 91 per cent of those in the Dublin area had experienced at least one other incident in the three-year period, compared to 75 per cent of those outside the Dublin area.

The QNHS results confirm a generally higher repeat victimisation rate within specific crime categories in Dublin among individuals and private households. Dubliners who had been victims of burglary, vehicle-related crime and assault on one occasion are more likely than the population generally to experience a repeat of the same incident. The greater risk of repeat victimisation in Dublin was not found for vandalism, theft with violence or non-violent theft, however (Central Statistics Office, 1999a).

Reporting Rates for Other Incidents Experienced in Three-year Period

Ireland has traditionally been identified as a low-crime country. For instance, in her review of the common characteristics of countries with low crime rates throughout the world, Adler (1983) chose Ireland (along with Switzerland) as representatives of low-crime countries in Europe. In common with other countries, the crime rate increased rapidly in the post-World War II period, but less rapidly than in England and Wales and Northern Ireland, and with a later starting period (Brewer et al., 1997). There was a six-fold increase in recorded crime over the 30-year period from 1961–1991, with the key period of change being the late 1960s, during which the number of recorded offences doubled (McCullagh, 1996; Rottman, 1989; Brewer at al, 1997).

Ireland's status as a low-crime country has been based on a comparison of police statistics across countries, however. Breen and Rottman (1985), drawing on data from the 1982/83 Crime Victimisation Survey, questioned this low-crime reputation with respect to property crime: the incidence of burglary, vehicle theft and vandalism per 10,000 households was significantly higher in the Republic than in England and Wales. Breen and Rottman argue that the comparability of police crime statistics across jurisdictions is reduced by differences in the counting procedures used (Breen and Rottman, 1985). In addition, if there are national differences in reporting rates, this further reduces the comparability of police statistics across jurisdictions.

As noted in Chapter 1, however, the early 1980s was a period when recorded crime rates in Ireland were at their highest. A comparison of the QNHS results with those from Breen and Rottman suggests that since the early 1980s there has been a substantial fall in the risk of vehicle-related crime and a rise in the risk of vandalism while the risk of burglary has remained essentially unchanged (Breen and Rottman, 1985, Table 3.1; Central

Statistics Office, 1999a).[7] The recently published figures on victimisation risk from the QNHS crime and victimisation module seem to reaffirm Ireland's status as having a lower crime rate than England and Wales.[8]

Compared to the British figures for 1997, households in Ireland faced a slightly higher risk of burglary with entry (3.4 compared to 3.2 per cent), but a considerably lower risk of vandalism (4.8 compared to 8.2 per cent). Households owning vehicles had a lower risk of vehicle theft in Ireland (1.6 compared to 2.1 per cent) and a much lower risk of theft from a vehicle (4 compared to 10.2 per cent). The risk of crime faced by adult individuals was also lower in Ireland. Although the categories are not identical (since the BCS figures are broken down in greater detail) the following gives an indication of the differences: 0.5 per cent of adults in Ireland were victims of theft with violence, compared to 0.8 per cent in England and Wales who were victims of mugging;[9] 0.9 per cent were victims of non-violent theft, compared to 1.1 per cent who were victims of stealth theft from the person in England and Wales; and 0.5 per cent were victims of assault (excluding domestic and sexual), compared to 1.3 per cent in England and Wales who were victims of stranger assault (Central Statistics Office, 1999a; Mirrlees-Black et al., 1998, Table A5.1).

Breen and Rottman's point regarding the problems involved in relying on police crime statistics in comparing groups that may

---

[7] The percentage of households (not controlling for vehicle ownership) that had a vehicle stolen dropped from 4.5 to 1.2 per cent. Theft from a vehicle fell from 6.1 to 3.0 per cent. The risk of burglary dropped very slightly from 3.6 to 3.4 per cent of households, while vandalism increased from 3.9 to 4.8 per cent.

[8] Note, however, that the figures for England and Wales refer to the calendar year 1997, while those for Ireland refer to the year from late 1997 to late 1998. Crime rates in Britain, as measured by the British Crime Survey, had fallen between 1995 and 1997 (Mirrlees-Black et al., 1998) and may have continued to fall in 1998. However, this is the closest time period for which figures are available for the two jurisdictions.

[9] "Mugging" includes robbery and snatch theft from the person.

have different propensities to report crime is still valid, however. In the context of the present study, it would be important to know whether there are reporting differences between individuals and households, on the one hand, and businesses and organisations, on the other. We were able to do this, to a limited extent, with the data from the present survey.

The design of the classic victimisation surveys, such as the British Crime Survey and the 1998 QNHS crime module, allows for a good estimate of the extent of unreported crime against domestic targets. These surveys typically have a large sample size and a representative sample of individuals and households. Respondents are asked whether they experienced incidents of a particular type in the target period and, if yes, whether the incident was reported. On the other hand, those identified as victims of recorded crime in the target year provide the sampling frame in the present study. We have information on whether they experienced other incidents in the previous three years and, if so, whether they were reported. We can use this information to estimate "reporting rates" for different types of crime, but these rates cannot be taken as representative of the overall reporting rate in the population. The sample was selected from those who have reported a crime in a one-year period, and had the crime recorded as such in the Garda records. It is quite possible that they differ from those crime victims who did not report a crime, or where the incident was not recorded. For instance, they may live nearer to a Garda station, or have a generally more favourable attitude to the Gardaí, or have insurance which covers them against a greater range of losses, or the Gardaí may regard their complaint as more plausible. Nevertheless, while the reporting rates among the present sample may differ from those of crime victims as a whole, they can provide useful insights into differences in reporting rates by characteristics of the victim and characteristics of the incident. In particular, the present survey allows us to compare the reporting rates of crimes against individuals to those against institutions.

For each of the incidents listed in Figure 3.1, the respondent was first asked whether it occurred; and then asked the number of incidents.[10] The next question was whether the incident was reported, with categories "All", "Some" or "None". Where more than two incidents of a given type occurred, and "some" were reported we used an interpolation based on probability of reporting versus not reporting incidents of that type to estimate the number reported. The method is described in Appendix A. The "some" category was most likely to be used by institutions and for frequently occurring incidents such as shoplifting (classified under "other theft") or vandalism.

Table 3.14 shows the estimated total number of other incidents experienced by these crime victims in the three-year period, and the estimated percentage of these incidents that were reported. The table also shows the unweighted number of cases where an incident of each type occurred, on which these estimates are based. Where the number of cases is small (such as vehicle theft from institutions, aggravated burglary against individuals and aggravated theft from the person), the estimates should be interpreted with caution.

Overall, individuals reported 63 per cent of these other incidents, while institutions reported 34 per cent. In general, reporting rates are highest where the loss or damage is likely to be covered by insurance. Almost all incidents of vehicle theft were reported and over four out of five cases of theft from a vehicle and burglary. Virtually all cases of aggravated burglary directed

---

[10] As can be seen from section E of the questionnaire in Appendix B, a single number was provided for "assault with theft" (item A1), and the interviewer ticked a box to indicate whether it was a "burglary/robbery" or a "mugging/theft from the person". In the handful of cases where the victim experienced both mugging and aggravated burglary, an interpolation had to be used to estimate the number of each type. The method is described in Appendix A.

against institutions were reported, with the proportion being lower for aggravated burglary directed against individuals. Among individual victims, the reporting rates were lowest for those who felt that someone "absconded without paying money owed, or defrauded or embezzled money" from them or from someone else in the household. Reporting rates were also relatively low for individual victims of assault (66 per cent), aggravated theft from the person (51 per cent), other theft (47 per cent) and vandalism (44 per cent), and were very low (9 per cent) for fraud.

Table 3.14: Estimated Percentage of Other Incidents Occurring in Last Three Years That Were Reported by Victim Type

	Individual			Institution		
	Total Incidents	*% Reported*	*N cases (Unweighted)*	*Total Incidents*	*% Reported*	*N cases (Unweighted)*
Vehicle Theft	7,739	96%	61	1,091	100%	22
Theft from Vehicle	11,615	81%	84	6,516	81%	58
Fraud	7,071	9%	44	22,086	21%	140
Assault	5,935	66%	64	2,829	81%	45
Burglary	20,429	82%	133	32,494	83%	177
Aggravated Burglary	2,300	75%	29	1,603	99%	67
Theft from Person	5,416	61%	82	–	–	0
Aggravated Theft from Person	2,872	51%	39	699	96%	45
Other Theft	17,311	47%	120	146,014	19%	176
Vandalism	11,230	44%	94	21,541	39%	106
Any of these	91,917	63%	369	234,873	34%	279
Weighted N cases	*59,360*			*15,204*		

Notes: Weighted by Total Victim weight. "–" indicates this crime type not identified for institutions. Target crime not included.

Compared to the results from the QNHS for 1997/98, discussed in Chapter 1, the reporting rates are higher among the present sample of individual and household victims of recorded crime. This is particularly true of theft from a vehicle, where the victims in the 1996 survey reported 81 per cent of incidents, compared to 59 per cent for all victims in the QNHS survey, and theft without violence (61 compared to 49 per cent). Reporting rates were also somewhat higher for burglary (82 compared to 79 per cent) and vandalism (44 compared to 40 per cent). On the other hand, the reporting rate for vehicle theft was very similar in both surveys, and the reporting rate was lower in the present sample than in the QNHS survey for theft with violence (51 compared to 62 per cent).[11] A direct comparison is not possible for assault, since different definitions are used. It would seem, overall, that the reporting rates among the present sample of individuals and private households are higher than those found in the population generally.

The results in Table 3.14 indicate that crimes against individuals or private households are more likely to be reported than those targeting businesses or other organisations. When incidents of all types are taken into consideration, institutions are only about half as likely to report a crime (34 per cent) as individuals (63 per cent). This overall pattern is primarily driven by the very large number of incidents of other theft directed against institutions, and to a lesser extent by the number of cases of fraud and vandalism — all categories of crime where the reporting rate is low. The reporting rate for incidents of other theft — which includes shoplifting — is only 19 per cent.

There are important similarities with respect to major categories of property crime (individuals and institutions reported about

---

[11] Note that the estimate of the reporting rate of aggravated theft from the person is based on only 39 cases in the present sample, and is therefore subject to a wide margin of error.

the same proportion of vehicle thefts, thefts from a vehicle, and burglaries), and important differences with respect to violent crime. Crimes involving assault or threat were much more likely to be reported if they took place on the premises of a business or organisation. For instance, four-fifths of assaults and almost all aggravated thefts from the person taking place in this setting were reported, compared to two-thirds and half, respectively, of those directed against individuals.

Table 3.15 shows the main reasons for not reporting incidents to the Gardaí, as reported by the victim of the target incident. Again, the results need to be interpreted with caution, since the unreported "other incident" may have happened to someone else in the household or organisation. The percentages need not add to 100, because the individual or institution may have been the victim of several different types of crime in the three-year period and a "main reason for not reporting" was recorded for each separate type of unreported crime. The most common reason for not reporting crime is that the respondent considered it "not important enough". Over half of the individual victims and over three-quarters of the institutions gave this as the main reason for not reporting a particular type of incident.[12]

Other reasons frequently cited were that the "Gardaí could do nothing" (31 per cent of individual victims and 50 per cent of institutions), or that the "Gardaí would not be interested" (about one-quarter of victims of both types). The latter reflects situations where the victim regarded the incident as serious enough to report, but felt that the Gardaí would not see it as serious. Fear of reprisal, and not wanting to get the offender into trouble were relatively unimportant overall, and were given as reasons by fewer than one in twenty of the victims.

---

[12] Unfortunately, the number of cases where an incident was not reported is too small to provide a breakdown by the type of incident.

Table 3.15: Reason for Not Reporting Other Incidents in Last Three Years by Victim Type

	Individual	Institution	Total
Not important enough	56	77	63
Gardaí could do nothing	31	50	37
Gardaí would not be interested	24	25	24
Fear of reprisal	2	1	2
Didn't want person in trouble	5	1	4
Made private arrangement	2	9	4
Reported to another authority	3	1	2
Felt partly responsible	3	3	3
Other	16	9	14
Reason not given	5	11	7
Unweighted Cases	*179*	*162*	*341*
Weighted N cases	*16,343*	*7,169*	*23,511*

Notes: Weighted by Total Victim weight. Since more than one different type of crime may have gone unreported, the percentages need not add to 100.

A comparison of the reasons given by the present sample to those given by the QNHS victims suggests that the pattern of reasons for not reporting is very similar among victims of recorded crime and victims of all crime. For each of the five crime categories where this information was collected in the QNHS (burglary, theft of vehicle, theft from vehicle, theft with violence and assault) the most common reason for not reporting an incident was that the victim felt it was not serious enough, ranging from 28 per cent for assault to 55 per cent for theft from a vehicle. The next most common reason given was that the "Gardaí could do nothing/ lack of proof", ranging from 15 per cent for assault to 22 per cent for theft from a vehicle. In assault cases, 16 per cent of victims not reporting the incident felt that the Gardaí "would not do anything", with a substantial minority also giving this response in cases of burglary (11 per cent) and theft from a vehicle (14 per cent) (Central Statistics Office, 1999a).

The reasons for not reporting crime also conform to the pattern found internationally, where the belief that the incident was "not serious enough" or there was "no loss" was by far the most common reason for not reporting in all countries. The belief that the police could do nothing about what happened featured in just over one in ten incidents overall, but it was a more common response in Northern Ireland (Mayhew and van Dijk, 1997). The belief that the police "would not be interested" was not included as a specific reason on the International Crime Victim Survey questionnaire.

Reporting Rates by Region and Social Class

Table 3.16 examines the percentage of incidents reported by region and victim type. Because of the small number of cases in several categories, the ten crime categories have been collapsed to ensure that there are at least 30 unweighted cases for the estimate of the percentage reported.

Table 3.16: Percentage Reported of Other Incidents in Last Three Years by Victim Type and Region

	Individual		Institution	
	Dublin	*Elsewhere*	*Dublin*	*Elsewhere*
Violent crime	60%*	78%*	84%*	97%*
Vehicle crime	86%	89%	87%	79%
Burglary	83%	78%	81%	85%
Other Theft	46%	49%	23%	16%
Vandalism	58%*	30%*	44%	37%
Any of these	65%	56%	35%	32%

Notes: Weighted by Total Victim weight. Vehicle crime includes theft of vehicle and theft from vehicle. Violent crime includes assault, aggravated burglary, and aggravated theft from the person. Theft from person and fraud are not shown as separate categories, but are included in the total figure. * Indicates statistically significant difference between percentages for Dublin and elsewhere at p<.05 (two-tailed).

The overall difference in reporting rates by region is not statistically significant for either individual victims or institutions. The reporting rates for violent crime (assault, aggravated burglary and aggravated theft from the person) are higher outside the capital, however: among individual victims, about three-fifths of these incidents taking place in Dublin are reported, compared to nearly four-fifths taking place elsewhere in the country. On the other hand, reporting rates for vandalism are much higher in the Dublin area (58 per cent for individual victims) than in other parts of Ireland (30 per cent).

The QNHS results support the finding of very similar reporting rates in Dublin to those in the country as a whole among individuals and private households, but the QNHS survey did not find the same regional differences in reporting rates for violent crime or vandalism. Reporting of burglary in that survey was slightly higher in Dublin (82 per cent) than for the state (79 per cent). Reporting differences between Dublin and the country as a whole for other types of crime were smaller in magnitude (Central Statistics Office, 1999a).

Among institutions, overall reporting rates are very similar in the Dublin area and elsewhere in the country, and the differences are not statistically significant for vehicle crime, burglary, other theft or vandalism. Reporting rates for violent crime taking place on the premises or to an employee on duty tend to be higher outside Dublin.

Table 3.17 shows the reporting rates by social class of the individual victim. Those in the non-manual social classes are more likely to report crime overall (68 per cent) than those in the manual social classes (56 per cent). This holds true for vehicle crime (mainly driven by different reporting rates for theft from a vehicle), and other theft, but the reporting rates do not differ significantly for violent crime, burglary or vandalism. A similar overall pattern was found in the International Crime Victimisation Survey (van Dijk et al., 1991), with higher reporting rates by those victims with higher incomes, and by O'Connell and Whelan (1994) in the Dublin Crime Victimisation Survey, where reporting rates were highest for the self-employed and professionals. Van Dijk et al. (1991) argue that the relatively low reporting rate for the lowest income group is partly accounted for by the lower mean value of property they had stolen from them, as well as by lower rates of insurance cover.

Table 3.17: Estimated Percentage Reported of Other Incidents in Last Three Years by Social Class (Individual Victims)

	Non-manual	Manual	Total
Violent Crime	60%	75%	65%
Vehicle Crime	93%*	76%*	87%
Burglary	83%	82%	83%
Other Theft	57%*	35%*	46%
Vandalism	54%	35%	47%
Any of these	68%*	56%*	64%

Notes: Weighted by Total Victim weight. Vehicle crime includes theft of vehicle and theft from vehicle. Violent crime includes assault, aggravated burglary, and aggravated theft from the person. Theft from person and fraud are not shown as separate categories, but are included in the total figure. Cases where the social class is unknown (often those who have never worked) are not included in the table. * indicates statistically significant difference between percentages for non-manual and manual social classes at p<.05 (two-tailed).

Summary

Throughout this chapter, the focus has been on the victims of crime. The data were weighted so that the victim is counted only once, even if several incidents of a given type occurred in the target period. This is particularly important in the case of institutions and in the case of crimes such as shoplifting (included in the "other theft" category). There were two main sections in the chapter: the first part examined the characteristics of crime victims, and the second part explored the issue of repeat victimisation and reporting rates.

There were clear age and sex differences in terms of the individual crime victims. More of the victims of recorded crime were male than female. In the case of incidents such as burglary, vandalism and vehicle crime — which may affect several household members — the sex is that of the person reporting the crime. The risk of assault is highest for young males, while the risk of theft from the person and aggravated theft from the person is greater for women of all ages than it is for men. In general, the gap between male and female victimisation rates was larger among victims of recorded crime than among victims of all crime (whether reported and recorded or not) in the QNHS crime survey. This suggests that some of the observed differences by gender in the recorded statistics may be driven by differences in reporting patterns, or in the recording or classification of crimes based on the gender of the victim.

Apart from assault, those under age 35 tend to be under-represented among victims of recorded crime relative to their proportion of the population, while those age 35 to 49 tend to be over-represented. With the exception of aggravated burglary, those over age 65 are under-represented among victims of recorded crime. Part of the age pattern is undoubtedly driven by the relationship between age and vehicle ownership and between age and being a household head, but it may also be the case that younger victims are less likely to report crime. The QNHS crime victimisation results, which controlled for vehicle ownership, found a higher risk of both vehicle theft and theft from a vehicle in households where the reference person was under age 25, and also showed a higher risk of household burglary for young adult households (Central Statistics Office, 1999a, Table 1). The QNHS results confirm the lower risk of victimisation overall faced by those over age 65.

In social class terms, the risk of being a victim of crimes involving theft tends to be greater for those at the upper end (the professional/managerial class) than at the lower end (the semi-skilled and unskilled manual social classes), but the risk tends to be higher in general for the lower professional/managerial class than for the higher professional/managerial class. Assault, again, shows a different pattern: the risk of being a victim of assault is greatest for those in the skilled manual social class. The overall risk of being a crime victim tends to be at or below average for those in the semi-skilled and unskilled manual classes.

In terms of economic status, employees and the self-employed had a greater than average risk of being a victim of crime in all categories. Following from this, those living in households where the main source of income is from wages or from self-employment are at a greater risk of crime victimisation, while it tends to be lower than average for those in households where the main source of income is from social welfare (which includes social welfare pensions).

About four-fifths of crime victims are individuals or private households, while the remaining fifth are institutions. Among the institutional victims of crime, the most common are shops, particularly for fraud, other theft (which includes shoplifting) and aggravated burglary. Private sector businesses other than manufacturing, retail and public houses/restaurants are the most common in the vehicle theft category. Most institutional victims of crime tend to be small in terms of the numbers employed, with half or more in all categories having ten or fewer employees in the local branch or outlet where the incident occurred.

In the second part of the chapter, we drew on information regarding *other* criminal incidents suffered by the crime victims or someone else in their household or organisation in the three-year period from mid-1993 to mid-1996. These were incidents apart from the "target" crime reported in the year from November 1994 to October 1995, and on the basis of which the individual or institution was selected into the sample. This allowed us to examine the issue of repeat victimisation. The QNHS crime and victimisation module provides a better source of information on repeat victimisation for crimes targeting individuals and private households, because it has a larger sample size and is based on a survey of all households and individuals (not just victims of recorded crime). However, the present survey is unique in that it allows us to assess repeat victimisation of businesses and other organisations. For the purpose of this analysis, the sample was weighted by the victim weights, which give equal representation to victims reporting one crime and those reporting several crimes in the target period.

The extent of repeat victimisation in the sample was quite marked, particularly for institutions. Fifty-three per cent of the individual victims and 81 percent of the institutions that reported a crime in the target year had been victims of at least one other criminal incident in the three-year period.

Among individual victims, victims of burglary, theft from a vehicle and vandalism were most likely (about one-fifth) to have experienced another incident of the same type in the three-year period. The repeat incidents did not necessarily involve a second (or third) incident of the same type as the crime reported in 1994/95, however. While the extent of repeat victimisation is marked, then, it is not primarily based on repeated occurrences of the *same type* of incident. There was some tendency for the risk of repeat victimisation to be greater in Dublin, and for those in the non-manual social classes.

The extent of repeat victimisation is even greater for institutions than for individual victims: four-fifths of the institutions in the sample had experienced at least one other criminal incident in the three-year period. Repeat victimisation of institutions is quite general with respect to the type of incident, with burglary and other theft affecting over three-fifths of those reporting any crime type in the 1994/95 period. Sixty-nine per cent of the institutions selected into the sample in any crime category had at least one burglary or attempted burglary in the three-year period, and 60 per cent had been victims of at least one incident of other theft.

The risk of repeat victimisation was substantially higher for institutions in the Dublin area (91 per cent) than for those in other parts of the country (75 per cent).

We were able to examine variations in reporting rates across types of crime by looking at whether other incidents experienced by the victims or their household/organisation in the three-year period had been reported. Again, the QNHS results provide a better estimate of overall reporting rates for individuals and private households, because of the larger sample size and because the sample is not limited to those who reported at least one crime to the Gardaí. A comparison of reporting rates for the present sample to those for a national sample in the 1998 QNHS crime module showed that reporting rates on the part of the victims of recorded crime did indeed tend to be higher.

The main value of the analysis of reporting rates is that it allows us to compare the reporting patterns of institutions with those of individuals. Overall, institutions were likely to report a lower proportion of all criminal incidents. This was mainly due to the very low reporting rate of other theft, fraud and vandalism. Reporting of vehicle crime and burglary was high and very similar to the levels for individual victims, while reporting of violent crime was higher than among individual victims.

Chapter 4

Victims, Offenders and the Criminal Justice System

This chapter examines the interaction between crime victims and the offender, on the one hand, and with the criminal justice system, on the other. In many cases, especially those types of crime that are not witnessed by the victim, any knowledge of the offender on the part of the victim is mediated through the criminal justice system. The chapter begins by looking at the characteristics of the offender — where these are known to the victim — and the relationship between victim and offender. Often, as we will see, the offender is not identified, and the victim has no knowledge of who the offender might be. In other instances, and this is particularly true of assault, the offender is someone with whom the victim was acquainted prior to the incident. The second section of the chapter examines the contact between the victim and the Gardaí, including how the crime was reported and the level of satisfaction with the Garda service provided. Finally, the focus shifts to the outcome of the case and the level of satisfaction with the outcome on the part of crime victims.

The data in this chapter are weighted using the incident weights, so that each reported incident in 1994/95 is given equal weight.

Victims and Offenders

In this section, information on the offender is available only to the extent to which it is known to the victim. The respondent may know how many offenders were involved, their ages and sex, for instance, through witnessing the crime, or through being informed of this following Garda investigation. The information is far from complete, since in many cases the victim was not present at the time — particularly for offences such as vehicle theft and most burglaries. However, at least in terms of observable characteristics, the picture is more comprehensive than the available statistics on the sub-sample of offenders who have been convicted. Nevertheless, caution is advisable in interpreting these results, particularly for those categories of crime where few of the offenders are seen or subsequently identified: it could well be that young offenders (teenagers or children), for instance, are more likely to be observed than their adult counterparts.

Table 4.1 looks at the number of offenders involved in the incident, where this was known. In about half of the cases directed at individuals, the respondent does not know how many offenders there were. The proportion is much lower, at 29 per cent, for incidents targeted at institutions. This is further evidence of selectivity in the reporting of crimes by institutions: it seems that crimes that are witnessed are more likely to be reported. In almost nine out of ten reported cases of "other theft" directed at institutions, the number of offenders is known. Since it is unlikely that the offender is observed in such a high proportion of crimes such as shoplifting, this suggests that the reported instances of other theft are the subset of incidents where the offender is "caught in the act". Many cases of shoplifting are probably not discovered until later, during stocktaking, when there may seem to be little point in reporting them.

In crimes like vehicle theft, theft from a vehicle, burglary, and other theft — where the victim tends not to be present — the number of offenders tends to be unknown. In violent crimes, such as assault, aggravated burglary and aggravated theft from the person, the victim has witnessed the crime and can usually provide this information.

Table 4.1: How Many Offenders (Where Known to the Victim) by Crime and Victim Type (column percentages within victim type)

	Theft of Vehicle	Theft from Vehicle	Fraud	Ass-ault	Burg-lary	Agg. Burg-lary	Theft from person	Agg. theft from person	Other Theft	Van-dal-ism	Total
Individual											
Number of offenders known	26	38	*	100	47	82	65	93	43	53	51
Not Known	74	62	*	0	53	18	35	7	57	47	49
Weighted N Cases	12,953	16,510	240	6,875	17,445	391	3,083	6,123	10,726	5,680	80,027
Number, where known											
One	33	22	*	42	34	29	54	43	50	20	37
Two	31	57	*	18	49	53	39	37	24	39	38
Three plus	35	21	*	40	17	18	7	20	26	41	26
Weighted N Cases	3,339	6,264	170	6,875	8,234	322	2,006	5,666	4,578	3,011	40,466
Institution											
Number of offenders known	*	37	99	*	61	99	*	*	87	51	71
Not Known	*	63	1	*	39	1	*	*	13	49	29
Weighted N Cases	945	2,328	3,338	171	13,548	1,089	0	527	12,994	4,519	39,467
Number, where known											
One	*	0	70	*	39	30	*	*	45	12	42
Two	*	83	25	*	27	44	*	*	42	43	37
Three plus	*	17	5	*	33	26	*	*	12	44	21
Weighted N Cases	322	853	3,307	171	8,272	1,086	0	527	11,289	2,308	28,134

Note: Cases weighted to total number of incidents in 1995.

It is interesting that in burglaries of private residences, the burglars (at least where we have information on the numbers involved) are most likely to work in pairs, while either a lone burglar or three or more working together (useful in moving large quantities of merchandise) are more common in burglaries targeted at institutions.

Also worth noting is the fact that more assaults involve multiple assailants (58 per cent) than a lone assailant. Bearing in mind that the assault victim was accompanied by someone other than the assailant in 50 per cent of cases (see Table 2.11), this suggests that recorded assaults often involve groups. This may not generalise to all assault incidents, however: as noted earlier, witnessed assaults are probably more likely to be reported and recorded. Multiple assailants are also more common than a single assailant in cases of aggravated burglary and aggravated theft from the person.

Where the sex of the offender is known (Table 4.2), it is most likely to be male, particularly in the case of violent crime (ranging from 79 per cent for assault to almost all cases of aggravated burglary). Other theft is the only crime where more than one-third of the offenders are female, or a male and female working together. Fraud cases, however, also involve a sizeable proportion (29 per cent) of female offenders.

The age of the offender, in very broad categories, is shown in Table 4.3. Caution is advisable in interpreting these results since it is possible that respondents' assessment of the age of the offender is not accurate, with, for example, young teen offenders identified as children.

Table 4.2: Sex of Offender (Where Known) by Crime and Victim Type (column percentages within victim type)

	Theft of Vehicle	Theft from Vehicle	Fraud	Ass-ault	Burg-lary	Agg. Burg-lary	Theft from per-son	Agg. Theft from person	Other Theft	Van-dal-ism	Total
Individual											
Male	100	93	*	79	96	100	73	95	57	97	87
Female	0	0	*	7	4	0	19	3	29	0	7
Both	0	7	*	13	0	0	8	2	14	3	6
Weighted N Cases	1,924	6,264	170	6,863	6,651	322	1,943	5,470	4,193	3,011	36,812
Institution											
Male	*	100	71	*	97	98	*	*	58	97	78
Female	*	0	20	*	0	0	*	*	31	0	15
Both	*	0	9	*	3	2	*	*	11	3	7
Weighted N Cases	322	515	3,077	171	7,773	1,046	0	430	10,928	1,845	26,108

Note: Cases weighted to total number of incidents in 1995.

Table 4.3: Approximate Age of Offender (Where Known) by Crime and Victim Type (column percentages within victim type)

	Theft of Vehicle	Theft from Vehicle	Fraud	Ass-ault	Burg-lary	Agg. Burg-lary	Theft from per-son	Agg. Theft from person	Other Theft	Van-dal-ism	Total
Individual											
Child	0	0	*	0	0	0	5	0	27	5	4
Teenager	66	64	*	23	35	24	25	49	37	38	40
Adult	27	32	*	74	53	66	70	45	36	51	51
Mixed ages	8	4	*	3	13	10	0	6	0	6	5
Weighted N Cases	1,579	4,453	139	5,936	6,414	241	1,783	4,972	3,426	2,556	31,497
Institution											
Child	*	0	0	*	0	0	*	*	0	18	1
Teenager	*	100	17	*	46	21	*	*	33	52	38
Adult	*	0	81	*	47	77	*	*	67	19	57
Mixed ages	*	0	2	*	6	2	*	*	0	11	3
Weighted N Cases	54	515	2,233	171	5,929	836	0	387	9,028	1,682	20,835

Note: Cases weighted to total number of incidents in 1995.

Overall, where the age of offenders is known, they are most likely to be adult, but teenagers are responsible for about two-fifths of the incidents where the offender was identified, rising to two-thirds in the case of vehicle crime.[1] For aggravated theft from the person and other theft directed at individual victims, the offender is about as likely to be a teenager as an adult. According to respondents, over one-quarter of the incidents of other theft directed at individuals, and nearly one-fifth of the incidents of vandalism directed at institutions (where the offender is identified) are committed by children who have not yet reached their teens. Otherwise, the proportion of reported crime committed by children is five per cent or less.

Table 4.4 examines whether the offender is someone who was known to the victim prior to the incident, for the subset of cases where the offender was identified.

Table 4.4: Whether Offender Known to Victim by Crime and Victim Type (column percentages within victim type)

	Theft of Vehicle	Theft from Vehicle	Fraud	Assault	Burglary	Agg. Burglary	Theft from person	Agg. Theft from person	Other Theft	Vandalism	Total
Individual											
At least 1 known	31	18	*	58	36	11	3	10	22	35	29
Not Known	69	82	*	42	64	89	97	90	78	65	71
Weighted Cases	3,408	6,606	170	6,875	8,234	322	2,006	5,732	4,578	3,011	40,941
Institution											
At least 1 known	*	26	30	*	41	17	*	*	32	30	33
Not Known	*	74	70	*	59	83	*	*	68	70	67
Weighted Cases	591	853	3,307	171	8,941	1,098	0	527	11,468	2,568	29,522

Note: Table includes only cases where the offender was identified. Cases weighted to total number of incidents in 1995.

---

[1] Note, however, that there are very few vehicle crimes where the offender is identified.

In about 30 per cent of incidents targeted against individuals and one-third of the incidents directed at institutions, the victim knew at least one of the offenders. This increases to 58 per cent in the case of assault victims. This higher figure for assault is consistent with results internationally. In the United States, for instance, about half of all violent crimes were committed by someone whom the victim knew (Rand, 1999; Zimring and Hawkins, 1997).

Table 4.5 looks at the context in which the victim knew the offender: the closeness of the relationship prior to the incident. Apart from assault, the offender was not known to the victim, or was not identified, in the large majority of the incidents. In assault cases, the victim knew the offender prior to the assault in over half of the cases. The offender was a friend or acquaintance of the victim in one-tenth of these incidents, the spouse of the victim in 8 per cent of cases, a neighbour in a further one-tenth of the cases, and someone known by name in about one case in eight.

Table 4.6 looks at how the offender was known, for individual victims of crime, by sex of the victim. In general, female assault victims tend to have had a closer relationship with their assailants prior to the incident than male victims. In nearly half of the cases involving male victims, the assailant was not known to the victim, compared to slightly less than one-quarter of the cases involving female victims. The assailant was the spouse or another relative in 6 per cent of incidents involving a male victim, but in 39 per cent of incidents involving a female victim. Over one-quarter of the recorded assault cases against women are cases of domestic violence — where the assailant is the spouse. The assailant was a friend, acquaintance or neighbour in a further 18 per cent of incidents involving a male victim but in 36 per cent of cases where the victim was female.

Table 4.5: How Offender Known by Crime and Victim Type (column percentages within victim type)

	Theft of Vehicle	Theft from Vehicle	Fraud	Assault	Burglary	Agg. Burglary	Theft from person	Agg. Theft from person	Other Theft	Vandalism	Total
Individual											
Not Identified*	74	62	*	0	53	18	35	7	57	47	49
Not Known	18	32	*	42	30	73	63	83	33	35	36
Spouse	0	0	*	8	0	0	0	0	0	0	1
Relative	0	0	*	5	0	3	0	0	1	0	1
Work/business	1	0	*	3	1	0	0	0	3	0	1
Friend/acquaintance	1	2	*	10	3	0	1	1	2	0	3
Neighbour	3	0	*	11	5	0	0	0	2	4	3
Known by name	1	2	*	12	6	3	1	3	0	4	3
Known by sight	3	2	*	9	2	3	1	5	1	11	3
Weighted N Cases	12,953	16,510	240	6,875	17,445	391	3,083	6,123	10,726	5,680	80,027
Institution											
Not Identified*	*	63	1	*	39	1	*	*	13	49	29
Not Known	*	27	69	*	38	82	*	*	60	34	49
Through work/business	*	0	12	*	4	0	*	*	5	3	5
Friend/acquaintance	*	0	1	*	2	0	*	*	0	0	1
Neighbour	*	0	0	*	3	0	*	*	1	1	2
Known by name	*	0	9	*	12	6	*	*	7	10	9
Known by sight	*	10	9	*	3	10	*	*	9	3	6
Previous offender	*	0	0	*	0	1	*	*	3	0	1
Weighted N Cases	945	2,328	3,338	171	13,548	1,098	0	527	12,994	4,519	39,467

Note: Cases weighted to total number of incidents in 1995. * "Not Identified" includes cases where the offender was not seen by the victim at the time and was not subsequently identified by the Gardaí. "Not known" includes cases where offender was a stranger to the victim.

Table 4.6: How Offender Known to Individual Victims by Crime Type and Sex (column percentages within sex)

	Theft of Vehicle	Theft from Vehicle	Assault	Burglary	Agg. Burglary	Theft from person	Agg. Theft from person	Other Theft	Vandalism	Total
Male										
Not Identified	73	65	0	53	29	50	7	73	44	53
Not Known	14	30	47	33	57	50	73	21	38	31
Spouse	0	0	3	0	0	0	0	0	0	0
Relative	0	0	3	0	7	0	0	0	0	0
Through work/business	1	0	4	0	0	0	0	6	0	1
Friend/ acquaintance	2	0	10	3	0	0	3	0	0	2
Neighbour	4	0	8	7	0	0	0	0	5	4
Known by name	2	3	15	5	0	0	5	0	5	4
Known by sight	4	2	10	0	7	0	12	0	7	4
Weighted N Cases	*8,307*	*11,564*	*5,469*	*10,382*	*162*	*367*	*1,879*	*5,663*	*3,838*	*47,808*
Female										
Not Identified	76	58	0	53	10	33	8	40	54	44
Not Known	24	34	23	26	85	64	88	47	27	42
Spouse	0	0	26	0	0	0	0	0	0	1
Relative	0	0	13	0	0	0	0	3	0	1
Through work/business	0	0	0	3	0	0	0	0	0	1
Friend/ acquaintance	0	8	12	3	0	1	0	4	0	3
Neighbour	0	0	24	3	0	0	0	4	0	2
Known by name	0	0	0	7	5	1	3	0	0	2
Known by sight	0	0	3	6	0	1	2	2	19	3
Weighted N Cases	*4,646*	*4,459*	*1,406*	*7,064*	*229*	*2,693*	*4,244*	*5,062*	*1,842*	*31,708*

Note: Cases weighted to total number of incidents in 1995. Total includes figures for fraud.

Domestic assaults would have been included in the present sample if they were reported and either constituted an indictable assault or a non-indictable assault where proceedings were taken. It is generally acknowledged that the reporting rate for domestic violence is particularly low (Mirrlees-Black and Byron, 1999; Kelleher et al., 1995). The 1996 British Crime Survey had a special self-completion module on domestic violence (Mirrlees-Black and Byron, 1999). The results indicated, somewhat surprisingly, that the same proportions (4.2 per cent) of men and women age 16 to 59 had been physically assaulted by a current or former partner in the previous year. However, there were differences in the severity of the assault. Women were twice as likely as men to have been injured by a partner in the last year (2.2 per cent of women compared to 1.1 per cent of men), and were also more likely to have been assaulted three or more times (2.0 per cent compared to 1.5 per cent). Only 11 per cent of the domestic assaults that took place in the previous year had been reported to the police. An Irish study by Kelleher et al. (1995), based on a national survey carried out in 1994, found that 10 per cent of women who had been in an intimate relationship with men had been subjected to actual physical violence at some point, and 18 per cent had experienced some form of violence more broadly defined (including mental cruelty, threats of violence, sexual violence). Of those who had experienced any form of violence, 20 per cent had reported it to the police (Kelleher et al., 1995, p. 21). This figure is higher than that found in the 1996 BCS, but is not directly comparable because of the use of a different reference period: the British Crime Survey focused on the previous year, while the Irish study focused on lifetime experiences of violence. Nevertheless, both studies confirm the low reporting rate of domestic assaults.

Drugs and Crime from the Victim's Perspective

Public debate and media reports in recent years have had a good deal to say about the link between drugs and crime. A Department of Justice discussion paper on crime notes that:

> The growth in drugs misuse (mainly cannabis, ecstasy and heroin) in recent years is generally recognised . . . to represent the most insidious threat to our society. It destroys the lives of many young people, it promotes a criminal culture and its exploitation is the bedrock of a great deal of major organised crime. . . . The most serious problems with drug abuse are associated with heroin which not only damages the addicts themselves but also fuels a great deal of crime in Dublin and surrounding areas. (Department of Justice, 1997, p. 87)

The extent of the link between rising crime rates and drugs has been questioned, however, particularly with regard to the overall number of recorded indictable crimes. Brewer et al. (1997) note that the marked increase in crime in Ireland began in the mid-1960s, well before the "drug explosion" (p. 9).

The crime victims were asked whether they believed the incident was drug-related, and then whether they believed it was alcohol-related. In most cases, as can be seen from Table 4.7 and Table 4.8, the victims report that they do not know. Over three-fifths of individual victims and almost half of institutional victims do not have an opinion on whether the incident was drug-related. This is understandable for crimes where the victim was not present and where no offender was apprehended.

Of those who do have an opinion, more are inclined to believe that the incident was *not* drug related (22 per cent of individual and 30 per cent of institutional victims) than to believe that it was drug-related (16 per cent of individual and 24 per cent of institutional victims). Aggravated burglary directed at institutions is the only crime where more than half (56 per cent) of the victims believe the incident was drug-related, although the proportion of

individual victims of aggravated theft from the person who believe the incident was drug-related (42 per cent) is also substantial. Only one in ten assault victims but 27 per cent of individual
victims of aggravated burglary believe that the incident was drug-
related.

Table 4.7: Whether Respondent Believes Incident Drug-Related by Crime and Victim Type (column percentages within victim type)

	Theft of Vehicle	Theft from Vehicle	Fraud	Assault	Burglary	Agg. Burglary	Theft from person	Agg. Theft from person	Other Theft	Vandalism	Total
Individual											
Certain it was	1	4	*	4	9	0	5	20	4	2	6
Fairly certain it was	0	8	*	6	18	27	12	22	8	6	10
Don't know	86	73	*	26	52	56	68	44	64	65	62
Fairly certain it wasn't	7	6	*	14	4	0	8	11	12	17	8
Certain it wasn't	6	9	*	50	17	18	7	3	12	11	14
Weighted N cases	12,953	16,510	240	6,875	17,445	391	3,083	6,123	10,726	5,680	80,027
Institution											
Certain it was	*	6	7	10	11	30	*	*	12	1	11
Fairly certain it was	*	25	10	30	12	26	*	*	15	6	13
Don't know	*	68	32	10	56	31	*	*	30	66	46
Fairly certain it wasn't	*	0	20	0	12	4	*	*	12	15	12
Certain it wasn't	*	0	31	50	8	9	*	*	32	12	18
Weighted N cases	945	2,328	3,338	171	13,548	1,098	0	527	12,994	4,519	39,467

Note: Cases weighted to total number of incidents in 1995.

In terms of whether the crime was alcohol-related, the proportions of individual (64 per cent) and institutional victims (44 per cent) who do not to have an opinion are similar to those for the item on whether the crime was drug-related.

Table 4.8: *Whether Respondent Believes Incident Alcohol-Related by Crime and Victim Type (column percentages within victim type)*

	Theft of Veh-icle	Theft from Veh-icle	Fraud	Ass-ault	Burg-lary	Agg. Burg-lary	Theft from per-son	Agg. Theft from person	Other Theft	Van-dal-ism	Total
Individual											
Certain it was	4	4	*	43	2	6	1	1	0	20	7
Fairly certain it was	2	3	*	13	4	0	4	5	8	11	5
Don't know	86	78	*	18	59	68	64	56	66	47	64
Fairly certain it wasn't	3	4	*	4	15	12	21	14	10	15	9
Certain it wasn't	6	11	*	22	21	15	10	23	16	6	15
Weighted N cases	12,953	16,510	240	6,875	17,445	391	3,083	6,123	10,726	5,680	80,027
Institution											
Certain it was	*	0	8	*	7	0	*	*	3	12	6
Fairly certain it was	*	19	5	*	2	3	*	*	1	26	6
Don't know	*	71	26	*	56	51	*	*	32	41	44
Fairly certain it wasn't	*	10	25	*	25	26	*	*	15	14	19
Certain it wasn't	*	0	36	*	10	20	*	*	48	7	26
Weighted N cases	945	2,328	3,338	171	13,548	1,098	0	527	12,994	4,519	39,467

Note: Cases weighted to total number of incidents in 1995.

Of those with an opinion on whether alcohol was involved, more are inclined to believe that the incident was not alcohol-related (24 per cent of individual and 45 per cent of institutional victims), than to believe that is was alcohol-related (12 per cent for both categories of victim). Assault and vandalism are the two crime categories where a substantial proportion of victims believe the incident to be related to alcohol: 56 per cent in the case of assault; 38 per cent in the case of vandalism directed at institutions and 31 per cent in the case of vandalism directed at individuals.

Intimidation by Offender

One issue of concern to the Gardaí, in the context of providing support to victims of crime, was the adequacy of the protection they received from possible intimidation by the offender after the incident. The proportion of individual victims who felt intimidated by the offender (Table 4.9) was less than one in 14 for all categories of crime except assault.

Table 4.9: Whether Victim Intimidated by Offender by Crime and Victim Type (column percentages within victim type)

	Theft of Vehicle	Theft from Vehicle	Fraud	Ass-ault	Burg-lary	Agg. Burg-lary	Theft from per-son	Agg. Theft from person	Other Theft	Van-dal-ism	Total
Individual											
Yes	0	3	*	48	4	0	1	5	5	7	7
No	100	97	*	52	96	100	99	95	95	93	93
Weighted Cases	12,953	16,510	240	6,875	17,445	391	3,083	6,123	10,726	5,680	80,027
Institution											
Yes	*	0	4	*	7	6	*	*	13	3	8
No	*	100	96	*	93	94	*	*	87	97	92
Weighted Cases	945	2,328	3,338	171	13,548	1,098	0	527	12,994	4,519	39,467

Note: Cases weighted to total number of incidents in 1995.

In assault cases, nearly half of the victims experienced some form of intimidation by the offender, apart from the incident itself. The overall pattern was similar for institutional victims, with the exception of other theft, where intimidation was reported in one case in eight. This intimidation was most likely (70 per cent) to occur after reporting the crime. Cases where the victim was intimidated as a witness (9 per cent) or after sentencing (8 per cent) were less common (See Table 4.10).

Table 4.10: When Victim Intimidated by Offender by Crime and Victim Type (column percentages within victim type)

	Assault	Other	Total
Individual			
When reporting crime	25	25	25
After reporting	73	65	70
As witness	15	2	9
After sentencing	10	6	8
Other	14	13	13
Total Weighted Cases	3,315	2,545	5,860
Institution			
When reporting crime	*	36	35
After reporting	*	65	66
As witness	*	9	9
After sentencing	*	1	1
Other	*	8	8
Total Weighted Cases	102	3,078	3,180

Note: Only includes cases where offender intimidated victim. Cases weighted to total number of incidents in 1995.

Table 4.11 looks at whether victims who experienced intimidation felt that the protection available to them was adequate. Assault is the only crime category where there are enough cases experiencing intimidation to provide a separate breakdown in the table.

About one-third of the assault victims felt they received insufficient protection from the Gardaí, while almost 60 per cent felt that the protection provided by the Gardaí was adequate.

The actual numbers needing protection in court tended to be lower, since fewer cases had gone to court at the time of the interview. Two-fifths of assault victims felt that the protection provided in court was adequate, while one-fifth felt that it was not adequate.

Table 4.11: Whether Victim Felt Protection Was Adequate by Crime Type (column percentages)

	Assault	Other	Total
From Gardaí			
Yes	58%	39%	46%
No	35%	13%	22%
NA/Not Needed	8%	48%	32%
In Court			
Yes	44%	6%	20%
No	21%	7%	12%
NA/Not Needed	36%	87%	67%
Elsewhere			
Yes	31%	9%	18%
No	29%	11%	19%
NA/Not Needed	40%	80%	63%
Weighted N cases	3,418	5,623	9,041

Note: Includes only those victims intimidated by offender. Cases weighted to total incidents in 1995.

Nearly one-third of the assault victims felt that the protection available to them in other circumstances was adequate, with nearly as many feeling that it was not adequate. The kinds of things the victims had in mind here can be gauged from their responses to an open-ended question on how the level of protection might be improved. Only about one-fifth of the victims who experienced intimidation had a suggestion. These tended to revolve around a faster response time in coming to the scene of the crime, and getting the offenders arrested.

Victims and the Gardaí

As noted in the introduction, one of the goals of this research project was to assess the quality of service provided by the Gardaí to victims of crime and to discover ways in which the service might be improved. Previous research in Ireland has pointed to the generally positive perception of the Gardaí on the part of the public. Murphy and Whelan (1995) found that 85 per cent of the population felt that the Gardaí at their local station are approachable, and 89 per cent of those who had reason to contact the Gardaí within the past two years were satisfied with the service received. The QNHS module on crime found that 65 per cent of the national sample felt that the Gardaí were doing a good or very good job in controlling crime in their area, while only 9 per cent felt that they were doing a poor or very poor job (Central Statistics Office, 1999a). This section focuses on the interaction between the victims of recorded crime and the Gardaí and looks at the satisfaction of victims with various aspects of the service provided by the Gardaí. We begin by examining the initial contact between the victim and the Gardaí — how the crime was reported, whether the Gardaí came to the scene, whether a written statement was taken. Next we examine the level of satisfaction with this initial contact and with subsequent information provided on the progress of the case, and whether the respondent would be more or less inclined to report a similar incident in the future. We then turn to the respondent's view of how effective the Gardaí are in controlling crime in their area and to membership of, and perceptions of, Neighbourhood Watch and Community Alert Schemes.

As in the previous section, the cases are weighted by the incident weight, so that each criminal incident is given an equal weight in the analysis. The tables also distinguish between incidents targeted against institutions and those targeted against individuals.

Initial Contact with the Gardaí

We begin, in Table 4.12, by looking at how the crime was reported to the Gardaí. Most crime where the victim was an individual was reported by a telephone call to the local Garda station (35 per cent) or by a personal visit to the station by the victim (35 per cent). In 14 per cent of cases, the call was made by someone else (particularly in cases of assault — 34 per cent — or aggravated burglary — 41 per cent), while in 8 per cent of cases the crime was reported by dialling 999 (30 per cent in the case of aggravated burglary).

Where the target of crime was an institution, in contrast, a personal visit to the Garda station was rare (only 5 per cent of cases). In 56 per cent of cases, the crime was reported by a telephone call to the local Garda station, while in 13 per cent of cases the crime was reported by someone other than the victim. The use of monitored alarms accounted for 37 per cent of the reports in cases of aggravated burglary against institutions, but this was very rare in the case of crimes against individuals.

What is also very clear from this table is that only a very small proportion of crime in the categories covered in this report would be known to the Gardaí without having been reported by the victim or a witness. Only 3 per cent of crime against individuals and 4 per cent of crime against institutions is discovered by the Gardaí directly. It is also interesting to note that 2 per cent of crime against individuals is reported by informing a Garda on patrol, but that this increases to 13 per cent of theft from the person and 11 per cent of aggravated theft from the person. These are the crimes most likely to occur in busy urban areas where victims are more likely to encounter Gardaí on patrol.

Table 4.12: How Crime Was Reported by Crime and Victim Type (column percentages within victim type)

	Theft of Vehicle	Theft from Vehicle	Fraud	Assault	Burglary	Agg. Burglary	Theft from person	Agg. Theft from person	Other Theft	Vandalism	Total
Individual											
Called 999	7	4	*	6	18	30	3	4	5	6	8
Phoned local station	46	37	*	18	43	18	16	15	37	37	35
Informed Garda on patrol	0	2	*	1	0	3	13	11	1	1	2
Called to station	40	48	*	29	16	0	45	35	43	34	35
Someone else made call	4	3	*	34	19	41	17	27	8	20	14
Monitored alarm	0	0	*	1	0	0	0	0	0	0	0
Discovered by Gardaí	3	4	*	4	1	0	4	2	4	2	3
Other	0	1	*	4	2	0	3	3	3	0	2
Don't know	0	1	*	2	2	9	0	2	0	1	1
Weighted N Cases	12,953	16,510	240	6,875	17,445	391	3,083	6,123	10,726	5,680	80,027
Institution											
Called 999	*	10	4	*	10	19	*	*	7	4	8
Phoned local station	*	61	66	*	50	14	*	*	64	55	56
Informed Garda on patrol	*	0	1	*	0	2	*	*	2	4	1
Called to station	*	29	8	*	2	1	*	*	4	3	5
Someone else made call	*	0	8	*	16	19	*	*	11	14	13
Monitored alarm	*	0	0	*	15	37	*	*	2	11	8
Discovered by Gardaí	*	0	5	*	4	3	*	*	4	7	4
Other	*	0	7	*	0	4	*	*	4	1	2
Don't know	*	0	1	*	4	0	*	*	1	0	2
Weighted N Cases	945	2,328	3,338	171	13,548	1,098	0	527	12,994	4,519	39,467

Note: Cases are weighted to the total number of incidents in 1995 (incident weight).

Table 4.13 looks at the number of Gardaí who came to the scene of the crime. This may not be relevant — such as in most cases where the victim went in person to the Garda station to report the crime. It was not relevant in 28 per cent of the incidents were the target was an individual, rising to about two-fifths of the incidents of vehicle theft, theft from the person and aggravated theft from the person.

Table 4.13: How Many Gardaí Came to Scene by Crime and Victim Type (column percentages within victim type)

	Theft of Veh-icle	Theft from Veh-icle	Fraud	Ass-ault	Burg-lary	Agg. Burg-lary	Theft from person	Agg. Theft from per-son	Other Theft	Van-dal-ism	Total
Individual											
None	8	19	*	7	5	0	10	4	9	6	9
One	17	12	*	17	22	0	24	20	21	17	18
Two	22	23	*	37	53	59	27	29	34	35	34
More than two	0	5	*	13	6	32	1	4	2	11	5
Can't recall /DK	9	8	*	7	2	9	0	4	6	3	6
Not relevant	43	33	*	20	11	0	39	39	28	29	28
Weighted N cases	*12,953*	*16,510*	*240*	*6,875*	*17,445*	*391*	*3,083*	*6,123*	*10,726*	*5,680*	*80,027*
Institution											
None	*	4	8	*	2	0	*	*	7	0	4
One	*	43	38	*	30	7	*	*	29	38	31
Two	*	34	41	*	52	60	*	*	51	52	49
More than two	*	0	2	*	9	32	*	*	5	5	7
Can't re-call/DK	*	0	7	*	6	1	*	*	4	5	5
Not relevant	*	19	4	*	1	0	*	*	4	0	3
Weighted N cases	*945*	*2,328*	*3,338*	*171*	*13,548*	*1,098*	*0*	*527*	*12,994*	*4,519*	*39,467*

Note: Cases are weighted to the total number of incidents in 1995 (incident weight).

In general, at least one Garda is more likely to come to the scene of the crime where the victim is an institution than where the victim is an individual. In 87 per cent of incidents where the victim is an institution, at least one Garda went to the scene of the crime, with the usual number of Gardaí going to the scene being two. This was true in only 57 per cent of the cases were the target was an individual.

Gardaí are most likely to go to the scene of a burglary or aggravated burglary, or, where the victim is an institution, to the scene of vandalism. In nearly all cases of aggravated burglary, at least two Gardaí went to the scene.

Table 4.14 shows whether a written statement was taken by the Gardaí from the crime victim. A written statement was taken in about the same proportion of cases targeting an individual and cases directed against institutions: 55–59 per cent.

Table 4.14: Whether Written Statement Was Taken by Crime and Victim Type (column percentages within victim type)

	Theft of Veh- icle	Theft from Veh- icle	Fraud	Ass- ault	Burg- lary	Agg. Burg- lary	Theft from per- son	Agg. Theft from per- son	Other Theft	Van- dal- ism	Total
Individual											
Yes	45	52	*	87	47	76	61	62	53	61	55
No	40	37	*	11	48	18	25	27	38	28	36
Cant recall	15	11	*	2	5	6	14	11	9	10	9
Weighted Cases	12,953	16,510	240	6,875	17,445	391	3,083	6,123	10,726	5,680	80,027
Institution											
Yes	*	79	73	*	57	70	*	*	58	47	59
No	*	11	21	*	33	17	*	*	36	26	30
Cant recall	*	10	5	*	10	13	*	*	7	27	11
Weighted Cases	945	2,328	3,338	171	13,548	1,098	0	527	12,994	4,519	39,467

Note: Cases are weighted to the total number of incidents in 1995 (incident weight).

In roughly 10 per cent of cases, the victim cannot recall whether or not a written statement was taken. A written statement was most likely to be taken in cases of assault (87 per cent) and aggravated burglary (70–76 per cent).

Satisfaction with Garda Service

Table 4.15 looks at the percentage of crime victims who were satisfied with various aspects of the Garda service. The percentages show those who were "fairly satisfied" and "very satisfied". Cases where an item is not applicable (e.g. the Gardaí did not come to the scene, or the victim had no questions) are not included in the calculation of the percentages. In general, the level of satisfaction is quite high. Over 80 per cent of individual victims are satisfied with the speed with which the initial call was answered, and the politeness of the Gardaí. Over 70 per cent are satisfied with the speed with which the Gardaí came to scene, the understanding of the problem shown by the Gardaí, and the answers to the victim's questions. Over two-thirds of the individual victims are satisfied with the thoroughness of the Gardaí.

In the case of institutional victims, the level of satisfaction with the thoroughness and politeness of the Gardaí, their understanding of the problem, and their answers to questions tends to be higher than for the corresponding items where the victim is an individual. Institutional victims tend to be less satisfied than individual victims with the speed with which the initial call was answered and the speed with which the Gardaí came to the scene. Nevertheless, over 70 per cent of institutional victims are satisfied with all of these aspects of the Garda service.

Table 4.15: Per Cent Satisfied with Aspects of Garda Service by Crime and Victim Type (column percentages within victim type)

	Theft of Veh- icle	Theft from Veh- icle	Fraud	Ass- ault	Burg- lary	Agg. Burg- lary	Theft from per- son	Agg. Theft from per- son	Other Theft	Van- dal- ism	Total
Individual											
Speed Answer Call	78	85	*	87	79	76	86	93	81	82	82
Speed Came to Scene	81	77	*	84	74	82	89	90	76	70	78
Thoroughness	71	65	*	66	71	63	73	72	72	63	69
Politeness	94	92	*	84	95	88	91	96	96	84	93
Understanding shown	81	76	*	70	74	70	84	84	87	78	79
Answers to questions	80	78	*	67	77	78	81	85	83	73	78
Info on progress	33	30	*	55	24	41	15	30	27	37	31
Info on outcome	28	28	*	32	15	24	11	21	21	32	24
Weighted N (Min)	*7,509*	*8,503*	*131*	*4,669*	*13,165*	*289*	*1,021*	*2,945*	*5,594*	*3,736*	*47,561*
Institution											
Speed Answer Call	*	68	82	*	71	78	*	*	76	84	75
Speed Came to Scene	*	66	81	*	67	77	*	*	72	96	73
Thoroughness	*	78	84	*	68	78	*	*	79	77	74
Politeness	*	100	98	*	96	97	*	*	95	96	95
Understanding shown	*	96	92	*	90	82	*	*	92	82	89
Answers to questions	*	76	87	*	87	80	*	*	91	82	85
Info on progress	*	0	43	*	37	41	*	*	53	53	41
Info on outcome	*	0	40	*	33	29	*	*	39	37	33
Weighted N (Min)	*783*	*1,794*	*2,433*	*171*	*10,263*	*1,012*	*0*	*461*	*11,020*	*3,841*	*31,779*

Note: Cases are weighted to the total number of incidents in 1995 (incident weight). Number of cases varies by item since cases where item is not applicable are excluded.

The two aspects of Garda service with which both individual and institutional victims were least likely to be satisfied are the provision of information on the progress of the case and on the outcome of the case. Only a third of individual victims were satisfied with the information made available to them on the progress of the case, and only a quarter were satisfied with the information made available to them on the outcome of the case. Institutional victims tend to be slightly more satisfied, with 41 per cent satisfied with information on the progress of the case and a third satisfied with information on the outcome of the case. Individual victims of theft from the person show the lowest level of satisfaction with the information provided on the case, while victims of assault tend to be most satisfied with information on the progress of the case (55 per cent) and information on the outcome of the case (32 per cent).

Table 4.16 provides some further insight into why the level of satisfaction with information on the case might be low. Only 38 per cent of the individual victims and 44 per cent of the institutional victims were contacted by the Gardaí at any time since reporting the crime. Generally, victims of violent crime were more likely to have been contacted by the Gardaí. Seventy per cent or more of the individual victims of assault and aggravated burglary were contacted by the Gardaí after reporting the crime, and 59 per cent of the institutional victims of aggravated burglary were contacted. The figure is only 34 per cent for individual victims of aggravated theft from the person, however.

Table 4.16: Whether Contacted by Gardaí since Reporting Crime by Crime and Victim Type (column percentages within victim type)

	Theft of Veh-icle	Theft from Veh-icle	Fraud	Ass-ault	Burg-lary	Agg. Burg-lary	Theft from per-son	Agg. Theft from per-son	Other Theft	Van-dal-ism	Total
Individual											
Yes	42	26	*	70	35	76	24	34	34	46	38
No	55	68	*	29	63	18	75	64	62	51	59
DK/ Can't recall	3	6	*	1	2	6	1	2	4	3	3
Weighted Cases	12,953	16,510	240	6,875	17,445	391	3,083	6,123	10,726	5,680	80,027
Institution											
Yes	*	21	54	*	48	59	*	*	41	48	44
No	*	79	36	*	47	38	*	*	52	41	49
DK/ Can't recall	*	0	10	*	5	3	*	*	7	11	7
Weighted Cases	945	2,328	3,338	171	13,548	1,098	0	527	12,994	4,519	39,467

Note: Cases are weighted to the total number of incidents in 1995 (incident weight).

Victims were asked whether, as a result of their experience, they would be more inclined are less inclined to report a similar crime in future. Table 4.17 shows the results. The majority, about 60 per cent, said that there would be no difference.

Table 4.17: Whether More Inclined to Report Similar Crime in Future by Crime and Victim Type (column percentages within victim type)

	Theft of Vehicle	Theft from Vehicle	Fraud	Assault	Burglary	Agg. Burglary	Theft from person	Agg. Theft from person	Other Theft	Vandalism	Total
Individual											
More inclined	20	24	*	39	35	27	31	26	33	34	29
No difference	73	70	*	30	59	56	54	65	57	52	61
Less inclined	7	7	*	31	6	17	14	9	10	14	10
Weighted Cases	12,953	16,315	240	6,863	16,493	391	3,043	6,058	10,521	5,495	78,373
Institution											
More inclined	*	0	51	*	36	36	*	*	33	36	35
No difference	*	96	45	*	59	58	*	*	63	61	60
Less inclined	*	4	3	*	5	6	*	*	4	3	6
Weighted Cases	945	2,328	3,225	171	12,599	1,098	0	527	12,813	4,519	38,224

Note: Cases are weighted to the total number of incidents in 1995 (incident weight).

However, 29 per cent of individual victims and 35 per cent of institutional victims said that they would be more inclined to report crime to the Gardaí in future. This is much higher than the 10 per cent of individual victims and 6 per cent of institutional victims who said that they would be less inclined to report a similar crime in future. Individual victims of assault are more polarised in their response to this item: 39 per cent said that they would be more inclined to report a similar incident in the future, 30 per cent said there would be no difference, and 31 per cent said they would be less inclined to report a similar incident in the future. This suggests that the experiences of victims of assault during and after reporting the crime is more varied than those of other crime victims.

Table 4.18 examines the crime victim's perspective on how good a job is done by the Gardaí in controlling crime in the areas where they live. In general, their perceptions of the performance of the Gardaí in terms of crime prevention tend to be positive rather than negative.

Table 4.18: How Good a Job Done by Gardaí in Crime Control by Crime and Victim Type (column percentages within victim type)

	Theft of Veh-icle	Theft from Veh-icle	Fraud	Ass-ault	Burg-lary	Agg. Burg-lary	Theft from per-son	Agg. Theft from person	Other Theft	Van-dal-ism	Total
Individual											
Very good	15	19	*	15	24	22	23	21	32	20	21
Fairly good	54	52	*	43	32	50	46	44	42	40	44
Neither good/bad	21	16	*	10	25	3	11	16	6	19	17
Fairly poor	3	7	*	15	9	9	15	13	10	11	9
Very poor	7	6	*	18	11	16	5	7	9	10	9
Weighted Cases	12,656	16,510	240	6,677	16,421	368	3,020	5,862	10,317	5,581	77,651
Institution											
Very good	*	38	39	*	16	22	*	*	28	40	26
Fairly good	*	37	41	*	49	31	*	*	45	23	42
Neither good/ bad	*	19	10	*	15	14	*	*	15	9	14
Fairly poor	*	6	7	*	13	24	*	*	11	13	12
Very poor	*	0	2	*	8	9	*	*	2	14	6
Weighted Cases	945	2,328	3,264	171	13,548	1,082	0	527	12,813	4,359	39,036

Note: Cases are weighted to the total number of incidents in 1995 (incident weight).

Overall, about two-thirds of the crime victims (both individuals and institutions) believe the Gardaí are doing either a very good or a fairly good job in controlling crime. On the other hand, 18 per cent believe the Gardaí are doing a very poor or fairly poor job.

The most positive rating comes from individual victims of other theft: nearly one-third believe the Gardaí are doing a very good job, while a further 42 per cent believe the Gardaí are doing a fairly good job. Amongst institutional victims, the most positive ratings come from victims of theft from vehicles, fraud and vandalism, where about two-fifths of victims believe the Gardaí are doing a very good job. The least positive ratings come from individual victims of assault and of aggravated burglary, of whom 16 to 18 per cent believed the Gardaí are doing a very poor job.

A question on public perceptions of how good a job is done by the Gardaí in controlling crime in the local area was included on the QNHS crime module. Some caution is required in comparing the results to those of the present study because of the difference in timing of the surveys (1996 for the present survey and 1998 for the QHNS), and a difference between the labelling of the neutral response categories ("neither good nor bad" in the present survey and "average" on the QNHS). We might expect crime victims to have a less favourable assessment of police effectiveness in controlling crime than the general population. However, the percentages giving a positive rating to the work of the Gardaí in controlling crime is very similar to that found for a national sample (including non-victims) in the QNHS crime module (Central Statistics Office, 1999a). On the other hand, the victims of recorded crime in the present study are more likely to give a negative evaluation and less likely to give a neutral response: 17 per cent of individual victims rate the Garda performance as "neither good not bad", compared to 26 per cent of the national sample who rate Garda performance as "average". Nine per cent of the victims believe the Gardaí are doing a poor job (compared to 7 per cent of the national sample) and 9 per cent of victims rate the Garda performance as "very poor" (compared to 3 per cent of the national sample). The more negative perception of Garda performance in crime control compared to a national sample is understandable, given their experience of victimisation. However, the similar proportions giving a positive rating on crime control is somewhat surprising.

A similar question was included in the 1996 International Crime Victim Survey (Mayhew and van Dijk, 1997). This was a survey of the general population across 11 industrial countries, and not just of crime victims. The proportion of victims in the present survey judging Garda performance favourably (66 per cent) is on a par with the figures for the general population in Scotland (69 per cent), and England and Wales (68 per cent), although lower than the favourable ratings in Canada (80 per cent) and the US (77 per cent) (Mayhew and van Dijk, 1997). The present findings are also consistent with the generally positive view of the Gardaí on the part of the public in Ireland found by Murphy and Whelan (1995).

Court Services

Table 4.19 looks at whether special court services for crime victims were, or would have been, useful. Such services would include advice on what to expect during the court case, and support if called on as a witness for the prosecution. Only those victims involved in cases that have already gone to court are included in this table. Generally, individual victims tend to perceive these types of services as being more useful than institutional victims.

Nearly half of the individual victims and about a third of the institutional victims feel that such services would be useful, but a substantial proportion (17 per cent of individual victims and 26 per cent of institutional victims) are not sure. Victims of assault are most likely to feel that special court services would be useful (70 per cent), while victims of theft from a vehicle are least likely (16 per cent).

Table 4.19: Whether Special Court Services for Victims Useful by Crime and Victim Type (column percentages within victim type)

	Theft of Veh- icle	Theft from Veh- icle	Fraud	Ass- ault	Burg- lary	Agg. Burg- lary	Theft from person	Agg. Theft from person	Other Theft	Van- dal- ism	Total
Individual											
Yes	31	16	*	70	59	54	25	41	44	46	46
No	66	51	*	18	30	46	30	36	43	33	37
Not sure	3	33	*	13	11	0	45	23	13	21	17
Weighted Cases	*2,803*	*3,133*	*39*	*4,980*	*3,910*	*126*	*677*	*1,401*	*1,389*	*1,657*	*20,113*
Institution											
Yes	*	0	31	*	24	39	*	*	53	27	35
No	*	100	54	*	22	31	*	*	43	58	38
Not sure	*	0	15	*	54	31	*	*	5	15	26
Weighted Cases	*0*	*147*	*1,032*	*136*	*4,320*	*433*	*0*	*226*	*3,788*	*1,965*	*12,047*

Note: Cases are weighted to the total number of incidents in 1995 (incident weight). Table includes only cases that went to court.

Neighbourhood Watch and Community Alert

Neighbourhood Watch and Community Alert schemes involve co-operation between local communities and the Gardaí for the purpose of crime prevention. Neighbourhood Watch schemes are found in urban areas, while Community Alert schemes are the rural equivalent. Table 4.20 looks at the proportion of crime victims who were living in Neighbourhood Watch or Community Alert areas. Note that even for institutional victims, this refers to where the respondent lives, and not to the area where the institution is located.

Table 4.20: Whether Living in Neighbourhood Watch/Community Alert Area by Crime and Victim Type (column percentages)

	Theft of Veh-icle	Theft from Veh-icle	Fraud	Ass-ault	Burg-lary	Agg. Burg-lary	Theft from per-son	Agg. Theft from person	Other Theft	Van-dal-ism	Total
Individual											
Yes	50	50	*	52	51	44	57	48	50	56	51
No	30	37	*	41	38	50	30	28	34	28	35
Don't Know	20	13	*	7	11	6	13	24	16	17	15
Weighted N cases	12,953	16,510	240	6,875	17,445	391	3,083	6,123	10,726	5,680	80,027
Institution											
Yes	*	65	55	*	60	56	*	*	64	56	60
No	*	25	35	*	32	32	*	*	35	30	33
Don't Know	*	10	9	*	8	12	*	*	2	14	7
Weighted N cases	945	2,328	3,338	171	13,548	1,098	0	527	12,994	4,519	39,467

Note: Cases are weighted to the total number of incidents in 1995 (incident weight). * indicates too few sample cases to provide a breakdown.

A little over half of the individual crime victims and 60 per cent of institutional respondents live in areas covered by these schemes. This rate is in keeping with the estimated 54 per cent of households nationally in areas covered by Neighbourhood Watch and Community Alert in 1996–97, ranging from 43 per cent in the Eastern Region to 62 per cent in the Dublin Region (McKeown and Brosnan, 1998). There is little difference in the proportion by crime category, but individual victims of aggravated burglary are somewhat less likely to live in Community Alert or Neighbourhood Watch areas. One in eight of the crime victims did not know whether their area was covered by such a scheme. The figure was one in five for victims of vehicle theft and almost one-quarter for victims of aggravated theft from the person.

Table 4.21 looks at whether the victims believe that such schemes are useful in either preventing crime or in helping them feel more secure. About 60–65 per cent of victims believe that the schemes are effective in each of these ways. Victims of other theft are most likely to believe that the schemes are effective. Individual victims of aggravated burglary are least likely to believe that the schemes are effective either in helping to prevent crime (36 per cent) or in helping them feel more secure (23 per cent). The proportion of assault victims who believe the schemes are effective in either of these ways is also lower than average.

Table 4.21: Per Cent Believing that Neighbourhood Watch/ Community Alert Helps Prevent Crime or Feel More Secure by Crime and Victim Type (column percentages)

	Theft of Vehicle	Theft from Vehicle	Fraud	Assault	Burglary	Agg. Burglary	Theft from person	Agg. Theft from person	Other Theft	Vandalism	Total
Individual											
Prevents crime	60	58	*	51	67	36	64	68	78	72	65
Helps feel secure	59	61	*	47	61	23	62	69	83	54	62
Weighted N cases	5,867	6,241	100	2,698	7,585	127	1,216	1,913	4,742	2,627	33,113
Institution											
Prevents crime	*	77	74	*	52	74	*	*	73	72	64
Helps feel secure	*	59	67	*	52	68	*	*	64	70	59
Weighted N cases	268	922	1,613	153	7,812	489	0	292	6,859	1,844	20,252

Note: Cases are weighted to the total number of incidents in 1995 (incident weight). Table includes only those living in an area covered by these schemes.

Outcome of the Case

Table 4.22 turns to the outcome of the case, based on information provided by the crime victims. Perhaps what is most striking in the table is the proportion of victims who did not know the outcome of the case. This is particularly true of individual victims. In 32 per cent of cases targeted against individuals, the victim did not know whether or not the offender had been caught, reaching over 40 per cent in the case of theft from the vehicle and theft from the person.

Table 4.22: Outcome of Case by Crime and Victim Type (column percentages within victim type)

	Theft of Veh-icle	Theft from Veh-icle	Fraud	Ass-ault	Burg-lary	Agg. Burg-lary	Theft from per-son	Agg. Theft from person	Other Theft	Van-dal ism	Total
Individual Victim											
Offender apprehended	8	16	*	78	23	44	10	20	21	51	25
Offender not Apprehended	59	40	*	12	44	18	46	41	51	39	43
Don't know whether apprehended	34	44	*	9	33	38	44	39	28	10	32
Total Weighted Cases	12,953	16,510	240	6,875	17,445	391	3,083	6,123	10,546	5,680	79,848
Offender apprehended and . . .											
Case being processed	0	6	*	21	24	20	0	4	9	5	14
Cautioned/ Juvenile Diversion	0	24	*	4	7	0	12	5	30	22	13
Not proceeded – other	15	4	*	11	0	33	12	16	18	9	9
Prosecuted but acquitted	0	0	*	9	0	0	0	0	0	4	3
Custodial sentence	24	21	*	18	33	34	12	31	8	13	21
Non-custodial sentence (fine, suspended sentence)	45	7	*	33	10	0	0	10	9	19	19
Don't know outcome	15	37	*	4	26	13	63	34	25	28	22
Total Weighted Cases	979	2,601	100	5,378	3,979	171	322	1,241	2,251	2,912	19,933
Offender Not Apprehended . . .											
Case Open	7	12	*	1	19	*	6	10	27	22	15
Case Closed	29	12	*	42	7	*	16	13	14	8	16
Don't know if case open/closed	64	76	*	56	74	*	78	76	60	69	69
Total Weighted Cases	7,629	6,611	101	846	7,660	69	1,412	2,500	5,257	2,205	34,391

Table 4.22 (continued)

	Theft of Vehicle	Theft from Vehicle	Fraud	Assault	Burglary	Agg. Burglary	Theft from person	Agg. Theft from person	Other Theft	Vandalism	Total
Institution											
Offender apprehended	*	13	64	*	44	33	*	*	68	30	50
Offender not apprehended	*	30	22	*	48	47	*	*	29	56	38
Don't know whether apprehended	*	57	15	*	9	19	*	*	3	14	12
Total Weighted Cases	945	2,328	3,338	171	13,548	1,098	0	527	12,813	4,519	39,285
Offender Apprehended and . . .											
Case being processed	*	*	16	*	19	20	*	*	14	0	15
Cautioned/ Juvenile Diversion	*	*	0	*	6	0	*	*	14	12	10
Not proceeded — other	*	*	12	*	8	4	*	*	7	32	10
Prosecuted but acquitted	*	*	3	*	0	0	*	*	4	5	5
Custodial sentence	*	*	5	*	29	59	*	*	10	5	16
Non-custodial sentence (fine, suspended sentence)	*	*	28	*	7	3	*	*	15	41	16
Don't know outcome	*	*	35	*	31	13	*	*	35	5	30
Total Weighted Cases	292	293	2,120	153	5,924	367	0	300	8,683	1,370	19,501
Offender Not Apprehended . . .											
Case Open	*	*	33	*	13	30	*	*	16	23	17
Case Closed	*	*	20	*	17	13	*	*	21	30	22
Don't know if case open/closed	*	*	47	*	70	58	*	*	63	46	61
Total Weighted Cases	278	706	726	17	6,462	517	0	131	3,709	2,526	15,072

Note: * indicate too few cases to provide breakdown. Cases weighted to total number of incidents in 1995.

Of the 25 per cent of cases where the victim knows that the offender was apprehended, one-fifth of the victims had no further information regarding the outcome of the case. Of the 43 per cent of individual victims who know that the offender was *not* apprehended, over two-thirds do not know whether the case was open or closed.

In a quarter of the cases involving individual victims and half of the cases involving institutions, the offender was apprehended. The offender was most likely to be apprehended in assault cases (78 per cent) and in cases of fraud and other theft directed against institutions (64 and 68 per cent respectively). The high figures for these types of crime, together with the low reporting rates noted in Chapter 3, again suggest that reported cases are but a small and selective subset of all such incidents. The high figure for assault is influenced by the fact that the offender was known to the victim in over half the cases, and that the sample of non-indictable assaults was drawn from cases where proceedings were initiated. The fact that the sample does not include non-indictable incidents unless proceedings were taken also accounts for the relatively high proportion of vandalism incidents where the offender was apprehended (51 per cent for individual targets and 30 per cent among institutional targets). The offender was least likely to be apprehended in the case of theft of vehicle (8 per cent).[2]

Turning now to the subset of cases where the offender was apprehended, in one in five incidents directed against individuals and one in six targeted against institutions, the offender had received a custodial sentence by the time of the interview, with similar proportions resulting in a non-custodial sentence. The proportion resulting in a custodial sentence was highest for aggravated burglary (34 per cent for individual victims and 59 per cent for institutional victims). About one-fifth of the assault cases where the offender was apprehended resulted in a custodial sentence at the time of the interview, while one third resulted in a non-custodial sentence. In those cases where the victim knows that the offender was not apprehended (two-fifths of the incidents

---

[2] The sample includes cases of non-indictable vehicle takings even if no proceedings were taken.

targeted against individuals and over one-third of those where the victim was an institution), most of the victims (61 to 69 per cent) did not know whether the case was open or closed.

Table 4.23 examines another aspect of the outcome of the case — whether any stolen property was recovered.

Table 4.23: Whether Property Recovered by Crime and Victim Type (column percentages)

	Theft of Veh-icle	Theft from Veh-icle	Fraud	Ass-ault	Burg-lary	Agg. Burg-lary	Theft from per-son	Agg. Theft from person	Other Theft	Van-dal-ism	Total
Individual, property stolen and . . .											
All recovered	28	7	*	*	0	0	3	9	11	*	10
Some recovered	37	18	*	*	15	11	31	23	17	*	22
None recovered	35	75	*	*	85	89	66	68	73	*	68
Weighted N Cases	*12,953*	*15,881*	*240*	*119*	*14,559*	*310*	*2,963*	*5,862*	*10,394*	*674*	*63,956*
Institution, property stolen and . . .											
All recovered	*	4	30	*	9	6	*	*	54	*	29
Some recovered	*	27	19	*	13	11	*	*	7	*	12
None recovered	*	69	51	*	78	82	*	*	39	*	59
Weighted N Cases	*945*	*2,182*	*3,058*	*0*	*12,364*	*984*	*0*	*527*	*12,615*	*910*	*33,584*

Note: * indicate too few cases to provide breakdown. Cases weighted to total number of incidents. Incidents where no property was stolen are excluded.

We saw in Chapter 2 that some property is stolen in about four-fifths of incidents overall, but with much lower proportions in the case of assault (fewer than one case in twenty) and vandalism (about one incident in eight). No stolen property is recovered in 68 per cent of crime against individuals and 59 per cent of crime targeted against institutions. The crime categories where at least some property is likely to be recovered are theft of vehicle, fraud, and reported instances of other theft where the victim is an institution. Property is least likely to be recovered in cases of burglary and aggravated burglary.[3]

The overall level of satisfaction with the outcome of the case is not high, but institutions tend to be more satisfied than individuals (Table 4.24).

Table 4.24: Satisfaction with Outcome of Case by Crime and Victim Type (column percentages within victim type)

	Theft of Vehicle	Theft from Vehicle	Fraud	Assault	Burglary	Agg. Burglary	Theft from person	Agg. Theft from person	Other Theft	Vandalism	Total
Individual											
Very satisfied	10	16	*	20	4	19	12	9	7	19	12
Fairly satisfied	24	6	*	14	17	14	7	10	8	21	14
Neither	27	25	*	10	25	5	48	28	35	25	26
Fairly dissatisfied	18	28	*	13	21	14	23	26	23	13	21
Very dissatisfied	21	25	*	43	33	47	10	26	27	23	28
Weighted N cases	*8,459*	*8,630*	*162*	*6,184*	*10,427*	*241*	*1,468*	*3,454*	*7,464*	*4,911*	*51,400*
Institution											
Very satisfied	*	0	26	*	4	13	*	*	26	18	16
Fairly satisfied	*	15	28	*	24	23	*	*	20	8	20
Neither	*	15	17	*	29	20	*	*	20	44	25
Fairly dissatisfied	*	44	17	*	23	27	*	*	16	7	19
Very dissatisfied	*	26	12	*	20	17	*	*	17	22	20
Weighted N cases	*569*	*999*	*2,579*	*171*	*10,989*	*796*	*0*	*430*	*11,463*	*3,574*	*31,571*

Note: Includes only cases where outcome is known. * indicates too few cases to provide breakdown. Cases weighted to total number of incidents in 1995.

---

[3] In cases of vehicle theft, the recovered property may have been something other than the vehicle itself. In cases of "other theft" property would typically be recovered when the offender was apprehended. We saw evidence earlier (Table 4.1) that other theft tends to be reported – particularly by institutions – only when the offender is seen.

About a quarter of individual victims and just over a third of institutional victims are fairly satisfied or very satisfied with the outcome, while nearly half of individual victims and almost two-fifths of the institutional victims are fairly dissatisfied or very dissatisfied. Among individual victims, victims of assault and aggravated burglary are the most polarised, with both the highest percentage very satisfied (19–20 per cent) and the highest percentage very dissatisfied (43–47 per cent). One-third of the victims of domestic burglary are also very dissatisfied with the outcome of the case. Among institutional victims of crime, victims of fraud are the most satisfied (26 per cent very satisfied and 28 per cent fairly satisfied) followed by victims of other theft (26 per cent very satisfied and 20 per cent fairly satisfied).

As can be seen from Table 4.25, the main reasons for satisfaction, among those who were satisfied with the outcome, tend to be the recovery of property, followed by the arrest of the offender. For institutional victims, the ordering of reasons for satisfaction is slightly different. The arrest of the offender is the main reason for satisfaction, more often than the recovery of property. As we might expect, for those crimes involving violence or where property is rarely stolen, the reason for satisfaction tends to be the arrest and conviction of the offender (assault, aggravated burglary, aggravated theft from the person, vandalism).

Table 4.26 examines the main reason for dissatisfaction with the outcome of the case on the part of those who were dissatisfied. For individual victims, failure to arrest and the fact that property was not recovered (or that the victim was not compensated) are about equally important. These are the main reasons for dissatisfaction in roughly 60 per cent of cases where the victim was dissatisfied with the outcome.

Table 4.25: Main Reason for Satisfaction with Outcome of Case by Crime and Victim Type (column percentages within victim type)

	Theft of Vehicle	Theft from Vehicle	Fraud	Assault	Burglary	Agg. Burglary	Theft from person	Agg. Theft from person	Other Theft	Vandalism	Total
Individual											
Arrest	1	18	*	38	21	57	14	31	0	41	21
Conviction	5	18	*	39	11	43	14	37	20	12	17
Recovery of property/ compensation	83	36	*	1	43	0	57	11	36	21	39
Do not know	4	9	*	4	0	0	0	0	0	7	4
Other	8	19	*	18	25	0	14	22	44	19	19
Total Weighted Cases	2,862	1,925	31	2,101	1,944	80	282	602	898	1,964	12,688
Institution											
Arrest	*	*	46	*	33	32	*	*	37	37	38
Conviction	*	*	22	*	7	56	*	*	16	20	15
Recovery of property/ compensation	*	*	21	*	29	4	*	*	37	43	32
Do not know	*	*	0	*	0	8	*	*	0	0	0
Other	*	*	11	*	31	0	*	*	11	0	15
Total Weighted Cases	23	147	1,388	0	3,093	290	0	226	5,063	945	11,175

Note: Includes cases where victim is "very satisfied" or "fairly satisfied" with outcome. * indicates too few cases to provide breakdown. Cases weighted to total number of incidents in 1995.

Table 4.26: Main Reason for Dissatisfaction with Outcome of Case by Crime and Victim Type (column percentages within victim type)

	Theft of Vehicle	Theft from Vehicle	Fraud	Assault	Burglary	Agg. Burglary	Theft from person	Agg. Theft from person	Other Theft	Vandalism	Total
Individual											
Failure to arrest	52	33	*	16	33	16	5	30	12	23	29
Property not recovered/ no compensation	36	21	*	0	31	31	52	24	71	11	30
Failure to proceed	2	16	*	6	7	46	8	11	6	36	10
Failure to convict	4	8	*	17	8	0	17	13	0	3	8
Sentence too lenient	2	0	*	38	8	0	0	4	0	14	8
Garda disinterest/ did not keep informed	0	22	*	2	10	0	13	11	11	13	10
Other	5	0	*	21	4	8	4	7	0	0	5
Total Weighted cases	*3,297*	*4,516*	*100*	*3,466*	*5,656*	*149*	*475*	*1,743*	*3,664*	*1,741*	*24,805*
Institution											
Failure to arrest	*	38	19	*	39	66	*	*	22	51	35
Property not recovered/ no compensation	*	38	26	*	23	7	*	*	17	16	19
Failure to proceed	*	0	12	*	20	5	*	*	34	0	22
Failure to convict	*	0	0	*	0	5	*	*	5	18	4
Sentence too lenient	*	0	19	*	4	0	*	*	0	0	3
Garda disinterest/ did not keep informed	*	0	16	*	10	8	*	*	11	0	9
Other	*	25	8	*	4	8	*	*	10	15	8
Total Weighted Cases	*546*	*591*	*753*	*171*	*4,719*	*334*	*0*	*131*	*3,636*	*1,042*	*11,922*

Note: Includes only cases where victim dissatisfied with outcome. * indicates too few cases to provide breakdown. Cases weighted to total number of incidents in 1995.

In 10 per cent of cases, dissatisfaction was attributed to Garda disinterest and failure to keep the victim informed. These were not pre-coded options, since they refer more to the processing of the case by the Gardaí than to its outcome. This was the main reason offered in 22 per cent of cases of theft from a vehicle. Failure to proceed was the most frequently cited reason for dissatisfaction in cases of aggravated burglary and vandalism, while lenient sentencing was the most frequently cited reason in assault cases.

For institutional victims, the failure to arrest and the failure to proceed with the case are cited more often than the failure to recover property. This probably reflects the fact that many crimes (such as shoplifting) are only reported when the offender is "caught in the act". In these cases, property would typically be recovered at the time the offender is apprehended. The failure to arrest the offender was the most important reason for about two-thirds of the victims of aggravated burglary, half of the victims of vandalism, and about two-fifths of the victims of burglary and theft from a vehicle.

Summary

This chapter began by examining the characteristics of the offender, to the extent that these were known to the victim. In half of the crimes against individuals and about 70 per cent of the crimes against institutions, the victim knew how many offenders were involved — the victim had either witnessed the incident or was aware of the number of offenders (if any) subsequently charged with the crime. For individual victims, then, the offender is often unknown — even to the extent that they do not know how many offenders were involved in the incident, their ages or sex. This is particularly true of the type of crime where the victim is not present, such as vehicle theft, and theft from a vehicle. It is interesting, however, that the offender is identified in a larger proportion of burglaries against institutions (61 per cent) than of burglaries against individuals (47 per cent). This may be because institutions are more likely to be protected by security cameras and monitored alarms.

Where the sex of the offender is known, it is most likely to be male. Other theft directed at institutions (a category that includes shoplifting) is the only crime category where more than one-third of the offenders are female. About one-fifth of the identified perpetrators of fraud against institutions are female.

Assault is the only crime where the victim (prior to the incident) knew the offender in more than half of the cases. In assaults of male victims, the offender tended to be less closely linked to the victim than in assaults against females. Only about one-quarter of female assault victims had been assaulted by a stranger (compared to nearly half of male victims); and in about a quarter of cases involving female victims, the assault was perpetrated by the spouse of the victim.

Most individual victims (62–64 per cent) and a substantial proportion of institutional victims (44–46 per cent) do not know whether drugs or alcohol were a factor in the incident that the survey focused on. Of those who did have an opinion, more were inclined to believe that the incident was not drug- or alcohol-related, than to believe that it was. There were certain exceptions, however: over half of the victims of aggravated burglary directed at institutions and over two-fifths of the individual victims of aggravated theft believed that the incident was drug-related. In the case of alcohol, the strongest link, from the victim's perspective, was between alcohol and assault (56 per cent) and alcohol and vandalism (31–38 per cent).

Intimidation by the offender (apart from the incident itself) occurs in less than one case in ten for all crime categories except assault. Nearly half of the assault victims experienced some form of intimidation from the offender. This was most likely to occur at some time after reporting the crime. One-third of assault victims who had been intimidated felt that the protection provided to them by the Gardaí was not adequate, and one-fifth would have appreciated more protection in court. Few of the respondents had any suggestions for improving the level of protection, however. Those who did have suggestions tended to focus on the speed with which the Gardaí arrived at the scene of the crime, and getting the offenders off the streets.

The second main section of this chapter examined the interaction between the crime victims and the Gardaí, and the level of satisfaction with the service provided by the Gardaí. The Gardaí are dependent on the public for information about crime: only three to four per cent of the crimes covered in this report were discovered by the Gardaí independently. Most crime against institutions is reported by a phone call to the local Garda station, while crime against individuals is likely to be reported either by a phone call to the local station, or by a personal visit by the victim to the station. In cases of assault and aggravated burglary where the victim is an individual, the call to the Gardaí is likely to be made by someone other than the victim. In over a third of the cases of aggravated burglary against institutions, the Gardaí are alerted by a monitored alarm.

Gardaí are more likely to come to the scene of the crime where the victim is an institution than in cases where the victim is an individual. They are also slightly more likely to take a written statement in cases where the victim is an institution, although in assault cases a written statement from the victim is taken in almost nine out of ten cases. The overall level of satisfaction with the service provided by the Gardaí is high for the speed with which a call is answered, the speed with which the Gardaí come to the scene, the thoroughness and politeness of the Gardaí, the understanding shown of the problem faced by the victim and answers to the victims' questions. Institutional victims tend to be slightly less satisfied than individual victims with the speed with which the call is answered or the speed with which the Gardaí come to the scene. However, they tend to be slightly more satisfied with the thoroughness, politeness, and understanding of the Gardaí, and the answers provided to their questions.

Levels of satisfaction tended to be a good deal lower when it came to information provided to the victim on the progress of the case and on the outcome of the case. A little over a third of individual victims, and somewhat over two-fifths of institutional victims were contacted by the Gardaí at some stage after reporting the crime. This lack of contact following report of the crime is no doubt the reason for the lower levels of satisfaction with the extent to which the victims are kept informed. Feedback was found to be an important determinant of general attitudes towards the Gardaí in a postal survey of burglary victims in the Limerick/ Tipperary area (Kevlin, 1998): those who were satisfied with the way in which they had been kept informed during the investigation held more positive attitudes towards the Gardaí after the incident.

Contrary to what we might expect, given that our sample have all experienced crime, the overall rating of how good a job is done by the Gardaí in controlling crime tends to be positive. Two-thirds of the victims (both individual and institutional) feel that the Gardaí are doing a good job in controlling crime, and only 18 per cent feel that the Gardaí are doing a poor job.

The majority of victims would be at least as likely to report a similar incident in the future, although the proportion of assault victims who would be less inclined to do so was relatively high, at about one-third. We saw in the previous section that nearly half of assault victims were intimidated by the offender at some stage since the crime occurred, with just over a third experiencing intimidation after reporting the crime. Assault victims who experienced intimidation were also more likely than other victims to feel that the protection provided by the Gardaí and the protection provided in court was inadequate. A higher proportion (about two-fifths) of assault victims were very dissatisfied with the outcome of the case. In this section, it is clear that their level of satisfaction with various aspects of the Garda service tends to be at least as high as that of other crime victims, and they tend to be more satisfied with information on the progress of the case. It seems therefore, that the reluctance to report a future incident is probably due to a combination of factors, including intimidation by the offender, a feeling that protection is not adequate, and dissatisfaction with the outcome of the case. It does not appear to be due to dissatisfaction with the service provided to the victim by the Gardaí who first dealt with the case.

Special court services to victims are seen as potentially more useful by individual victims − particularly victims of assault − than by institutional victims. Many victims whose cases have gone to court are uncertain as to the usefulness of such services, however. This probably reflects the fact that victims of crimes like vehicle theft are rarely called upon to appear in court cases involving the incident in question, since (as we saw in Chapter 2), they rarely witness the event.

Neighbourhood Watch and Community Alert are run jointly by the Gardaí and local communities and have crime prevention as one of their main aims. About half of the individual victims lived in areas covered by one of these schemes, with little variation across crime category. Nearly two-thirds of the individual crime victims felt that the schemes were useful in preventing crime, and a slightly lower proportion felt that the schemes helped them feel safer. Victims of aggravated burglary who lived in an area covered by these schemes were much less likely to feel that they were effective in either preventing crime or in helping them feel secure, however. This is in marked contrast to the individual victims of non-aggravated burglary − the other "home-based" crime category − who were very close to the overall figure for crime victims in terms of the percentage feeling the schemes were effective.

The third main part of the chapter focused on the outcome of the case. A relatively high proportion of individual victims (nearly one-third) did not know whether the offender had been apprehended. In one-quarter of the cases directed against individuals and half of the cases against institutions, the offender had been apprehended. There is some evidence that the apparently higher "apprehension rate" of offenders who commit crimes against institutions may be an artefact of differential reporting. For instance, in two-thirds of the cases of "other theft" against institutions, the offender is apprehended. It is highly unlikely that two-thirds of the *actual* cases in a category of crime that includes shoplifting result in the offender being caught. We saw in Chapter 3 that institutions tend to report a lower proportion of crimes than individuals in the "other theft" and vandalism categories. What is much more likely is that these types of incidents are only reported when the institution can identify the offender.

At least some stolen property was recovered in about one-third of the incidents involving theft targeted against individuals and about two-fifths of those directed against institutions. Property is most likely to be recovered in cases of vehicle theft — which includes "unauthorised takings" in the present sample — and reported cases of fraud and other theft directed against institutions. Property is least likely to be recovered in cases of burglary and aggravated burglary.

Institutional victims tend to be more satisfied than individual victims with the outcome of the case, although the overall level of satisfaction tends to be low. About a quarter of the individual victims and one-third of the institutional victims feel either "fairly satisfied" or "very satisfied" with the outcome. The main reasons for satisfaction or dissatisfaction tended to centre on the arrest and/or conviction of the offender in the case of violent crime, and the recovery/non-recovery of property for non-violent crimes involving theft. Perhaps surprisingly, the arrest and/or conviction of the offender appears relatively more important to institutional victims of crime, while the recovery of property appears relatively more important to individual victims of crime. This may arise if institutional victims believe that a single offender is responsible for repeated instances of the same type of offence (such as shop-lifting or fraud), or where institutions are better able to bear the financial costs of crime. Certainly, as we will see in Chapter 5, for the reported incidents covered here, the median net cost per incident to the institutional victims was appreciably the same as the median cost to the individual victim. Individual victims may also have a greater sentimental attachment to the property stolen.

The next chapter explores the impact of crime on the victims. It will include an examination of the extent to which the victims' experience of the criminal justice system — their interaction with the Gardaí and the outcome of the case — mediate the impact of the crime in terms of psychological distress.

Chapter 5

The Impact of Crime on Victims

The seriousness of crime has at least two dimensions: its "wrong-fulness" and its "harmfulness" to the victim (see discussion in O'Connell and Whelan, 1996). In this study, we have focused on the impact of crime on the victim rather than evaluations of crime seriousness by the public generally. Skogan (1994) suggests that the seriousness of crime to victims has a number of elements: the intrusiveness of the incident, and the seriousness of the harm to the victim in three areas: physical, financial, and emotional. Intrusiveness refers to the extent to which the incident invades areas considered private and safe: principally the body itself, but also the home. For this reason, burglary is generally rated as among the more serious incidents.

It is difficult, and perhaps not very productive, to devise an overall rating of the seriousness of the ten crime categories discussed in this study. This is because the seriousness of crimes in a particular category will depend on the mix of types of crime included. Some assaults or threats, for instance, may be rated as less serious by the victim than some instances of vandalism, depending on the perceived severity of the physical threat, on the one hand, and the value to the victim of the damaged property, on the other. Moreover, it would be difficult to arrive at a common scale to compare a given financial cost to a certain level of injury or psychological distress (but see Miller et al., 1996, for an attempt at this in the context of the United States).

Some of the difficulties involved are illustrated by the "seri-ousness" rankings of crimes in the International Crime Victim Surveys. Beginning in the 1992 wave, victims were asked to assess the seriousness of the incidents (unreported as well as reported) they had experienced. Seriousness was rated on a scale from 1 to 3, with higher scores indicating greater seriousness. The mean scores for different offence types, and the ranking of offences in terms of seriousness tended to be very similar across countries (Mayhew and van Dijk, 1997). Overall, across countries and tak-ing account of data from both the 1992 and 1996 wave, the crimes ranked as most serious tended to be vehicle theft, robbery and burglary with entry (with an average score of 2.3). Motorcycle theft, assault/threats, and sexual offences were ranked next with an average score of 2.1. Attempted burglary, theft of personal property and bicycle theft ranked next with scores of 1.8 to 1.9. Theft from garages (1.7), theft from a car (1.6) and damage to a car (1.6) were ranked less seriously (Mayhew and van Dijk, 1997).[1]

The similar overall seriousness ratings of sexual offences and assaults/threats, on the one hand, and motorcycle thefts, on the other, depends very much on the range of incidents that are in-cluded. These average figures for seriousness are not likely to be representative of the seriousness of *reported* crime, however, par-ticularly where a relatively low proportion of all offences in a category are reported, as in cases of assault and sexual assault. The seriousness of a criminal incident has been consistently found to be one of the main determinants of whether or not it is reported to the police (Mirrlees-Black et al., 1998; Mayhew and van Dijk, 1997). Reported assaults, then, are likely to be the subset of more serious incidents in that category.

The survey data analysed in this report allowed us to examine three aspects of the seriousness of the crime, from the victim's

---

[1] Average figures calculated from Table 4, in the website summary of the report at http://ruljis.leidenuniv.nl/user/jfcrjk/www/ICVS.

perspective: the physical injury involved, the financial costs, and the emotional impact on the victim. These issues are examined in the first three sections of the chapter. In the fourth section, the focus shifts to victims' perceptions of risk and of their own safety. The final section presents an analysis of the extent to which the psychological impact of the crime is mediated by the victims' experience of the criminal justice system.

The sample data for the first three sections of this chapter are weighted to the total number of incidents recorded by the Gardaí in 1995. In the fourth section, where the focus is on perceptions of crime overall, we use the victim weights so as to provide figures for comparison to sources based on a national population survey. The victim weights give equal representation to each person reporting a crime in the target year, irrespective of the numbers of crimes reported. The final section, which is based on a multivariate analysis of factors associated with the distress experienced by individual victims of crime, is based on the unweighted sample data.

Physical Injury

Overall, crimes where the target is an individual are more likely to result in physical injury than those where the target is a business or institution (Table 5.1). However, physical injury is present in only a minority of crimes: about one-tenth of the incidents where the victim is an individual and one in twenty of the incidents where the victim is an institution.

Physical injury is most likely to occur in assault (91 per cent), aggravated theft from the person (30 per cent), and aggravated burglary (24 per cent). In almost one-quarter of assault cases, at least one other person besides the respondent was physically injured.

Table 5.1: Whether Someone Was Physically Injured by Crime and Victim Type (column percentages within victim type)

	Theft of Vehicle	Theft from Vehicle	Assault	Burglary	Agg. Burglary	Theft from person	Agg. Theft from person	Other Theft	Vandalism	Total
Individual										
None	100	100	9	100	76	91	70	98	99	89
Respondent only	0	0	61	0	21	8	26	2	1	8
Other person only	0	0	6	0	0	1	1	0	0	1
Respondent and other	0	0	23	0	3	0	3	0	0	2
Total Weighted cases	12,953	16,510	6,875	17,445	391	3,083	6,123	10,726	5,680	79,787
Institution										
None	*	100	*	98	87	*	*	92	100	96
Respondent only	*	0	*	0	13	*	*	3	0	2
Other person only	*	0	*	2	0	*	*	3	0	2
Respondent and other	*	0	*	0	0	*	*	2	0	1
Total Weighted cases	945	2,328	171	13,548	1,098	0	527	12,994	4,519	36,129

Note: Sample weighted to total incidents in 1995. Fraud victims not included in table. * indicates too few cases to provide breakdown.

The seriousness of physical injury can be gauged by the type, if any, of medical treatment required. Only 2 per cent of crime resulted in injuries requiring hospitalisation, rising to 9 per cent in the case of aggravated burglaries against individuals, and 24 per cent in the case of assault (Table 5.2). A further 47 per cent of the assault cases required medical attention short of hospitalisation. Aggravated theft from the person rarely resulted in injuries requiring hospitalisation.

*Table 5.2: Seriousness of Physical Injury by Crime and Victim
Type (column percentages within victim type)*

	Theft of Vehicle	Theft from Vehicle	Assault	Burglary	Agg. Burglary	Theft from person	Agg. Theft from person	Other Theft	Vandalism	Total
Individual										
No injury	100	100	9	100	76	91	70	98	99	89
Cuts/bruises	0	0	20	0	3	4	18	0	0	3
Needed medical attention but not hospitalisation	0	0	47	0	12	4	11	2	0	5
Needed overnight hospital stay	0	0	12	0	0	0	0	0	1	1
Hospital, >1 night	0	0	12	0	9	1	1	0	0	1
Total Weighted cases	*12,953*	*16,510*	*6,875*	*17,445*	*391*	*3,083*	*6,123*	*10,726*	*5,680*	*79,787*
Institution										
No injury	*	100	*	98	87	*	*	92	100	96
Cuts/bruises	*	0	*	2	3	*	*	7	0	3
Needed medical attention but not hospitalisation	*	0	*	0	10	*	*	0	0	1
Hospital, >1 night	*	0	*	0	0	*	*	2	0	1
Total Weighted cases	*945*	*2,328*	*171*	*13,548*	*1,098*	*0*	*527*	*12,994*	*4,519*	*36,129*

Note: Sample weighted to total incidents in 1995. Fraud victims not included in table. * indicates too few cases to provide breakdown.

Comparing the figures on the treatment received by assault victims in Table 5.2 to those from the Quarterly National Household Survey (QNHS) crime module for victims of assault, it is clear that the injuries sustained by victims of recorded assault are more likely to require medical attention.[2] Sixty-four percent of the as-

---

[2] Note that domestic assaults were explicitly excluded from the QNHS survey, but these incidents would be included in the present sample if they were reported and recorded as an indictable incident or a non-indictable incident where proceedings were taken.

sault victims in the QNHS survey had either no injury or injuries that did not require medical attention, compared to 29 per cent of victims of recorded assault. Twenty-nine percent of the QNHS assault victims (compared to 47 per cent here) required some medical attention but not a hospital stay, and 7 per cent (compared to 24 per cent) required a hospital stay (Central Statistics Office, 1999a).

Table 5.3: Whether Injury Resulted in Permanent or Recurring Problems by Crime and Victim Type (column percentages within victim type)

	Theft of Vehicle	Theft from Vehicle	Assault	Burglary	Agg. Burglary	Theft from person	Agg. Theft from person	Other Theft	Vandalism	Total
Individual										
No injury	100	100	9	100	76	91	70	98	99	89
Injury, not permanent	0	0	70	0	18	8	21	2	0	8
Permanent/ recurring problem	0	0	21	0	6	1	8	0	1	3
Total Weighted cases	12,953	16,510	6,875	17,445	391	3,083	6,123	10,726	5,680	79,787
Institution										
No injury	*	100	*	98	87	*	*	92	100	96
Injury, not permanent	*	0	*	2	9	*	*	7	0	3
Permanent/ recurring problem	*	0	*	0	4	*	*	2	0	1
Weighted N Cases	945	2,328	171	13,548	1,098	0	527	12,994	4,519	36,129

Note: Sample weighted to total incidents in 1995. Fraud victims not included in table. * indicates too few cases to provide breakdown.

Table 5.3 looks at another aspect of the seriousness of the injury: whether the injuries were permanent or led to recurring problems for the individual. This was true of 3 per cent of all crimes where the target was an individual and 1 per cent of crimes where the target was an institution. One-fifth of the assault cases, a little fewer than one in ten cases of aggravated theft from the person and about one in twenty cases of aggravated burglary resulted in injuries that still affected the victim at the time of the interview.

Table 5.4: *Nature of Recurring/Permanent Injury by Crime and Victim Type (column percentages within victim type)*

	Theft of Veh-icle	Theft from Veh-icle	Ass-ault	Burg-lary	Agg. Burg-lary	Theft from person	Agg. Theft from person	Other Theft	Van-dal-ism	Total
Individual										
None	100	100	79	100	94	99	92	100	99	97
Back or limb pain	0	0	5	0	0	0	0	0	1	1
Headaches	0	0	5	0	0	0	3	0	0	1
Loss/damage to sight/hearing	0	0	2	0	3	0	0	0	0	0
Numbness/loss of feeling	0	0	4	0	0	0	0	0	0	0
Scars	0	0	1	0	3	0	3	0	0	0
Broken bones/teeth	0	0	3	0	0	0	1	0	0	0
Needed surgery	0	0	3	0	0	0	0	0	0	0
Other	0	0	2	0	3	1	2	0	0	0
Total Weighted cases	12,953	16,510	6,875	17,445	391	3,083	6,123	10,726	5,680	79,787
Institution										
None	*	100	*	100	96	*	*	98	100	99
Back or limb pain	*	0	*	0	0	*	*	0	0	0
Headaches	*	0	*	0	1	*	*	2	0	1
Loss/damage to sight/hearing	*	0	*	0	0	*	*	0	0	0
Numbness/loss of feeling	*	0	*	0	3	*	*	0	0	0
Scars	*	0	*	0	0	*	*	2	0	1
Total Weighted cases	945	2,328	171	13,548	1,098	0	527	12,994	4,519	36,129

Note: Sample weighted to total incidents in 1995. Fraud victims not included in table. * indicates too few cases to provide breakdown.

The nature of these injuries, as can be seen from Table 5.4, usually involves pain (back, limb pain or headaches) or numbness and loss of feeling. Up to two types of injury were coded in this table, so that some of those experiencing headaches, for instance, may also experience numbness or loss of feeling. Five per cent of assault cases left the victim with headaches up to two years later; 5 per cent resulted in back or limb pain; and 4 per cent led to numbness or loss of feeling. In 3 per cent of assault cases, the victims suffered from broken bones or broken teeth. Three per cent also needed some form of reconstructive surgery, such as repair to a broken nose.

Financial Costs

Table 5.5 examines the total financial loss, before taking account of insurance receipts, by crime type and the type of victim. This represents only the direct financial cost. If an amount were to be attached to the pain and trauma to the victims, the costs would likely be considerably higher. For instance, in a US study of the cost of crime, the researchers found that the cost of criminal victimisation (taking account of property and productivity losses and outlays for medical expenses) amounts to an annual "crime tax" of roughly $425 per man, woman, and child in the United States. When the values of pain, long-term emotional trauma, disability, and risk of death are put in dollar terms, the costs rise to $1,800 per person (Miller et al., 1996).

The figures in Table 5.5 are not directly comparable to the published Garda figures on the value of property stolen in the course of burglary, robbery and larceny. Respondents in the present survey were instructed to include the cost of damage, any medical treatment that was required as a result of the incident, costs associated with, for example, renting a car, and with time lost from work as a result of the incident. In addition, respondents in the present survey appear to discount the value of stolen property that was recovered very soon after the incident: in the case of shoplifting, this may happen before the offender has left the store.

Table 5.5: Total Financial Cost of Crime, by Crime and Victim Type

	Theft of Vehicle	Theft from Vehicle	Fraud	Ass-ault	Burg-lary	Agg. Burg-lary	Theft from per-son	Agg. theft from person	Other Theft	Van-dal-ism	Total
Individual											
No financial cost	5	6	*	48	7	12	5	12	5	12	10
Less than £300	16	47	*	39	35	44	89	79	65	55	45
£300–£499	8	15	*	5	15	3	3	4	17	17	12
£500–£999	16	20	*	6	14	6	1	4	8	8	12
£1,000–£4,999	41	10	*	1	26	20	0	1	5	5	16
£5,000–£9,999	13	2	*	0	2	12	1	0	0	3	3
£10,000 or more	1	0	*	0	1	3	0	0	0	0	0
Median	£3,000	£150	*	£150	£400	£150	£150	£150	£150	£150	£150
Total	*12,885*	*16,048*	*240*	*6,219*	*16,816*	*391*	*3,003*	*5,928*	*9,932*	*5,680*	*77,141*
Institution											
No financial cost	*	0	34	*	1	14	*	*	45	7	20
Less than £300	*	33	47	*	30	43	*	*	34	36	33
£300–£499	*	7	10	*	12	13	*	*	5	16	9
£500–£999	*	20	2	*	10	12	*	*	10	8	10
£1,000–£4,999	*	30	5	*	33	10	*	*	6	25	20
£5,000–£9,999	*	10	0	*	9	1	*	*	0	2	4
£10,000 or more	*	0	2	*	4	5	*	*	0	5	4
Median	*	£750	£150	*	£750	£150	*	*	£150	£400	£150
Total	*676*	*2,182*	*3,160*	*68*	*12,975*	*1,082*	*0*	*527*	*12,237*	*4,088*	*36,994*

Note: Sample weighted to total incidents in 1995. * indicates too few cases to provide breakdown.

The median figure given in the table is simply the mid-point of the median category for each crime category. The median financial cost of crime overall is under £300, for both individual and institutional victims. The most costly type of crime is theft of vehicle, with a median total cost in the £1,000 to £4,999 range; followed by theft from a vehicle directed against institutions and burglary targeted against institutions, both with median costs in the £500–£999 range.

Perhaps surprisingly, a greater proportion of incidents where the target is an institution (20 per cent) involved no financial loss than the corresponding proportion where the target was an individual or private household (10 per cent). The figure is highest for "other theft" at 45 per cent, followed by fraud where about one-third of cases result in no financial loss. In all probability, this arises because these crimes tend to be reported only when the offender is "caught in the act" and prevented from actually stealing or defrauding the organisation − an explanation which received some support from the finding in Chapter 4 that the offender is identified in a substantial proportion of reported incidents of fraud and other theft against institutions.

The QNHS figures on the financial cost of domestic burglaries indicated a substantially higher proportion involving no financial cost (29 per cent compared to 7 per cent in the present sample). Given that 21 per cent of the QNHS burglaries were not reported, this points to the role of the seriousness of the loss in the reporting of crime (Central Statistics Office, 1999a).

In cases where there was a financial loss, it is likely to be greater for institutions. While 45 per cent of incidents where the victim was an individual involved a loss of less than £300, the figure is 33 per cent for institutions. Over one-quarter of the incidents targeted against institutions involved financial losses in excess of £1,000 compared to one-fifth of incidents where the victim was an individual.

As we might expect, theft of vehicle involves the greatest cost among incidents targeted against individuals (with over half resulting in losses over £1,000), followed by burglary (29 per cent over £1,000) and aggravated burglary (35 per cent over £1,000). The most costly incidents for institutions tend to be burglary (46 per cent over £1,000), and thefts from a vehicle (40 per cent over £1,000). However, vandalism can also be extremely costly for institutions: nearly one-third of the incidents of recorded vandalism involved a loss of £1,000 or more. It is also interesting that aggravated burglaries against institutions tend to be dominated by those involving relatively small amounts: over half involve amounts of £300 or less, while only one in six involves an amount of £1,000 or more.

Table 5.6: Whether Victim Insured Against Loss by Crime and Victim Type

	Theft of Veh-icle	Theft from Veh-icle	Fraud	Ass-ault	Burg-lary	Agg. Burg-lary	Theft from per-son	Agg. theft from person	Other Theft	Van-dal-ism	Total
Individual											
Yes	86	63	*	19	61	49	10	14	28	64	52
No	14	37	*	81	39	51	90	86	72	36	48
Total	*12,953*	*16,510*	*201*	*6,795*	*16,843*	*380*	*3,083*	*5,993*	*10,521*	*5,680*	*78,959*
Institution											
Yes	*	64	23	*	65	70	*	*	61	77	61
No	*	36	77	*	35	30	*	*	39	23	39
Total	*945*	*2,328*	*3,175*	*171*	*13,041*	*1,082*	*0*	*527*	*12,813*	*4,519*	*38,598*

Note: Sample weighted to total incidents in 1995. * indicates too few cases to provide breakdown.

The net loss to the victim depends on whether some of the loss can be recouped from insurance. Table 5.6 indicates that institutions are more likely (61 per cent, compared to 52 per cent for individuals) to have been covered against the financial cost of the incident.[3] The differences are not as great as we might expect, however. In the case of theft from vehicle and burglary, in particular, the proportion of individuals and institutions with insurance cover is very similar at around 61–65 per cent. Institutions are more likely than individuals to have cover against other theft and aggravated burglary, however, and somewhat more likely to have cover against vandalism.

The relatively high proportion of individual victims uninsured against burglary (almost two-fifths) is of interest. It is frequently assumed that the reporting rate for burglary is high because reporting is a precondition for insurance claims. The fact that over one-third of the individual victims reporting burglary were *not* insured indicates that entitlement to insurance payments is only a partial explanation of high reporting rates.

Table 5.7 shows the net financial loss to the victim when insurance payments are taken into account. Again, the table shows the percentage where the cost falls into each range and the median (the mid-point of the median category).

The median net cost remains under £300 overall, but now the only crime category with a higher median is burglary directed against institutions, where the median net cost to the crime victim is in the £300 to £499 range. It is clear, then, that insurance companies pay for a substantial proportion of the cost involved in vehicle theft, theft from the vehicles owned by institutional victims, and domestic burglaries.

---

[3] In the case of crimes resulting in injury requiring medical treatment, someone with medical insurance that covers the cost of treatment is considered to be insured against the financial cost.

Table 5.7: Financial Cost Net of Insurance Cover by Crime and Victim Type

	Theft of Vehicle	Theft from Vehicle	Fraud	Assault	Burglary	Agg. Burglary	Theft from person	Agg. theft from person	Other Theft	Vandalism	Total
Individual											
No financial cost	20	19	*	47	17	26	8	14	9	18	19
Less than £300	35	55	*	41	44	41	87	79	66	61	53
£300–£499	11	11	*	5	14	3	2	3	15	12	11
£500–£999	13	9	*	6	13	6	1	4	5	6	9
£1,000–£4,999	17	5	*	0	10	9	0	0	5	2	7
£5,000–£9,999	3	2	*	0	0	12	1	0	0	1	1
£10,000 or more	0	0	*	0	1	3	0	0	0	0	0
Median	£150	£150	*	£150	£150	£150	£150	£150	£150	£150	£150
Total	*12,870*	*16,510*	*240*	*6,528*	*16,751*	*391*	*3,060*	*5,993*	*10,521*	*5,617*	*78,481*
Institution											
No financial cost	*	27	37	*	11	34	*	*	52	31	31
Less than £300	*	26	45	*	38	39	*	*	31	36	34
£300–£499	*	7	10	*	7	13	*	*	3	11	7
£500–£999	*	20	2	*	9	5	*	*	7	3	8
£1,000–£4,999	*	20	4	*	28	6	*	*	7	10	16
£5,000–£9,999	*	0	0	*	5	2	*	*	0	3	2
£10,000 or more	*	0	2	*	3	2	*	*	0	5	2
Median	*	£150	£150	*	£400	£150	*	*	£0	£150	£150
Total	*945*	*2,182*	*3,191*	*153*	*12,745*	*1,065*	*0*	*527*	*12,597*	*4,445*	*37,848*

Note: Sample weighted to total incidents in 1995. * indicates too few cases to provide breakdown.

Nearly one-third of the incidents targeted at institutions involve no net financial loss, compared to about one-fifth of incidents where the victim is an individual. Overall, 8 per cent of incidents where the victim is an individual result in a net financial loss greater than £1,000, with the proportion tending to be higher for vehicle theft (one-fifth costing over £1,000) and aggravated burglary (about one-quarter costing over £1,000). Among institutional victims, over one-third of burglaries and one-fifth of the incidents of theft from a vehicle involve net financial losses of £1,000 or more.

Other Effects of Crime on Victims

Apart from physical injury and the financial costs of crime, victims can also be affected in other ways. Victimisation can result in psychological distress and increased suspicion, or victims may respond by restricting their activities. Table 5.8 examines the extent to which the crime had these types of effects on the victim at any stage: increase in suspicion; psychological distress (increased anxiety, trouble sleeping, trouble concentrating); feeling that they themselves were to blame for the incident; restricting their daily activities (going out less often); or any impact on work (loss of time at work, losing or leaving a job, closing a business). These effects of crime have implications that go beyond the victims. To the extent that crime results in an increase in suspicion, it has a negative impact on the quality of the interaction between individuals in an area. As well as the pain it causes to the victim, psychological distress has an impact on their responses to, and interactions with, others.

Table 5.8: Other Effects of Crime on Respondent by Crime and Victim Type (column percentages within victim type)

	Theft of Veh-icle	Theft from Veh-icle	Fraud	Ass-ault	Burg-lary	Agg. Burg-lary	Theft from per-son	Agg. theft from person	Other Theft	Van-dal-ism	Total
Individual											
None of these	51	37	*	13	19	12	9	15	32	36	30
More suspicious	29	45	*	53	63	67	75	69	46	47	51
Psych. distress	19	33	*	76	50	76	60	69	37	39	43
Self-blame	10	27	*	13	27	14	37	22	24	5	21
Go out less often	1	7	*	46	12	29	20	44	9	8	14
Impact on work	7	10	*	39	4	14	3	8	4	7	9
Other	6	7	*	21	16	15	5	5	7	10	10
Weighted N Cases	*12,953*	*16,510*	*240*	*6,875*	*17,445*	*391*	*3,083*	*6,123*	*10,726*	*5,680*	*80,027*
Institution											
None of these	*	16	37	*	41	7	*	*	47	56	41
More suspicious	*	78	60	*	45	90	*	*	50	30	49
Psych. distress	*	29	16	*	45	74	*	*	22	24	34
Self-blame	*	44	22	*	11	7	*	*	9	3	12
Go out less often	*	0	0	*	10	12	*	*	8	0	7
Impact on work	*	16	2	*	7	24	*	*	5	14	8
Other	*	20	1	*	3	12	*	*	0	7	4
Weighted N Cases	*945*	*2328*	*3338*	*171*	*13548*	*1098*	*0*	*527*	*12994*	*4519*	*39467*

Note: Sample weighted to total incidents in 1995. * indicates too few cases to provide breakdown. Percentages need not sum to 100 since more than one effect may have been experienced.

In general, as shown in Table 5.8, more of the crimes directed at individuals (70 per cent) than at institutions (59 per cent) result in effects of this type. The most common effect is an increase in suspicion (about 50 per cent for both individuals and institutions), rising to over two-thirds of cases of aggravated burglary, and theft from the person (aggravated and non-aggravated) directed at individuals, and theft from a vehicle and aggravated burglaries directed at institutions. Two-fifths of the individual victims and one-third of the institutional victims experienced psychological distress. Psychological distress is particularly common among victims of violent crime (assault, aggravated burglary and aggravated theft from the person). Individual victims are more likely to blame themselves (21 per cent) than are institutional victims (12 per cent), although the figure is highest for institutional victims of theft from vehicles (44 per cent). Individual victims of assault and aggravated theft from the person were most likely to have restricted their activities by going out less often at some stage since the incident (44 and 46 per cent respectively).

Of course, these effects on the victim may be temporary. Table 5.9 examines the proportion of individual respondents who were still affected in these ways at the time of the interview, by the time that had elapsed since the incident.

Table 5.9: Lasting Effects on Individual Respondent by Time Elapsed since Incident (column percentages within time elapsed)

	8–12 months	13–16 months	17 or more months	Total
Not affected in these ways	52	48	57	53
More suspicious	37	46	37	40
Psychological distress	25	26	21	24
Go out less often	8	9	7	8
Weighted Cases	17,384	25,169	29,478	72,032

Note: Sample weighted to total incidents in 1995. This table only includes cases where the date the incident was reported is known. Percentages need not sum to 100 since more than one effect may have been experienced.

Cases where information on the date of the incident was not available — mainly non-indictable assault, vehicle theft and vandalism — are not included in Table 5.9. The elapsed time could have ranged from 8 to 24 months, depending on when in the target year the incident occurred, and on whether the interview took place early or late in the fieldwork period. By the time of the interview, the percentage of victims remaining more suspicious had fallen from 51 to 40 percent, and there were even larger drops, in relative terms, in the percentage experiencing psychological distress (43 to 24 per cent), and going out less often (14 to 8 per cent).

However, the actual amount of time that had elapsed in the eight to 24 month range did not appear to be important. There is no tendency for those more recently victimised at the time of the interview to be more affected than those for whom the experience was more remote in time. The most likely explanation is that short-term psychological effects are likely to have disappeared by eight months after the incident, but that effects which persist for eight months are likely to be still present up to two years later.

Table 5.10 examines the extent to which the incidents still affected the victims at the time of the interview by type of incident and type of victim. About two-fifths of both individual and institutional victims remain more suspicious of others. The proportion still suffering from psychological distress has fallen to about one-quarter for individual victims and one-fifth for institutional victims. Half or more of the victims of assault, aggravated burglary and aggravated theft from the person continue to experience psychological distress. One-tenth of individual victims still go out less often, but this rises to about one-third of victims of assault and of aggravated theft from the person. The impact on "going out" for victims of aggravated burglary is lower but still substantial (21 per cent), which is understandable given that the burglary is most likely to have occurred in their homes, so that staying in is less likely to be seen as protective.

Table 5.10: Lasting Effects on Respondent by Crime and Victim Type (column percentages within victim type)

	Theft of Vehicle	Theft from Vehicle	Fraud	Assault	Burglary	Agg. Burglary	Theft from person	Agg. theft from person	Other Theft	Vandalism	Total
Individual											
None of these	73	53	*	24	39	33	25	23	56	49	47
More suspicious	21	37	*	48	50	53	62	63	36	37	41
Psych. distress	10	24	*	49	24	59	35	54	16	26	26
Self-blame	1	9	*	1	12	6	17	9	12	1	8
Go out less often	1	5	*	33	8	21	17	31	5	8	10
Impact on work	0	1	*	8	1	3	0	2	0	0	1
Other	3	3	*	8	15	6	2	3	4	8	6
Weighted N Cases	12,953	16,510	240	6,875	17,445	391	3,083	6,123	10,726	5,680	80,027
Institution											
None of these	*	28	47	*	49	22	*	*	56	70	51
More suspicious	*	53	52	*	40	77	*	*	42	28	42
Psych. distress	*	19	8	*	29	41	*	*	13	13	21
Self-blame	*	14	6	*	0	4	*	*	2	0	2
Go out less often	*	0	0	*	7	7	*	*	8	0	5
Impact on work	*	0	0	*	0	8	*	*	2	0	1
Other	*	15	1	*	1	9	*	*	0	4	2
Weighted N Cases	945	2,328	3,338	171	13,548	1,098	0	527	12,994	4,519	39,467

Note: Sample weighted to total incidents in 1995. * indicates too few cases to provide breakdown. Percentages need not sum to 100 since more than one effect may have been experienced.

Table 5.11 examines whether the lasting effects of crime vary by the sex of the victim for incidents directed at individuals. Women are more likely than men to remain more suspicious, suffer psy-

chological effects or to restrict their activity. Over one-third of female victims reported still experiencing psychological distress
compared to one-fifth of male victims; while 13 per cent of
women continue to go out less often, compared to 8 per cent of
male victims. In the case of violent crime (assault, aggravated
theft from the person and aggravated burglary) the proportion of
victims who still experience psychological distress is very high for
both sexes (42–44 per cent for males and 59–70 per cent for females).

*Table 5.11: Lasting Effects on Individual Respondent by Crime
Type and Sex (column percentages within sex)*

	Theft of Veh-icle	Theft from Veh-icle	Fraud	Ass-ault	Burg-lary	Agg. Burg-lary	Theft from per-son	Agg. theft from person	Other Theft	Van-dal-ism	Total
Male											
None of these	76	61	*	32	48	57	67	43	73	45	57
More suspicious	20	31	*	45	48	36	22	40	27	41	35
Psych. distress	9	23	*	44	14	43	22	42	3	28	20
Go out less often	0	5	*	33	3	36	11	26	0	11	8
Weighted Cases	*8,307*	*11,564*	*178*	*5,469*	*10,382*	*162*	*367*	*1,879*	*5,663*	*3,838*	*47,808*
Female											
None of these	75	43	*	19	34	15	24	16	41	64	40
More suspicious	22	57	*	61	54	65	67	73	46	28	51
Psych. distress	12	30	*	69	39	70	36	59	31	23	36
Go out less often	1	4	*	32	15	10	18	34	10	0	13
Weighted Cases	*4,646*	*4,459*	*62*	*1,406*	*7,064*	*229*	*2,693*	*4,244*	*5,062*	*1,842*	*31,708*

Note: Sample weighted to total incidents in 1995. * indicates too few cases to provide breakdown. Percentages need not sum to 100 since more than one effect
may have been experienced.

Table 5.12 shows the lasting effect of crime by the age group of the individual victim. There is some support for the idea that elderly crime victims are more likely to restrict their activities in response to crime. Seventeen per cent of the victims age 65 or over, compared to about 9–10 per cent of victims in other age groups, are likely to go out less often as a result of the experience. There is no tendency for psychological distress or suspicion to be more prevalent among elderly crime victims, probably reflecting the fact that the elderly face a lower overall risk of violent crime, since assault and aggravated theft from the person tend to be concentrated in the younger age groups.

Table 5.12: Lasting Effects on Individual Respondent by Age Group (column percentages within age group)

	Under Age 35	Age 35-49	Age 50-64	Age 65 and over
Not affected in these ways	47	53	50	49
More suspicious	43	37	44	44
Psychological distress	27	26	25	26
Go out less often	9	9	10	17
Weighted Cases	*26,962*	*30,891*	*14,441*	*7,109*

Note: Sample weighted to total incidents in 1995. Percentages need not sum to 100 since more than one effect may have been experienced.

Who Provided Support to Victims?

Table 5.13 looks at who provided support to cope with the effects of the crime by crime type and victim type. Since up to three responses are recorded, the percentages do not necessarily add to 100. Forty-three per cent of individual victims and just over two-thirds of institutional victims felt that they did not want or need any support to cope with the effects of the crime. Among individuals, victims of vehicle crime and other theft are least likely to want or need support. However, the proportion not wanting support falls to less than one-quarter in the case of violent crime (assault, aggravated theft from the person and aggravated burglary) against individuals and to one-third in the case of aggravated burglary of institutions.

Table 5.13: Who Provided Support by Crime and Victim Type (column percentages within victim type)

	Theft of Veh-icle	Theft from Veh-icle	Fraud	Ass-ault	Burg-lary	Agg. Burg-lary	Theft from per-son	Agg. theft from person	Other Theft	Van-dal-ism	Total
Individual											
No support received	1	1	*	0	2	6	1	1	2	0	1
No support wanted	56	60	*	14	34	12	28	22	52	49	43
Family	36	36	*	79	44	56	57	63	27	43	44
Friends	19	14	*	62	42	44	46	46	26	27	31
Gardaí	18	18	*	39	31	41	26	38	23	31	26
Other	2	1	*	8	3	24	3	7	0	0	3
Weighted Cases	12,953	16,510	240	6,875	17,445	391	3,083	6,123	10,726	5,680	80,027
Institution											
No support received	*	0	2	*	0	1	*	*	1	1	1
No support wanted	*	84	73	*	61	33	*	*	71	66	67
Family	*	16	9	*	25	59	*	*	14	14	19
Friends	*	16	6	*	16	31	*	*	4	11	11
Gardaí	*	0	21	*	25	41	*	*	17	26	21
Other	*	0	1	*	0	14	*	*	2	9	2
Weighted Cases	945	2,328	3,338	171	13,548	1,098	0	527	12,994	4,519	39,467

Note: Sample weighted to total incidents in 1995. * indicates too few cases to provide breakdown.

In terms of who provides support, family (44 per cent), friends (31 per cent), and the Gardaí (26 per cent) are the most important sources for individual victims. For institutional victims of crime, the Gardaí are about as important as family members in providing support (about one-fifth of cases overall).

Contact with the Victim Support organisation, included in the "other" row in Table 5.12, was low.[4] It should be recalled, however, that the crimes on which the survey is based occurred in 1994/95. A higher level of contact could be expected today with an expansion of the Victim Support network and development of automatic referral by the Gardaí.

Perceptions of Crime and Fear of Crime

A considerable amount of research has focused on the fear of crime as a problem in its own right, distinct from criminal victimisation itself. Research has tended consistently to find that levels of fear of crime are greater than levels of victimisation, that fear is only weakly predicted by risk of victimisation in the aggregate (see review by Hale, 1996), and that certain groups (women and the elderly, in particular) experience greater levels of fear of crime than others (Borooah and Carcach, 1997; Skogan, 1986; Hale, 1996; Hough, 1995; Smith and Tortensson, 1997).

Skogan (1986) links levels of fear of crime to processes of community decline. Factors such as disinvestment, demolition and construction, property speculation and deindustrialisation all contribute to the destabilisation of neighbourhoods through their impact on the number of people moving into and out of the area. Instability weakens informal social control, contributing to increased crime levels. The resulting fear leads to a physical and psychological withdrawal from the community on the part of residents. This further reduces levels of informal social control, resulting in increased levels of crime, which feed back into greater levels of fear and withdrawal.

---

[4] Seven per cent of aggravated burglary victims had contact with the organisation, 3 per cent of aggravated theft victims and 2 per cent of burglary victims.

From this perspective, the fear of crime need not be linked directly to personal experiences of crime. Indeed, a perception of high risk or vulnerability is likely to lead to avoidance strategies that reduce the probability of becoming a victim. Young (1994, p. 114) notes that the "supposed low risk status of groups such as women and the elderly is in part a function of their high level of avoidance tactics". Furthermore, fear is heightened in certain environments, and residents may respond by avoiding "risky" situations. Hough (1995) found that anxiety about crime was increased where people saw "signs of crime" in their neighbourhoods, such as vandalism and litter. Borooah and Carcach (1997), using Australian data, also find that unfavourable perceptions about one's area of residence served to increase fear of personal crime. Moreover, they found that those whose fear of crime is greater than their risk of personal victimisation (older adults and women) adopted a constrained lifestyle which led them to avoid the outcome they feared; while those whose risk of personal victimisation was greater than their fear of crime (younger and male adults) tended to adopt an unconstrained lifestyle that increased their risk of becoming victims.

The lack of correspondence between victimisation and fear may also be due to the mediation of cognitive processes. Winkel (1998) argues that the link between victimisation and enhanced fear is mediated by the person's assessment of the likelihood of becoming a victim, on the one hand, and their view of the seriousness of the impact of being a victim, on the other. In a study using data from the Netherlands, he found that victimisation tends to increase perceived victimisation risk, but to reduce the perceived negative impact. In other words, those who have been victims of crime perceive a higher risk of future victimisation than non-victims do; but their view of the impact of victimisation is less negative. These tendencies tend to neutralise each other, so enhanced fear does not result from victimisation (Winkel, 1998).

The conceptualisation and measurement of "fear of crime" has been criticised by a number of authors (Farraro and LaGrange, 1987; Farrall et al., 1997; Gilchrist et al., 1998), who point out that there is often a lack of conceptual clarity as to the meaning of the term, and that different results can be obtained in quantitative and qualitative surveys (Farrall et al., 1997; Gilchrist et al., 1998). Farraro and LaGrange (1987, p. 71) note that "the phrase 'fear of crime' has acquired so many divergent meanings that its current utility is negligible". This is reflected in the variety of measures of "fear of crime", ranging from perceived risk of becoming a victim of specific incidents, how "worried" the person is that specific incidents will happen to them, to the more "formless" feeling of not being safe in certain circumstances (walking alone after dark, home alone at night, and so on). Despite the difficulties in measuring the concept, however, and the often counter-intuitive relationship between fear and victimisation, fear of crime is as real as crime itself and constrains many more lives than are directly victimised by criminal incidents.

In this section, we explore the perceptions of crime held by crime victims. Unlike the previous section, which dealt with the impact of crime on the victim, we are not able to attribute these perceptions to the experience of crime, since we have no information on whether the perceptions changed as a result of the crime. For some of the items, however, we do have information from other sources on the perceptions held by the population generally. Moreover, we are able to examine whether the perceptions of crime and perceptions of the risk of victimisation vary by the type of crime and by characteristics of the victim.

In order to facilitate comparisons between crime victims and the national population, we use the victim weights here (see Chapter 1 and Appendix A). These weights give equal representation to each individual or institution reporting a crime in the target year, irrespective of the number of crimes reported. The "total victim weight" described in Chapter 1 is used for figures in the total column of the tables. These weights take account of the fact that victims may have reported more than one type of crime, so that the total number of victims is less than the sum of the victims in each category.

Perception of Risk

Table 5.14 looks at the percentage of individual victims who feel that certain incidents are "very likely" or "likely" to happen to them in the next 12 months. Overall, apart from sexual assault (11 per cent) and assault in the home (5 per cent), the percentage who feel that they are likely to be crime victims is quite high; ranging from 29 per cent for vandalism of the home to 61 per cent for theft of property from a vehicle, with a figure of 57 per cent for having a vehicle stolen, 49 per cent for burglary, and 46 per cent for being mugged or having a pocket picked.

The perception of risk varies by the nature of the initial victimisation, but the link is relatively weak. Reading across the rows in Table 5.14, it is not always those who reported a particular type of crime in the target year who perceive the greatest risk of that type of incident. There is a tendency for victims of a particular crime to be more likely than average to believe that a similar incident will happen in the next 12 months, but the perception of risk appears to be more generalised. This is particularly true of victims of aggravated theft from the person, who have a higher than average perception of the risk of all types of incidents (apart from burglary). The relatively weak link between the crime reported in the target period and the perceived risk of victimisation is not surprising in the light of the results on repeat victimisation in Chapter 3. There it was noted that about half of the individual victims had experienced at least one *other* criminal incident in a three-year period, and that other incident was very likely to have been of a different type.

Table 5.14: Per Cent of Individual Victims Believing Certain Incidents Likely in Next 12 Months by Crime Type (column percentages)

	Theft of Vehicle	Theft from Vehicle	Assault	Burglary	Agg. Burglary	Theft from person	Agg. Theft from person	Other Theft	Vandalism	Total
Break-in at home	50	52	26	58	55	43	50	47	40	49
Vandalism to home	29	22	18	39	49	25	33	23	26	29
Vehicle stolen	56	64	29	48	55	50	59	65	57	57
Property stolen from vehicle	52	79	40	50	60	53	68	65	57	61
Mugged/pocket picked	44	48	40	38	52	47	69	51	35	46
Sexually assaulted	11	8	10	9	13	12	18	15	9	11
Assault at home	5	9	8	3	13	2	6	1	3	5
Assault outside home	19	33	47	24	32	24	45	30	27	31
Threatened/harassed by strangers	27	43	62	37	35	41	59	45	37	42
Weighted cases (minimum)	*10,366*	*11,966*	*3,385*	*8,541*	*107*	*1,716*	*3,169*	*6,486*	*4,570*	*39,712*

Note: Sample weighted to total victims in 1995. Number of cases varies by item since cases where item is not applicable (e.g. do not own a vehicle for vehicle crime) or response is "don't know" are excluded. There are too few cases to provide separate figures for victims of fraud, but these are included in the total.

Table 5.15 shows the percentage of individual victims believing each type of incident is likely to occur in the next 12 months for males and females separately. Male and female crime victims are fairly similar in terms of the percentages believing that burglary, vandalism, assault and threats or harassment by strangers are likely to occur in the next 12 months. However, women show a somewhat higher level of concern with respect to vehicle crime, and a considerably higher level of concern regarding personal theft (muggings and pickpocket), and sexual assault.

Table 5.15: Per Cent of Individual Victims Believing Certain Incidents Likely in Next 12 Months by Sex and Crime Type (column percentages)

	Theft of Vehicle	Theft from Vehicle	Assault	Burglary	Agg. Burglary	Theft from person	Agg. Theft from person	Other Theft	Vandalism	Total
Male										
Break-in at home	48	54	29	53	51	25	52	49	46	50
Vandalism to home	34	20	14	38	47	25	27	21	30	28
Vehicle stolen	60	62	31	44	57	16	56	61	63	55
Property stolen from vehicle	53	80	41	41	65	28	56	62	61	58
Mugged/pocket picked	49	37	36	34	33	0	64	41	35	39
Sexually assaulted	4	2	7	6	0	0	0	7	4	4
Assault at home	7	6	6	6	0	0	4	3	2	6
Assault outside home	21	29	48	25	15	0	51	21	23	29
Threatened/harassed by strangers	31	39	66	39	15	22	75	32	35	40
Weighted N Cases (min)	6,405	8,645	3,148	4,909	85	213	887	3,783	3,208	25,126
Female										
Break-in at home	54	47	18	65	58	45	49	44	29	50
Vandalism to home	20	25	37	40	51	24	35	26	19	30
Vehicle stolen	49	75	9	55	51	54	60	71	44	61
Property stolen from vehicle	50	82	35	66	51	56	73	68	49	66
Mugged/pocket picked	35	76	56	45	64	53	72	60	33	56
Sexually assaulted	22	26	20	15	23	13	27	23	20	22
Assault at home	0	17	15	0	21	3	6	0	6	5
Assault outside home	16	42	42	23	41	28	42	40	34	33
Threatened/harassed by strangers	19	54	49	35	46	43	51	59	40	44
Weighted N Cases (min)	3,961	2,835	237	3,631	23	1,479	2,282	2,703	1,362	14,032

Note: Sample weighted to total victims in 1995. Number of cases varies by item since cases where item is not applicable (e.g. no vehicle) or response is "don't

It is significant, and worrying, that over one-fifth of the women believe it likely that they will be sexually assaulted in the next 12 months. Overall, the high perceived level of risk is likely to be influenced by the victims' personal experience of crime. This would be consistent with the finding below that crime victims report a higher incidence of community problems and local crime than a national sample.

The 1998 QNHS crime module contained an item on whether individuals were worried that they themselves or someone else in their household may become a victim of crime, with response categories "Yes — personal injury", "Yes — property theft/ damage", "Yes — both personal and property" and "No". The question wording and categories are not directly comparable to the set used in the present survey. However, the QNHS results point to the generally high level of concern about crime in the population and confirm the greater level of concern among women than among men. Nationally, 63 per cent of women and 49 per cent of men were worried that they themselves or someone in their household would become a victim of crime (Central Statistics Office, 1999a, Table 13).

Table 5.16 shows the percentage believing incidents of different types are likely to occur in the next 12 months by age group. In general, there is a tendency for the perception of risk to increase with the age of the victim, even for those types of crime where younger adults are more frequently victimised, such as assault and theft from the person. The increase in fear with age is particularly marked in the case of break-ins at home: 67 per cent of those over age 65 believe that this is likely to occur in the next 12 months, compared to 49 per cent in the 35 to 64 age group and 45 per cent of those under age 35. The fear of sexual assault, which is low in any case, and the fear of being threatened or harassed by strangers, both decline with age.

Table 5.16: Per Cent of Individual Victims Believing Certain Incidents Likely in Next 12 Months by Age Group

	Age Under 35	Age 35-64	Age 65+
Break-in at home	44%	49%	67%
Vandalism to home	26%	28%	37%
Vehicle stolen	59%	53%	67%
Property stolen from vehicle	66%	57%	65%
Mugged/pocket picked	46%	46%	49%
Sexually assaulted	13%	10%	6%
Assault at home	2%	7%	8%
Assault outside home	32%	27%	38%
Threatened/harassed by strangers	50%	38%	32%
Weighted N Cases (Minimum)	*16,926*	*31,380*	*1,595*

Note: Sample weighted to total victims in 1995. Number of cases varies by item since cases where item is not applicable or response is "don't know" are excluded. The weighted number of cases is the minimum across items.

Crime and Other Problems in Neighbourhood

Tables 5.17 and 5.18 explore the perceptions of crime and other social problems in the area where the respondent lives, with the corresponding figures from a national sample taken from the *1995 Living in Ireland Survey*. Table 5.17 shows the percentage of individual victims reporting certain problems as "very common" in the area where they live. Most of these are more in the nature of public order issues or factors affecting the quality of the environment, rather than crimes *per se*: graffiti on walls and buildings, teenagers hanging around on the street, rubbish and litter lying about, homes and gardens in bad condition, vandalism, people being drunk in public, and drug use. Skogan (1986) has pointed to the importance of such aspects of neighbourhood environment in contributing to (and reflecting) a physical and psychological withdrawal from the community on the part of residents. This in turn leads to a weakening of informal social controls, to a reduced capacity on the part of residents to deal with community problems, and — by reducing guardianship — contributes to increased crime levels. Hough (1995) used these types of measures as indicators of "signs of crime" in a neighbourhood, which were found to heighten anxiety about crime among residents.

Table 5.17: Per Cent of Individual Victims Reporting Certain Problems Very Common in Area Where They Live by Crime Type

	Theft of Vehicle	Theft from Vehicle	Assault	Burglary	Agg. Burglary	Theft from person	Agg. Theft from person	Other Theft	Vandalism	Total	National Sample
Graffiti	11	4	10	11	3	8	8	11	7	7	2%
Teens hanging around	16	20	42	35	18	18	26	23	30	24	7%
Rubbish & litter	14	14	30	13	19	15	15	19	21	15	5%
Homes/ gardens bad condition	8	4	9	5	22	3	7	6	3	5	1%
Vandalism	6	5	16	9	9	7	8	15	11	9	4%
People drunk in public	8	7	24	7	9	8	5	12	15	9	2%
Drug use	7	17	17	14	15	9	21	13	23	13	
Weighted Cases (minimum)	12,150	15,100	6,350	15,460	287	2,992	5,798	9,535	5,191	57,029	2,504,128

Note: Sample weighted to total victims in 1995. Figures for individual victims of fraud are included in the total. Figures for the national sample come from the *1995 Living in Ireland Survey* (Callan et al., 1996 and 1999).

Compared to the national sample, the proportion reporting all problems is higher for victims of crime. The difference is particularly marked with respect to "teenagers hanging around in public" (24 per cent of the victim sample compared to 7 per cent of the national sample) and "rubbish and litter lying about" (15 per cent compared to 5 per cent). The general pattern across items is similar to that in the national sample, however, with the most frequently mentioned problem being "teenagers hanging around in the streets", and the least frequent "homes and gardens in bad condition". Thirteen per cent of the crime victim sample reports that drug use is very common in the area where they live — higher than the 9 per cent reporting people being drunk in public as very common. Unfortunately, we do not have corresponding figures on drug use in the neighbourhood for the national sample.

Generally, assault victims are most likely to report these problems as very common in their areas, particularly "teenagers hanging around in the streets" and "people being drunk in public". One exception is "homes and gardens in bad condition", where aggravated burglary victims are most likely (22 per cent) to see the problem as "very common". It is surprising that victims of vandalism are very close to the average victim in terms of the proportion who see graffiti and vandalism as very common in their areas, although the proportions are higher than for the national sample.

Table 5.18 looks at the perception of the amount of crime in the area where the respondent lives, compared to the rest of Ireland. If people's perception of the risk of crime was "accurate" we might expect the rating of their area by a national sample to follow a fairly normal distribution, with roughly equal proportions feeling that their area had more and less crime than the country as a whole.[5] In contrast, we would expect a sample of crime victims to report their neighbourhoods as having somewhat more crime than average. This is not the case, even for victims of crime: they tend to perceive their own areas as "safer" than elsewhere. Overall, crime victims do not feel they live in "high crime" areas. The crime victims, like residents of relatively high-crime areas studied by Brewer et al. (1997) in Belfast, are adopting a frame of reference that places their own area in a favourable light. About three-quarters of individual victims feel that the level of crime in their areas is about the same or less than in Ireland as a whole, with only one in ten feeling that there is a lot more crime in their area.

---

[5] This might not hold true for street crime occurring in non-residential areas.

Table 5.18: Amount of Crime in Area Compared to Rest of Ireland by Crime and Victim Type (column percentages within victim type)

	Theft of Vehicle	Theft from Vehicle	Fraud	Assault	Burglary	Aggravated Burglary	Theft from person	Aggravated theft from person	Other Theft	Vandalism	Total	National Sample
Individual												
A lot more	18	6	*	11	12	10	6	11	8	5	10	2
A bit more	8	26	*	12	13	15	18	24	14	10	15	9
Same	48	26	*	36	41	38	33	45	34	43	38	27
A bit less	17	26	*	22	26	35	28	13	25	31	25	28
A lot less	8	15	*	18	8	3	15	7	18	12	12	34
Weighted N Cases	10,149	14,419	240	6,049	16,140	355	2,780	5,864	9,859	4,857	54,982	2,527,152
Institution												
A lot more	*	0	4	*	3	4	*	*	0	2	2	
A bit more	*	10	15	*	21	18	*	*	19	19	16	
Same	*	43	25	*	36	43	*	*	26	19	29	
A bit less	*	29	34	*	29	26	*	*	28	31	31	
A lot less	*	18	22	*	11	9	*	*	26	29	22	
Weighted N Cases	928	1,701	2,417	122	8,126	828	0	421	6,246	3,317	14,810	

Note: Sample weighted to total victims in 1995. * indicates too few cases to provide breakdown. Figures for the national sample come from the 1995 *Living in Ireland Survey* (Callan et al., 1996 and 1999).

Institutional victims of crime tend to rate the areas where they live a little more positively, with only 2 per cent feeling that there is a "lot more" crime in the area where they live. This is because the crime the victim reported typically occurred at the place of business rather than at the place of residence. Even for the individual victims, however, only 10–12 per cent of victims of "home-based" crimes like burglary and aggravated burglary rate their area as having "a lot more" crime than the country as a whole.

Compared to the national sample (from the *1995 Living in Ireland Survey*), however, the perception of the level of crime is greater among crime victims. Only 2 per cent of the national sample feel that there is "a lot more" crime in the area where they live, compared to 10 per cent of the individual crime victim sample. Victims of vandalism are most like the national sample, with only 5 per cent feeling that levels of crime in their areas are a good deal higher than elsewhere. Victims of vehicle theft are most likely to feel they live in areas where there is a "lot more" crime (18 per cent). Despite the greater perceived frequency of public order problems in the areas where they live (Table 5.17), assault victims do not differ appreciably from crime victims generally in terms of their assessment of the relative amount of crime in their areas.

Perceptions of Safety

Table 5.19 shows the percentage of victims who feel very unsafe in their own area in certain circumstances. Again, we are unable to say whether the feelings of safety are linked to the experience of being a crime victim or are an objective assessment of the level of risk they face. The table shows the percentage who feel very unsafe in their own area walking alone by day, walking alone by night, home alone by day or home alone at night.

Table 5.19: Per Cent Who Feel Very Unsafe in Own Area by Crime and Victim Type (column percentages)

	Theft of Veh-icle	Theft from Veh-icle	Fraud	Ass-ault	Burg-lary	Agg. Burg-lary	Theft from per-son	Agg. theft from person	Other Theft	Van-dal-ism	Total
Individual											
Walking alone — day	3	0	*	0	0	9	0	3	0	1	1
Walking alone by night	16	8	*	14	13	36	18	26	7	6	12
Home alone by day	3	0	*	0	0	9	0	1	1	1	1
Home alone — night	6	1	*	3	3	28	6	7	1	2	3
Weighted N Cases (minimum)	12,179	15,120	240	6,304	16,205	343	2,952	5,929	10,006	5,235	58,177
Institution											
Walking alone — day	*	0	0	*	0	0	*	*	0	0	0
Walking alone by night	*	10	2	*	3	5	*	*	4	7	6
Home alone by day	*	0	0	*	0	2	*	*	0	0	0
Home alone — night	*	0	2	*	1	5	*	*	0	8	2
Weighted N Cases (minimum)	928	1,701	2,545	122	8,320	841	0	495	6,019	3,380	15,120

Note: * indicates too few sample cases to provide breakdown. Sample weighted to total victims in 1995. Number of cases varies by item since cases where item is not applicable or response is "don't know" are excluded

As we might expect, the perceived risk is greatest for walking alone by night and lowest for home alone by day and walking alone in the area by day. What is striking in the table is that individual victims of aggravated burglary feel the least safe. Nine per cent feel very unsafe walking alone by day, compared to 1 per cent overall, while 36 per cent feel very unsafe walking alone by night, compared to 12 per cent overall. Nine percent feel very unsafe home alone by day, compared to one per cent overall, while

28 per cent feel very unsafe home alone at night, compared to 3 per cent overall. The dramatic reduction in their sense of safety may be linked to the experience of being put at risk in their own homes and to their personal vulnerability — we saw in Chapter 3 that half of them are over age 65. This is in marked contrast to the sense of safety experienced by victims of burglary, which is very close to the average for all crime victims.

Victims of aggravated theft from the person are the second most likely to feel unsafe walking alone at night (26 per cent), but the feelings of insecurity at home are much less than those of victims of aggravated burglary. In contrast to other victims of violent crime, assault victims do not differ from crime victims generally in terms of feeling unsafe in each of these circumstances.

Table 5.20 indicates that, as we would expect based on previous research findings, female crime victims experience greater feelings of insecurity both walking alone at night and home alone at night. The sense of insecurity associated with walking alone at night is greatest for women who have been victims of aggravated burglary (47 per cent). Male victims of aggravated burglary (who tend to be elderly) also experience substantially greater levels of insecurity, with one in six feeling very unsafe walking alone at night; and one in seven very unsafe home alone at night.

The QNHS crime module had a comparable question put to all respondents (whether victims of crime or not) on how safe they felt walking around in their own area after dark, and on how safe they felt home alone at night. A comparison of these results with the figures for victims of recorded crime shown in Table 5.19 indicates that the victims are considerably more likely to feel very unsafe. Nine per cent of women in the QNHS survey and 1.5 per cent of men felt very unsafe walking around in their own area after dark, while 1.7 per cent of women and 0.3 per cent of men felt very unsafe home alone at night (Central Statistics Office, 1999a). It is not possible to say whether the heightened level of concern among the victims in the present survey is a direct result of the experience of being a crime victim, or reflects an accurate assessment of the level of risk they face in their home areas. It is clear however, that a sizeable minority of victims of recorded crime experience a much-reduced sense of safety in comparison to the general population.

Table 5.20: Per Cent of Individual Victims Who Feel Very Unsafe in Own Area by Crime Type and Sex (Column Percentages)

	Theft of Vehicle	Theft from Vehicle	Assault	Burglary	Agg. Burglary	Theft from person	Agg. theft from person	Other Theft	Vandalism	Total
Male										
Walking alone by day	5	0	0	0	7	0	3	0	2	1
Walking alone by night	12	0	10	9	17	11	18	6	9	7
Home alone by day	4	0	0	0	6	0	0	2	2	1
Home alone – night	4	0	0	3	14	11	0	2	2	2
Weighted N Cases (minimum)	7,667	10,323	5,164	9,502	120	357	1,752	5,357	3,463	34,813
Female										
Walking alone by day	0	0	1	0	10	0	3	0	0	1
Walking alone by night	22	26	30	19	47	19	29	7	0	21
Home alone by day	0	0	1	0	10	0	2	0	0	0
Home alone – night	8	5	16	3	36	5	10	0	0	6
Weighted N Cases (minimum)	4,512	4,310	1,140	6,702	224	2,572	4,177	4,649	1,771	22,811

Note: Number of cases varies by item since cases where item is not applicable or response is "don't know" are excluded. Sample weighted to total victims in 1995.

Multivariate Model of Distress

The impact of different aspects of criminal victimisation on psychological distress are examined in this section. How important are features of the incident itself, characteristics of the victim, the outcome of the case, and satisfaction with the Garda service in explaining variations in distress? The focus is on individual victims, since they experienced higher levels of distress than institutional victims. The effects of these different aspects of the crime and its outcome can be separated statistically by using multivariate analytical techniques. The unweighted sample data are used here in order to obtain the correct standard errors for testing the significance of effects of the different aspects of the experience on the level of distress suffered by the victim.

The measure of distress was constructed based on whether, as a result of the incident, the respondents experienced the following at any time since it happened, and whether they still experienced them:

- Became more anxious or fearful;

- Had trouble sleeping;

- Went out less often or became reluctant to go out alone;

- Had trouble concentrating.

The four items, and the two dimensions ("experienced at any time", and "still experienced") provided an eight-item scale with a reliability of .81, and a range from 0 (did not at any time experience any of the four effects) to 8 (still experiencing all four effects).

Ordinary Least Squares Regression was used to develop the model, which is shown in Table 5.21. The first model looks at how levels of distress vary by the crime type. The reference type is "theft of vehicle". Assault, aggravated burglary and aggravated theft from the person clearly stand out as having a score on the eight-point scale that is more than two points higher than for vehicle theft. Levels of distress are also higher than vehicle theft for victims of personal theft, burglary and vandalism.

Table 5.21: Multivariate Models of Distress Experienced by Individual Crime Victims

	Model 1	Model 2	Model 3	Model 4	Model 5	Model 6
Constant	.487*	.202	–.194	.225	–.161	.807**
Theft from Vehicle	.357	.353	.481	.497	.531	
Fraud	.942	.428	.567	.416	.372	
Assault	2.394**	–.050	.185	.042	.119	
Burglary	.791**	.708*	.636*	.594*	.594*	
Agg. Burglary	2.559**	1.301**	.944	.869	.916	
Theft from Person	1.207**	.689*	.466	.495	.458	
Agg. Theft from person	2.162**	1.021**	.873*	.830*	.815*	.503*
Other Theft	.344	.131	.103	.067	.083	
Vandalism	.717*	.591	.723*	.669	.702*	
Victim present		.530*	.424*	.375	.380	.396*
Assaulted/threatened		.622*	.725**	.779**	.763**	.728**
Injured		1.102**	1.037**	1.084**	1.095**	.893**
Permanent/recurring injury		.933**	.932**	.832*	.894**	.867**
Intimidated by offender		.494	.588*	.525	.537	
Net loss < £300		.069	–.016	.019	.041	
Net loss £300–£500		.344	.286	.275	.300	
Net loss £500+		.377	.456	.462	.500*	.389*
Victim is female			.743**	.801**	.802**	.822**
Age 35–44			.075	.035	.039	
Age 45–64			.432*	.348	.301	
Age 65+			.617*	.628*	.615*	.633**

Table 5.21 (continued)

	Model 1	Model 2	Model 3	Model 4	Model 5	Model 6
All property recovered				.251	.285	
Offender apprehended				.575	.512	.437**
Offender convicted				−.382	−.277	
Offender − no sentence				−.591	−.472	
DK if apprehended				−.065	−.103	
Apprehended, DK outcome,				.103	.171	
DK if case open/closed				.011	.009	
Satisfaction with outcome				−.172*	−.146	−.206**
Garda follow-up contact					−.037	
Satisfaction − information					−.138	
Satisfaction − service					.170	
Adjusted R-squared	.18	.25	.28	.29	.30	.29

Note: Models are based on the unweighted sample of individual victims (N=636). An asterisk (* or **) indicates that the coefficient is statistically significant (two-tailed test): * = p<.05; ** = p< .01.

It was clear in Chapter 2 that a sizeable minority of individual victims of crimes classified as aggravated burglary and aggravated theft from the person felt that there had been no assault or threat involved in the incident. The victim's perception of whether assault or threat was involved in the incident is added in the second model. Also added are measures of whether the victim was present, whether any injury resulted, whether the injury led to permanent or recurring problems, whether the victim was intimidated by the offender at any stage since the incident, and the net financial loss that resulted. Being present at the time, being assaulted or threatened, incurring injury, and incurring injuries leading to permanent or recurring problems all significantly in-

crease the levels of distress. Subsequent intimidation by the offender and the financial loss involved have no additional effect. It
is interesting that crimes where the victim is present lead to
greater distress, even in the absence of assault or threat. The absence of a link between financial loss and distress may be due to
the fact that the categories we used are very broad. When these
items are added, the level of distress remains higher for victims of
burglary, aggravated burglary and aggravated theft from the person, but the other crime categories are no longer significantly different from theft of vehicle.

The third model adds characteristics of the victim. Women and
those over age 45 experience greater levels of distress than men
and those under 35 (the reference categories), even when characteristics of the incident are controlled, perhaps reflecting their
greater sense of vulnerability. When characteristics of the incident
and characteristics of the victim are controlled, only burglary and
aggravated theft from the person are associated with higher levels
of distress than theft of vehicle (the reference category in the top
panel).[6]

The fourth model adds features of the outcome of the case:
whether all property was recovered; whether the offender was
apprehended; whether the offender was convicted (received a
custodial or non-custodial sentence), or received no sentence (was
acquitted or the case was not proceeded with); and the victim's
overall satisfaction with the outcome of the case (measured on a
five-point scale). Included as controls in this block are measures of
not knowing whether the offender was apprehended, not knowing the outcome of the case (but knowing the offender was appre-

---

[6] Separate models (not shown) found that the time elapsed since the incident,
social class of the victim, and whether the victim had experienced other criminal
incidents in the three-year period from mid-1993 to mid-1996 had no additional
impact on the levels of distress experienced. The absence of an effect of repeat
victimisation may reflect the fact that the question wording for the distress items
referred to distress arising from the target incident.

hended), and not knowing whether the case was open or closed. The reference category in terms of the outcome are cases where the victim knows the offender was not apprehended. Only the victim's overall satisfaction with the outcome has a significant impact on levels of distress, with greater satisfaction associated with reduced distress. Since satisfaction with the outcome is associated with the recovery of property, the case going to court, and the offender being convicted,[7] it is likely that satisfaction is capturing those aspects of the outcome of the case which are important to different victims.

The fifth model examines the impact of aspects of the service provided by the Gardaí: whether the victim was contacted by a member of the Garda Síochána at some time since reporting the incident, the level of satisfaction with the information provided after reporting, and the level of satisfaction with aspects of the service provided by the Gardaí at the time of the incident. Satisfaction with the information provided is measured by a two-item scale, re-scaled so that it ranges from 1 (very dissatisfied on both items) to 5 (very satisfied on both items). The two items are satisfaction with information on progress with the case and satisfaction with information on the outcome of the case.[8] Satisfaction with the service provided by the Gardaí who first handled the case is measured by a seven-item scale, re-scaled so that it ranges from 1 (very dissatisfied on all items) to 5 (very satisfied on all items).[9] The seven items are: satisfaction with the speed with which the initial call was answered, the speed with which the Gardaí came to the scene, the thoroughness of the Gardaí, their politeness, their understanding of the victim's situation, the an-

---

[7] Correlations between overall satisfaction and these elements of outcome are in the region of .2. Even when the measure of overall satisfaction is omitted, none of the other items in this block reaches statistical significance.

[8] The correlation between the two items is .71, resulting in a reliability coefficient (alpha) of .82.

[9] The reliability coefficient (Cronbach's alpha) for this scale is .89.

swers they provided to victim's questions, and overall satisfaction with the Gardaí who first handled the case. The service provided by the Gardaí does not have a significant impact on the level of distress experienced by the victims.

The final model was developed by sequentially eliminating the non-significant coefficients in the model so as to provide a more parsimonious representation of the most important determinants of the level of distress experienced by crime victims. Distress is greater where the victim was present at the time, was assaulted or threatened, even if no injury resulted. Short-term injury and injuries leading to permanent or recurring problems each significantly add to the level of distress experienced by crime victims. Higher levels of distress are also associated with incidents where the net loss to the victim was over £500. Even when these aspects of the crime are controlled, however, victims of aggravated theft from the person experience more distress than victims of other types of crime.

Women and the elderly experience greater levels of distress, even when aspects of the incident are taken into account. Interpreting the coefficients for the outcome of the case, a "neutral" level of satisfaction with the outcome (a score of 3 on the 5-point scale) would be enough to counteract the amount of distress associated with the offender being caught. This means that the victims tend to be more distressed if the offender is apprehended but the outcome of the case is not satisfactory to them.

Overall then, victims are most affected by what happens at the time of the incident itself, particularly the threat posed to them personally in terms of assault, threat, or injury. To a lesser extent, being present at the time, and suffering a financial loss over £500 tend to increase distress. Characteristics of the victim also make a difference: those who are likely to feel most vulnerable — women and the elderly — experience greater levels of distress than men or younger adults. The intervention of the criminal justice system is less important on the whole in terms of the level of distress experienced by crime victims. There is some increase in distress associated with the offender being apprehended, and a reduction in distress where the victim is satisfied with the outcome, but the size of these effects is smaller than the impact of aspects of the incident itself or characteristics of the victim.

Summary

In this chapter we explored the impact of crime on the victim in terms of physical injury, financial loss and psychological effects; as well as looking at their perceptions of crime more generally and the feelings of security in everyday situations. The majority of recorded criminal incidents do not result in injury to the victim. Injury results more often from crimes targeted against individuals (11 per cent of cases), than from those against institutions (4 per cent). Among individual victims, over nine out of ten recorded assault cases and between one-quarter and one-third of aggravated burglaries and cases of aggravated theft from the person result in physical injury. One quarter or less of these incidents leads to injuries that require hospitalisation, however, and the proportion leading to permanent or recurring problems ranges from 6–8 per cent for aggravated burglary and aggravated theft from the person to 21 per cent in the case of assault. The most common permanent or recurring problems involve pain (particularly back pain or headaches) and numbness. Overall, only 3 per cent of reported crime against individuals involved injuries resulting in permanent or recurring problems for the person affected.

About half of reported crime involves either no financial loss, or loss of less than £300. When insurance payments are taken into account, the proportion involving losses in this range increases to about two-thirds. It is difficult to say that losses of £300 or less are "not serious", without further knowledge of the victim's "ability to pay", and the total number of incidents of which they were victims in a given period. At the other end of the scale, 8 per cent of crime against individuals and 20 per cent of crime targeted against institutions involves net losses (after taking account of insurance receipts) of £1,000 or more.

Over one-quarter of individual crime victims continue to experience psychological distress (increased anxiety, loss of sleep or difficulty in concentration) up to two years after the event. These effects are most pronounced for victims of violent crime — assault, and particularly aggravated burglary and aggravated theft from the person — and affect a greater proportion of female than male victims. At the time of the interview, nearly one-third of assault victims (both male and female) continue to restrict their activities in that they go out less often. The same is true of one-third of the female victims and one-quarter of the male victims of aggravated theft from the person. There is also some evidence that elderly crime victims are more likely to restrict their activities (go out less often) as a result of the experience than their younger counterparts.

About two-fifths of individual crime victims and two-thirds of institutional victims did not need any support to cope with the effects of the incident. Of those who did need support, family, friends and the Gardaí were the main sources of that support. The role of the Gardaí in providing support and reassurance to crime victims is noteworthy, with about a quarter of individual crime victims saying that the Gardaí provided support. The appreciation of crime victims for the support provided by the Gardaí was very evident in these responses and also in further comments recorded on the questionnaires.

Crime victims generally perceive the risk of future victimisation as quite high. About half of the individual victims believed it likely their home would be broken into in the 12 months following the interview, over half of those who own vehicles believed it likely that the vehicle would be stolen or something taken from it, and just under half believed it likely that they would be mugged or have something stolen from their person. The fear of future victimisation appears to be quite generalised: while victims tend to believe the greatest risk is associated with the type of incident they already experienced, the extent to which this is the case is not as marked as we might expect.

Crime victims were compared to a national sample in terms of the proportions reporting certain social order problems as very common in the area where they lived. Graffiti, teenagers hanging around on the street, rubbish and litter lying about, homes and gardens in bad condition, vandalism, and people being drunk in public, were all more likely to be seen as very common by crime victims than by a national sample, with the proportion being highest among assault victims. This could arise if crime victims have a heightened awareness of social order problems, perhaps as a result of their experience, but it is more likely that these problems are in fact more common in their neighbourhoods.

Although crime victims are more likely than a national sample to believe that there is more crime in the area where they live than elsewhere in Ireland, the majority of victims feel that their home area is no worse than other parts of the country in terms of the amount of crime.

This perception does not always enhance their sense of safety, however. For instance, only 10 per cent of the victims of aggravated burglary feel there is a lot more crime in their areas than elsewhere; yet 36 per cent feel "very unsafe" walking alone in their areas at night, and 28 per cent feel very unsafe home alone at night. In general, the feeling of insecurity was greatest among victims of violent crime, particularly victims of aggravated burglary where the sense of insecurity was experienced in the home (particularly at night) as well as outdoors, and where half of the victims were over age 65.

The final section of the chapter presented a multivariate analysis of the factors associated with psychological distress among crime victims. The most important factors had to do with whether the incident involved assault or threat, or resulted in injury to the victim. Levels of distress were also higher where the victim was present at the time — even if not assaulted or threatened — and where the incident resulted in a financial loss over £500. Women and the elderly tended to experience greater levels of distress, as did victims in cases where the offender was apprehended but the victim was not satisfied with the outcome of the case. Satisfaction with the service provided by the Gardaí who first dealt with the case, and with the information subsequently provided on the progress and outcome had no additional effect on victim distress.

We have focused in this chapter on the impact of crime on the victims. The impact extends beyond those directly affected, however. About half of crime victims become more suspicious (with two-fifths remaining more suspicious over a year later) as a result of their experience. While suspicion is an understandable adaptation to the experience of victimisation, it does affect the quality of interaction between individuals. This general impact of crime on the overall quality of social relations, particularly the interactions between strangers, is something worthy of further consideration. As noted by the National Economic and Social Council (1996): "Crime impacts most seriously on the quality of life and the cohesion of society." It does so, not just by the distress it causes to victims, but also by the increase in suspicion, mistrust and fear that it engenders in society more broadly.

Chapter 6

Conclusion and Implications

So far in this report we have focused on the detailed results: the nature of the recorded criminal incident, the characteristics of victims, the victims' experience of the criminal justice system, and the impact the crime had on them. The emphasis in this chapter is on drawing together the results so as to highlight the new insights the study has provided into the reality behind the crime statistics and to inform crime policy.

This chapter begins with an overview of the main findings of the report, organised so as to underline the new information that the study has revealed about the nature of recorded crime in Ireland. It then moves on to draw out the implications of the findings in three areas: implications for the services to victims of crime; strategies for crime prevention; and implications for the compilation and interpretation of statistical information on crime in Ireland.

New Insights into Crime in Ireland

Recorded Crime in Context

Police crime statistics and victimisation surveys are the two types of data most often used in assessing the overall level and nature of crime in a population. In Chapter 1, it was argued that victimisation surveys are crucial in placing the recorded crime statistics in context. Victimisation surveys can give much higher estimates of the extent of criminal victimisation in a population than police crime statistics because they "capture" incidents that are not *reported* to the police as well as incidents that may not be *recorded* in the published police statistics. People decide not to report crimes for a variety of reasons: they do not consider the incident to be serious enough, they believe the police can do nothing about the incident, they may report it to another authority (such as a local authority, building or parking lot security personnel and so on) or they may believe the police would not be interested. A reported crime might not be recorded as a separate incident in the police statistics because the incident is not accepted by the police as constituting a crime, or because each reported crime might not be recorded as a separate incident in the published police statistics.

One of the main reasons that incidents which are accepted by the police as constituting a crime may still not be reflected in the published statistics is related to the way the figures for non-indictable crimes are compiled. Counts of non-indictable crimes — such as many cases of assault, vandalism and "unauthorised takings" of vehicles — have not routinely been published in the Garda statistics unless proceedings are taken in the case, usually when the offender is apprehended. Other differences may arise because of conventions adopted in the counting of incidents. For instance, a series of related incidents against the same victim attributable to a given offender — such as is often the case in domestic assault or sexual offences — may be counted by the police as a single incident.

In Ireland, as in other jurisdictions, The Quarterly National Household Survey (QNHS) module on crime victimisation gave a higher count of incidents than Garda crime figures for the corresponding period. We were able to compare the Garda figures (adjusted so as to exclude crimes targeted against businesses and other organisations) and the QNHS crime module results for seven categories of crime: vehicle theft, theft from a vehicle, burglary, vandalism, theft with violence, theft without violence and bicycle theft. Across these seven types of crime, the QNHS crime victimisation results gave a count which was about five times the Garda published statistics for the corresponding period. This figure is somewhat higher than the gap between police crime counts and victimisation survey results in England and Wales for the same set of crimes in 1997, where the ratio between the two figures was 4.1. However, the gap is slightly smaller in Ireland for vehicle theft, theft without violence and theft with violence; slightly higher for burglary and theft from a vehicle and considerably higher for vandalism and bicycle theft. If vandalism and bicycle theft are excluded, the ratio of the victim survey count to police counts is almost identical in Ireland to the figure for England and Wales, at 3.4.

The gap between the two figures should not be used to conclude that the Garda figures are "wrong" or that victim survey counts represent the "true" extent of crime. Instead, the two types of data give alternative accounts of the extent of crime. Both sources have their own strengths and weaknesses. Garda crime figures are based on information gathered at or close to the time of the incident, while the QNHS crime module asked respondents to recall incidents that took place up to one year ago. This may lead to recall problems, such as a tendency to "telescope" more distant incidents into the time frame covered by the survey, or a tendency to forget minor incidents. Incidents reported to the Gardaí are more carefully screened to ensure that they constitute a crime than can be accomplished in a victimisation survey. The published Garda figures include crimes targeted against businesses or other organisations, and against children, whereas victimisation surveys typically only cover crimes against private households and adult individuals. Further, victimisation surveys, like all sample surveys, may be subject to non-response bias if those actually responding to the survey differ in some way from those who do not participate. The results of victimisation surveys are also subject to sampling error.

The main strength of victimisation surveys is that they provide a count which is independent of victim reporting patterns or police recording procedures. Since methodologies can be standard-ised — or their differences clearly specified — across jurisdictions, they provide a means for comparing crime levels across different police jurisdictions. They can also prove crucial in the interpreta-tion of police crime statistics, by revealing the impact of changes in reporting rates on police counts of crime.

The gap between the Garda and QNHS victimisation survey results does point to the need to interpret the recorded crime figures in the light of the way in which they are collected and compiled. They are gathered and presented as part of the man-agement and administration of law enforcement, and, as such, they cannot be interpreted as if they were a complete count of all incidents that could be considered "criminal" in nature.

Victims and Incidents

The results of this study highlighted the implications of repeat victimisation, particularly as it affects institutions, for counts of victims and counts of incidents. The sample in the present study was drawn from Garda records of crimes committed between November 1994 and October 1995 (referred to as the target pe-riod). Since those reporting more than one crime in this period had a greater probability of being selected into the sample, it was necessary to control for this in order to draw conclusions about crime victims. This was done by using information on other criminal incidents reported by each sample member to derive a set of victim weights. These weights, in turn, permitted an esti-mate of the number of distinct victims reporting a given set of in-cidents.

The results suggested that the number of recorded incidents of crime is considerably higher than the number of distinct victims: for every 100 incidents across all categories, there are about 62 separate victims. The discrepancy is much less for particular categories of crime where a repeat of the same type of crime is less common, such as vehicle theft (96 victims per 100 incidents) and aggravated theft from the person (98 victims per 100 incidents). The gap between the number of victims and the number of incidents is greatest for other theft (the category that includes shoplifting: 70 victims for each 100 incidents). For burglary, there are an estimated 80 different victims for each 100 incidents. As noted earlier, since institutions face a higher level of repeat victimisation than individuals, the gap between the number of victims and the number of incidents is greatest for crimes targeted against institutions. It also means that while one-third of crimes are directed against institutions, they account for a smaller proportion (one-fifth) of those victimised in a given period.

The second point to emerge concerning repeat victimisation was that it tended not to be crime-specific: those experiencing more than one criminal incident in the three-year period did not necessarily experience a repeat of the same type of crime. For instance, about half of the individual victims had experienced more than one criminal incident in the three-year period; but the highest figure for a repeat of the *same type of incident* was 24 per cent for burglary. This combination of a relatively high rate of overall repeat victimisation with a lower rate within specific categories deserves further attention. It may well reflect important geographic patterns in the distribution of crime.

The third point worth noting was that the risk of repeat victimisation was higher for certain types of victim. As already noted, the risk was higher for institutions than for individual victims. The risk of repeat victimisation was higher in Dublin than elsewhere in the country — not surprising given the overall higher risk of crime in Dublin; and higher for individuals in non-manual social classes than for those in manual social classes.

Institutions as Targets of Crime

A particular strength of the present study was the inclusion of crimes against businesses and other organisations as well as crimes against individuals or private households: most crime victimisation studies focus only on private individuals and households. The neglect of crimes against businesses or other organisations has, until recently, extended to the literature on criminology (see discussions in Felson and Clarke, 1997; Bowers et al., 1998). A number of factors have contributed to this neglect, among them a sense that business can better "afford" the losses associated with crime than individual victims; the fact that much crime against businesses goes undetected at the time it is taking place (such as shoplifting and much fraud); a reluctance on the part of businesses to report certain types of crime (particularly fraud by employees and shoplifting). There are also a number of methodological problems that make businesses and other institutions more difficult to study than individuals. These include the difficulty in devising an adequate sampling frame for studies of risk-proneness; the sheer diversity in terms of types of organisation — ranging from schools to sports clubs, to shops, factories and banks — and in terms of the size of the organisation; and the problem of how to specify the unit in cross-sectional analyses (e.g. the local "branch" or the organisation as a whole) and, especially, in dynamic analyses, when organisations form, grow, merge, take on new functions and operations, or cease to operate.

The present study has side-stepped many of these problems by beginning with the recorded criminal incident itself, and moving from there to devise a set of weights (based on the number of incidents reported in a period) to characterise the victims. It has proven an important exercise in that it provided information that was not previously available in Ireland on the proportion of recorded criminal incidents that are directed against institutions (one-third) and the proportion of those victimised in a given year that are institutions (one-fifth). The discrepancy between the two figures arises because institutions are more likely than individuals to have been victimised repeatedly in a given period, so that they account for a larger proportion of the total incidents than of the total victims.

The study provided an overview of the types of organisations involved. Nearly two out of five were retail establishments. Almost one in ten was a public house or restaurant; 7 per cent were schools; 6 per cent were manufacturers; 3 per cent were banks or post offices and a quarter were other non-manufacturing private sector establishments. Two-fifths had between one and five employees, and a further 10 per cent were individuals working on their own account with no employees. The dominance of small-scale organisations among victims probably reflects the larger numbers of establishments of this size.

Recorded crime against institutions differs in some important respects from crime directed against individuals. First, there are differences with respect to the type of crime. Crimes against institutional targets account for over nine out of ten cases of recorded fraud, about three-quarters of aggravated burglaries, over half of the "other theft" category and over two-fifths of burglary and vandalism incidents. Across the categories covered in this study, property is stolen in more than four out of five recorded crimes against institutions – a slightly higher proportion than is true for individual victims. The stolen property is most likely to be retail or manufacturing stock or cash. Most recorded fraud crimes are directed against institutions, and the commonest cases are the use of stolen cheques or credit cards, cashing a cheque made out to someone else, and obtaining cash or goods under false pretences.

Second, as noted above, the extent of repeat victimisation is greater for institutions than for individuals. Four out of five of the businesses and organisations in the survey were victims of at least one other criminal incident in the three-year period from mid-1993 to mid-1996, compared to about half of the individual victims. Repeat victimisation was particularly common in the case of burglary, other theft, and fraud.

Third, recorded crime against institutions does not show the same "Dublin concentration" as crime against domestic or individual targets: 46 per cent of recorded crime against institutions took place in Dublin, compared to 63 per cent of the incidents against individuals. This does not appear to reflect reporting patterns: to the extent that we were able to check this with the present data, reporting rates by institutions are very similar overall in Dublin and other parts of the country. Aggravated burglary of institutions is exceptional in that it shows a high concentration in the Dublin area, with 84 per cent of recorded incidents taking place in Dublin city or county.

Fourth, the reporting of crime shows some important contrasts between individuals and institutions. We were able to estimate reporting rates for other incidents experienced by the victims in the three-year period from mid-1993 to mid-1996. These figures may not be fully representative, since our sample consisted of a group who, by definition, had reported at least one incident to the Gardaí; and, also, by definition, we could only look at reporting rates for the subset who had experienced more than one incident in a three-year period, since the target incident (the one on the basis of which the victim was selected into the sample) had to be excluded from the calculations. A comparison with figures from the QNHS for individuals and households suggested that the reporting rates tended to be higher among victims in the present sample.

Nevertheless, given the dearth of other data on the experience of crime by institutions, it is worth highlighting the results. Overall, institutions were only about half as likely to report a crime (34 per cent) as individual victims (63 per cent). Compared to individual victims, reporting rates were very similar (and high) for vehicle crime and burglary, and a little higher for crimes involving violence. However, reporting rates for the largest category of crime directed against institutions — other theft — was particularly low, at only 19 per cent. Reporting rates were also very low for fraud (21 per cent).

The results suggested that recorded incidents of "other theft" and fraud against businesses and other organisations are not representative of all such incidents. Not only are the reporting rates low, but the subset of incidents that are reported appear to differ from those that are not reported. A number of findings lead to this conclusion: the relatively large proportion of recorded fraud and other theft against institutions with no financial loss and the fact that the offender is identified in virtually all recorded fraud cases and almost nine out of ten recorded cases of other theft. This clearly suggests that only those incidents where the offender is "caught in the act" are reported to the Gardaí. Many cases of fraud and shoplifting may go undetected, or are not discovered until later — during stocktaking or when cheques or credit cards are discovered to have been stolen — when there may seem to be little point in reporting them. Given the very large number of "other theft" incidents directed against institutions which go unreported, the financial loss involved in the reported cases represents only the tip of the iceberg in terms of the cost of crime to businesses and other organisations.

This has two important implications for the representativeness of recorded crime figures in these categories: they will overstate the total proportion of cases where the offender is apprehended; and they will understate the loss to businesses and other organisations from these types of crime.

Finally, the impact of the crime on institutional victims differed in certain respects from the impact on individual victims. Permanent or recurring injury rarely results from crimes directed against institutions. Compared to individual victims, a larger proportion of recorded crime against institutions involves no loss (one-fifth, compared to one-tenth for individual victims), and a larger proportion results in losses in excess of £1,000 (over one-quarter compared to one-fifth for individual victims). Institutions are somewhat more likely to be insured against the financial loss, reducing the proportion of incidents with net losses in excess of £1,000 to one-fifth. Victims of crime against businesses or other organisations were considerably less likely than victims of crime directed against individuals to experience lasting psychological distress.

The Setting of Crime

The second chapter provided detailed information on the setting of crime, which is potentially crucial in developing an understanding of the "opportunity structure" of crime in Ireland, and in targeting crime prevention strategies. The results underlined the utility of a "routine activities" or "situational" perspective in understanding the pattern of crime.

Recorded crime shows a high concentration in the Dublin area compared to other broad regions of the country. This is consistent with findings elsewhere of higher crime rates in urban areas, attributable to the concentration of people and goods (particularly in the retail areas) and the weaker informal social control and "guardianship" of persons and property associated with the relative anonymity of the city. The types of crime that were particularly concentrated in the Dublin area suggested a targeting of businesses and their customers: aggravated burglary against institutions, theft from the person, and to a lesser extent, theft from a vehicle and vehicle theft.

The fact that recorded cases of assault and vandalism did not seem to be over-represented in Dublin relative to the population of this region (in contrast to the results from the QNHS (Central Statistics Office, 1999a)) is likely to be an artefact of the recording of non-indictable incidents in these categories. Cases of non-indictable vandalism and assault do not appear in the Garda statistics unless proceedings are taken. Proceedings may be taken less often in Dublin because the offender is less likely to be identified. This points to the danger involved in drawing conclusions from the recorded statistics when they do not include all reported incidents of crimes in certain categories.

Crime is not generally something that happens to people when they are "away from home", confirming the link between crime and "routine activities" that people engage in during their daily lives. Almost three-quarters of incidents occur in what individual victims consider to be their "own area", with more than half occurring at, or near, the home. Nearly nine out of ten of all crimes against institutional targets, apart from theft from a vehicle, take place on the premises of the organisation. The greater number of incidents taking place in or near the home is understandable, given that this is where people are likely to spend most of their time, and that burglaries against individual targets almost always affect the home, garage or garden shed. There are some exceptions, however: two-thirds of thefts from the person happen in a public place at some remove from the home; over half of the assault incidents happened either in a public place or in the vicinity of a public house or night club; and over half of the thefts from a vehicle occurred while the car was parked away from home.

The distribution of criminal incidents between day and night was more uniform than we might have expected at the outset. Over two-fifths of incidents targeted against individuals took place by day, while the division between day and night was about equal for those targeted at institutions. Some crimes are clearly daytime incidents, particularly those associated with businesses and their customers: this accounts for a sizeable proportion of other theft, aggravated burglary, aggravated and non-aggravated theft from the person, and, to a lesser extent, theft from a vehicle. On the other hand, assault, vandalism, non-domestic burglary and vehicle thefts are more likely to take place at night. About half of domestic burglaries take place during the day, particularly on weekdays when the home is most likely to be empty.

Material gain is clearly a major motivation for crime. Some property is stolen in over four-fifths of recorded criminal incidents across the categories covered in this study. Cash is the most frequently stolen type of property. Over one-quarter of incidents directed against individuals and nearly one-third of those directed against institutions involve the theft of cash, and the figure is over two-thirds for personal theft and aggravated burglary. Personal accessories, vehicles, tools or equipment, and retail or manufacturing stock are among the kinds of property taken in over ten per cent of all criminal incidents. The most common forms of fraud — the use of stolen cheques or credit cards and cashing a cheque made out to someone else — are indicative of links to the theft where these items were originally stolen. Obtaining cash under false pretences and the use of forged banknotes, each accounting for over one in seven incidents of fraud, would seem to suggest criminal activity of a different, and perhaps more "specialist" nature.

From the victim's perspective, one recorded incident in six involves some element of assault or threat, with the proportion being similar for crimes against individuals and against institutions. This most often takes the form of being pushed, dragged, kicked or punched. The threat or use of a weapon is most common in aggravated burglary (nearly three-quarters of the cases) and occurs in nearly one-third of the incidents of aggravated theft from the person, and nearly a quarter of assault cases. The weapon is usually a "blunt instrument" in assault cases, and either a knife or a gun in aggravated burglaries. The use of a syringe to assault or threaten the victim occurs in about one in eight cases of aggravated theft from the person and aggravated burglary.

The image of assault as involving a lone victim in a situation with nobody else around is not supported by the evidence. Only 17 per cent of victims were alone with the offender, and half of the assault victims were accompanied by someone they knew (apart from the offender) at the time. This may be an artefact of the reporting and recording process, however. Witnessed assaults are probably more likely to be reported, and the presence of a witness increases the credibility of the victim's complaint. Aggravated burglary against individual targets and aggravated theft from the person are more likely to involve a lone victim, however.

Victimisation Risk

An assessment of the risk of criminal victimisation for individuals was undertaken by comparing the profiles of victims of recorded crime to those of the general adult population from sources such as the *Labour Force Survey* and the 1995 *Living in Ireland Survey*. For this purpose, the sample was weighted so as to give equal representation to those reporting one crime and those reporting several crimes, providing a distribution similar to that obtained in classic victimisation surveys. It was not possible to assess risk for institutional victims, because of the absence of comparable population data covering all types of organisations. Note also that the risk referred to here is the risk of being a victim of a crime that is both *reported* and *recorded*: to the extent that there are differences in reporting by victims, or in recording by the Gardaí, associated with victim characteristics, the "true" distribution of risk may be different.

Victims of recorded crime do not tend to be the most vulnerable members of society. More victims are men than women, and more are people in their middle-years than are elderly. Moreover, those in the unskilled/manual and semi-skilled/manual social classes appear to be at lower risk of crime than those in the higher social classes. Although crimes against the elderly living in isolated rural areas have received a good deal of media coverage in recent years, the risk of being a crime victim is much greater in Dublin than in other parts of the country, and the overall risk of victimisation is lower for those over age 65.

The person reporting the crime is more likely to be male than female in most categories, and particularly in the case of assault.

Two exceptions are theft from the person and aggravated theft from the person, where there are more female than male victims. The general pattern of gender differences in risk of assault, theft from the person and aggravated theft from the person was confirmed in the QNHS results, but the gap between the risk faced by men and women was smaller in that survey (Central Statistics Office, 1999a). This may reflect reporting differences between men and women, or differences in the recording or classification of incidents based on the sex of the victim.

In terms of age, the overall risk is highest for those aged 35–49, followed by the 50–64 age group, with those aged 65 and over having the lowest risk. These figures do not control for such factors as vehicle ownership and being a head of household, however. Much of the risk pattern is driven by the fact that rates of vehicle ownership are highest in the middle age groups, and those under age 35 are less likely to be household heads — the person most likely to report a burglary in the household. The results from the QNHS suggested that young adults are at a higher risk of vehicle crime, when controls are included for vehicle ownership. In addition, the QNHS found a higher risk of burglary in households where the reference person is under age 25 (Central Statistics Office, 1999a).

In the case of recorded crime, the risk of assault is greatest for those under age 35, a finding that is consistent with the QNHS results. At the other end of the age distribution, the risk of domestic aggravated burglary — a very small category numerically but particularly distressing to victims in its impact — is greatest for those age 65 and over. This may partly reflect a deliberate targeting of elderly householders, particularly those living alone. It may also reflect the fact that older adults are out of the home less often, and are more likely to interrupt a burglar. The similarity in timing and regional distribution between domestic aggravated burglary and burglary provide some support for the latter explanation.

With the exception of assault, risk appears greater for those in the higher social class categories. Those in the higher professional/managerial class face the greatest risk of aggravated theft from the person, other theft and theft from a vehicle; while those in the lower professional/managerial social class face the greatest risk of vehicle theft, burglary and vandalism. The risk of assault is greatest for those in the skilled manual social class. An analysis by economic status or social class is not yet available from the QNHS, so it is not yet possible to say whether the pattern in the recorded statistics holds true for all criminal incidents, including those not reported or not recorded. There were some indications in the present study that those in the non-manual social class were more likely to report other criminal incidents they experienced in a three-year period, particularly vehicle crime and other theft.

Victims and Offenders

It is interesting that in a sizeable proportion of cases, particularly for individual victims, the victim had no information at all on the offender. In half of the crimes against individuals and over one-quarter of the crimes against institutions, the victim did not have any information on the offenders, even to the extent of not knowing how many offenders were involved. The victim did not witness the incident and was not aware of the number of offenders (if any) subsequently charged with the crime. This is particularly true of the type of crime where the victim is rarely present, such as vehicle theft, and theft from a vehicle.

Information on offenders obtained from the crime victims needs to be treated with care, since offenders who are witnessed or subsequently apprehended may not be representative of all offenders. Where the victim had some information on the offender, it emerged that crimes against individual victims were more likely to involve multiple offenders (nearly two-thirds of cases) than a lone offender (just over one-third); that the offender was more likely to be male (nearly nine out of ten cases) than female;

and that two-fifths of the offences were committed by teenagers, rather than adults. In crimes directed against institutions, a somewhat higher proportion of incidents where information is available on the offender involved a lone offender (about two-fifths), female offenders (15 per cent), and a slightly lower proportion involved teenagers or children. Other theft directed at institutions (a category that includes shoplifting) was the only crime category where more than one-third of the offenders were female, and about one-fifth of the identified perpetrators of fraud against institutions were female.

In nearly three-fifths of the assault cases, the offender was someone known to the victim. In assaults of male victims, the offender tended to be less closely linked to the victim than in assaults against females. Only about one-quarter of female assault victims had been assaulted by a stranger (compared to nearly half of male victims); and in just over a quarter of cases involving female victims, the assault was perpetrated by the victim's spouse. However, since domestic violence is known to have a low reporting rate, the proportion of assaults on women perpetrated by a spouse or partner is likely to be considerably higher in reality.

Victims and the Criminal Justice System

Crime victims were generally satisfied with the service provided by the Gardaí who first handled the case, but were dissatisfied with the follow-up information provided to them and with the outcome of the case.

Over three-quarters of victims were satisfied with the speed with which the initial call was answered, the speed with which the Gardaí came to the scene, the politeness and understanding of the problem shown, and the answers given to the victims' questions. Levels of satisfaction with the thoroughness of the Gardaí tended to be somewhat lower, albeit still relatively high. Two-thirds of victims felt that the Gardaí were doing a good job in controlling crime, and nine out of ten said that they would be as likely or more likely to report a similar incident in the future, although the proportion was lower (seven out of ten) for assault victims. We will return to the experience of assault victims, which seems to differ in a number of respects from that of other victims, in the discussion of services for crime victims, below.

Where respondents expressed dissatisfaction with the Garda service, it was with the information on the progress and on the outcome of the case, where only one-third and one-quarter, respectively, of the individual victims expressed satisfaction. Only about two-fifths of victims were contacted by the Gardaí after reporting the crime, and one-third of individual victims did not know whether the offender had been apprehended. Institutional victims of recorded crime seemed to be better-informed overall, but this may reflect the more selective reporting of incidents where the offender is "caught in the act", as noted earlier.

In one-quarter of the cases directed against individuals and half of the cases against institutions the offender had been apprehended. As noted above, the apparently higher "apprehension rate" of offenders who commit crimes against institutions may be an artefact of differential reporting: offences such as fraud and other theft, in particular, seem not to be reported by institutions unless the offender can be identified.

At least some stolen property was recovered in about one-third of the incidents involving theft targeted against individuals and about two-fifths of those directed against institutions. Property is most likely to be recovered in cases of vehicle theft — which includes "unauthorised takings" in the present sample — and reported cases of fraud and other theft directed against institutions. Property is least likely to recovered in cases of burglary and aggravated burglary.

Institutional victims tend to be more satisfied than individual victims with the outcome of the case, although the overall level of satisfaction tends to be low. About one-quarter of the individual victims and one-third of the institutional victims feel either "fairly satisfied" or "very satisfied" with the outcome. The main reasons for satisfaction or dissatisfaction tended to centre on the arrest and/or conviction of the offender in the case of violent crime, and the recovery/non-recovery of property for non-violent crimes involving theft.

The Seriousness of Crime

In this study we have focused on the impact of crime on the victim rather than evaluations of crime seriousness by the public generally. The survey data analysed in this report allowed us to examine three aspects of the seriousness of the crime, from the victim's perspective: the physical injury involved; the financial costs; and the emotional impact on the victim.

Overall, 7 per cent of the crimes against individual targets resulted in injuries requiring medical attention, with 3 per cent leading to permanent or recurring problems. The figures were lower, at 2 per cent and 1 per cent, respectively, for crimes targeting institutional victims. The crime categories most likely to cause injuries resulting in permanent or recurring problems for the victim were assault (one-fifth), aggravated burglary directed against individuals (6 per cent), and aggravated theft from the person (8 per cent).

In terms of the financial costs of crime, we measured only the direct financial costs, such as the value of property stolen or damaged, or out-of-pocket medical expenses. We did not attempt to include the costs of pain and suffering or loss of business in the case of institutional victims. Not did we attempt to put a value on the costs associated with crime prevention measures introduced as a result of the incident.

Looking only at direct costs, vehicle theft was by far the most expensive crime in terms of before-insurance costs, for individual victims, followed by burglary and aggravated burglary. However, the majority of victims were insured against the costs of vehicle theft, so that the net cost to the victim was much lower. The net cost (after insurance) to the victim was highest for aggravated burglary, with nearly one-quarter of the incidents resulting in losses of £1,000 or more. Contact thefts had the lowest costs among the property crimes, rarely resulting in losses over £300, but the victims tended not to be insured and so the cost was borne almost entirely by the victims.

Recorded crime against institutions tended to be more polarised, with both a higher proportion of incidents involving no financial cost (because the offender was caught) and a higher proportion involving costs over £1,000. Burglary, theft from a vehicle and vandalism resulted in the greatest before-insurance cost to institutional victims. About two-thirds of institutional victims were insured against theft from a vehicle and burglary, and three-quarters against vandalism, so that some of these losses could be recovered from insurance. However, burglary remained the most expensive incident, with losses of £1,000 or more in over one-third of the cases, after insurance.

As noted earlier, however, repeat victimisation is more common for institutional than for individual victims, particularly for "other theft", where the average number of incidents per victim was highest. This means that while the loss involved in one incident of shoplifting, for instance, is relatively low on average, the cumulative impact can be very significant.

The third dimension to the cost of crime is the emotional impact on the victim. At the time of the interview, which took place between eight months and two years after the incident, one-quarter of the individual crime victims and one-fifth of the institutional victims continued to experience psychological distress (increased anxiety, trouble sleeping, trouble concentrating). This persistent psychological distress was greatest for victims of violent crime: assault, aggravated burglary and aggravated theft from the person.

The multivariate analysis of factors associated with distress for individual victims showed that victims are most affected by what happens at the time of the incident itself. Of particular importance was whether the incident involved assault, threat, or injury. Being present at the time (even when not assaulted or threatened), and suffering a financial loss over £500 also tended to increase distress, but these effects were smaller. Characteristics of the victim also made a difference: those who are likely to feel most vulnerable — women and the elderly — experienced greater levels of distress than men or younger adults. The intervention of the criminal justice system was less important on the whole than aspects of the incident itself. There was some increase in distress associated with the offender being apprehended, but this was reduced where the victim was satisfied with the outcome of the case. Satisfaction or dissatisfaction with the service provided by the Gardaí had no additional impact on distress.

A broader impact of crime was the increased suspicion on the part of a substantial proportion of crime victims, particularly institutions. This inevitably has an impact on the quality of social interaction, and is likely to be most pronounced in urban areas where the majority of encounters in public places are with strangers. The atmosphere of mistrust and the forbidding and distancing effect of many of the security measures that businesses must introduce all contribute to an increase in urban tensions.

Allied to this are the costs in terms of loss of freedom on the part of those who have been victims, or on the part of those who fear becoming victims. A substantial minority of victims of violent crime restricted their activities by going out less often as a result of the incident. Assault victims — both male and female — were particularly affected in this respect, with about one-third claiming they still went out less frequently at the time of the interview.

In examining the total cost and net cost to the victim (after insurance receipts) in Chapter 5, it was clear, too, that insurance companies pay for a substantial proportion of the cost involved in vehicle theft, theft from the vehicles owned by institutional victims, and domestic burglaries. Since these costs are passed on to other potential victims, the financial costs of crime go well beyond the net loss to the victims.

Implications

The following sections will draw together the results in order to examine their policy implications in three areas: services for victims; strategies for crime prevention; and the development and interpretation of crime statistics for Ireland.

Services to Victims of Crime

There are three distinct areas where services to crime victims after reporting the crime need to be improved. First, there is a clear need to improve the follow-up information to victims on the progress and outcome of the case. As noted above, while victims generally showed high levels of satisfaction regarding the service provided by the Gardaí who first dealt with the case, this was not true of the information on the progress and outcome of the case that was subsequently provided to them. Providing follow-up information could prove time-consuming, and may seem of little benefit if there is no real progress to report: in most crimes, stolen property is not recovered and the offender is not apprehended. Nevertheless, if victims are to feel confident that the Gardaí are taking their complaints seriously, feedback after the event (even if it is negative) is important. Contact between police and victims after the crime is reported can be an important component of police–community relations, encouraging greater co-operation between the public and the Gardaí. Even if there is no progress to report in terms of identifying the offender, it sends a clear message that the problems of victims are important to the Gardaí. It can also have an important role in crime prevention, which will be discussed further below.

A second area where support could be provided for victims is during the court procedure. For the minority of cases where the victim goes to court, nearly half of the individual victims felt that special court services for crime victims were (or would have been) useful to them. This was particularly marked for victims of assault, where 70 per cent felt that such services would be useful, but the proportion was also relatively high for victims of burglary and aggravated burglary.

A third recommendation concerns the need for a review of services for victims of assault. It was clear that the experiences of assault victims are unique in a number of respects which have implications for the handling of these cases. Assault was the only category of crime covered in this report where the offender was someone known to the victim in over half (58 per cent) of the cases. Unlike other crimes, where intimidation by the offender was rare (less than one incident in ten), nearly half of the assault victims experienced some form of intimidation. This was most likely to occur at some time after reporting the crime. Although we do not have information on how serious or distressing the intimidation was for the victim, one-third of assault victims who experienced intimidation felt that the protection provided to them by the Gardaí was not adequate, and one-fifth would have appreciated more protection in court. Assault victims also emerged as having the highest proportion (one-third) who said they would be less likely to report a similar incident in the future. Since their overall level of satisfaction with the Gardaí who first handled the case is at least as high as that of other victims, this reluctance to report further incidents probably stems from a combination of their experience of intimidation by the offender, and their tendency to be less satisfied than other victims with the outcome of the case. There is clearly a need to review the follow-up services provided to victims of assault after the crime has been reported.

A new Garda policy on services to victims has been introduced (Garda Síochána, 1998b), and many of the commitments in the recently published Victim's Charter (Department of Justice, Equality and Law Reform, 1999) deal with support and information to be provided by the Gardaí who handle the incident.

Among the services promised in the Garda plan are a commitment to improving feedback to victims and enhancing victim support. This extended a pilot scheme of automatic notification of specific categories of crime to local branches of Victim Support. The categories of crime to be notified include assaults other than those of an indecent nature, robbery, residential burglaries, other burglaries involving an individual victim, kidnapping, abduction, larceny from the person, and hit-and-run accidents. The investigating Garda has discretion to refer any other crime where he or she feels that the victim would benefit from the support. Investigating Gardaí are now required to provide the injured party with written information about Victim Support, where a local branch exists. The victim is also to be supplied with a calling card showing the name of the investigating Garda and the name and telephone number of the Garda station. The local Garda Superintendent is required to write to the victim confirming these details. There is also a commitment to outlining the investigative process to victims and keeping them informed of the progress of the investigation and any subsequent trial process. In particular, victims are to be informed as a matter of course about the charging or cautioning of a suspect, the granting or withholding of bail, court hearings including their role as a witness, and trial outcomes. Where Gardaí are notified of offender releases, victims will be informed. Special provisions apply to the investigation of sexual offences.

This new Garda policy should go some way towards helping victims as regards what to expect in court, but cannot provide any ongoing support in court which might be construed as witness leading or coaching. Victim Support has developed a specific court witness service which provides court companions for victims of crime.

All of these changes — many of which were informed by earlier drafts of this report — seem to point in the right direction. The effectiveness of these measures, particularly as regards victim satisfaction with information on the progress and outcome of the case, and the provision of protection and support to victims of violent crime, needs to be evaluated and assessed on an ongoing basis. It is significant that a central role in providing support to crime victims — both counselling and the provision of assistance in court — is to be provided by a voluntary agency. It is important to ensure that Victim Support has the resources necessary to meet this role, on the one hand, and that there is continuing evaluation of its effectiveness in meeting the needs of crime victims, on the other.

Fear of Crime and Victim Empowerment

What may be the most debilitating consequence of crime is the fear and distress that it engenders in those who have been affected. We saw in Chapter 5 that over one-third of victims of aggravated burglary feel very unsafe walking alone in their own area by night, while nearly as many feel very unsafe alone in their homes at night. One-third of assault victims still go out less often up to a year after the incident.

However, fear of crime is more general than this. It is generalised beyond the type of incident experienced. We saw in Chapter 5 that crime victims perceived a heightened risk of incidents apart from the one they reported in 1994/95. In addition, research elsewhere indicates that those who have not been victims themselves can have their anxieties increased if someone they know has been a victim of crime (Gilchrist et al., 1998). Further, the results from the QNHS crime and victimisation module, referred to in Chapter 5, point to the high level of concern about crime among the population generally: 63 per cent of women and 49 per cent of men were worried that they themselves or someone in their household would become a victim of crime (Central Statistics Office, 1999a, Table 13).

Some general strategies to empower crime victims would include help with crime prevention, either in terms of practical assistance in installing improved locks or alarms, or providing information on things people can do to reduce their risk. Strategies which combine crime prevention objectives with other social objectives may be most successful. One example is the provision of emergency response phones for elderly persons which helps them retain their independence, security and peace of mind while living in their own homes.

Where it seems that a crime victim is overemphasising the level of risk, he or she can be helped to place the level of risk in perspective. There is evidence that people tend to do this in any case: we saw in Chapter 5 that crime victims tend to adopt a frame of reference which puts the crime risk of their own areas in a more favourable perspective, rarely believing that there is a "lot more" crime in their area than elsewhere in Ireland. It could be that those who are most anxious about crime are less successful at adopting the kinds of frames of reference that reduce their anxiety. It is worth investigating further the extent to which restorative justice initiatives, which bring offender and victim together in a controlled environment and can entail reparation of damage, could help alleviate the negative impact of the crime on the victim.

Another approach is to work to enhance a sense of community responsibility for crime prevention, through such programmes as Neighbourhood Watch and Community Alert. These are schemes designed primarily to encourage co-operation between the public and Gardaí in order to prevent crime and provide social reassurance for vulnerable members of the local community. Three-fifths of individual victims overall felt that these schemes were effective in preventing crime and in helping them feel more secure. However, a recent evaluation has highlighted the challenge of keeping schemes active, once initial enthusiasm and local crime problems have diminished (McKeown and Brosnan, 1998).

The proportion who felt Neighbourhood Watch/Community Alert schemes were effective was lower in the case of victims of aggravated burglary and assault, however. These are the groups

who experienced the greatest levels of psychological distress following the incident. It is worth investigating whether the schemes
can be strengthened in areas where elderly residents, in particular, have been victims of burglary or aggravated burglary. This
may be difficult to accomplish in communities that do not have a
stable core of residents. Some of the findings in Chapter 5 regarding the neighbourhoods in which victims of aggravated burglary, in particular, live (e.g. homes and gardens in bad condition)
are suggestive of neighbourhoods in decline. In such areas it may
be particularly difficult to establish effective Neighbourhood
Watch schemes.

In general, the empowerment of victims — and of those who
restrict their lifestyle out of fear of crime — needs to be approached on two fronts. One is to tackle the very real problem of
crime itself. But the second element is equally important. This involves a direct attack on the fear of crime. Great care must be
taken not to over-dramatise the problem of crime in order to make
political points or advance commercial concerns. The main way in
which crime is over-dramatised is the juxtaposition of high numerical figures which include many less serious incidents with
images and descriptions drawn from the much rarer, very serious
and threatening incidents. The problem of crime needs to be put
in perspective, and the risks weighed alongside the other threats
which people face in their everyday lives, such as road safety, illness, job loss and so on. For instance, in 1998, there were 429
deaths due to motor vehicle and traffic accidents, and a further
335 due to accidental falls (Central Statistics Office, 1999b). This
compares with a total of 83 for murder, manslaughter and dangerous driving causing death (Garda Síochána, 1999). The problem of the "fear of crime" is best tackled by a public information
campaign which combines information on specific things that
people can do in order to reduce their personal risk, while placing
the magnitude and seriousness of that risk in context.

Strategies for Crime Prevention

In drawing general policy conclusions from a piece of research, it is important to be aware of the limitations imposed by the research design. In the context of crime prevention, for instance, we cannot comment on the effectiveness of protective measures such as reinforced door locks or burglar alarms, because we have no comparable information for the population of non-victims.

There is also a danger that recommendations derived from a survey of victims will place an excessive emphasis on the role of victims, or potential victims, in crime prevention. Much of the recent crime prevention literature has emphasised "situational crime prevention" strategies (e.g. Brantingham and Brantingham, 1990; Clarke, 1980; Clarke, 1994; Clarke and Weisburd, 1994; Weisburd, 1997). This approach puts to one side concern with the characteristics and motivation of the offender, and instead focuses on the ways in which the opportunity for crime can be reduced. "Situational crime prevention" has drawn extensively on surveys of crime victims, which can be rich in detail regarding the criminal incident itself and on characteristics of victims, but have little, if any, information on the offenders. This can lead to a sort of "tunnel vision" focus on the victim and the incident, and a tendency to take for granted the motivations of the offender. At its extreme, this approach can end up placing the entire responsibility for crime prevention — sometimes shading into blame for the incident — onto the shoulders of crime victims themselves. There is a danger that such an approach would lead to an over-dramatisation of the problem of crime, and to exaggerated fears which lead people to restrict their activities unnecessarily.

Crime prevention strategies need in any event to be tailored to particular types of crime. Advice to minimise the risk of personal violence will differ in many respects from advice regarding property crime. Likewise within property crime, fraud will be different from burglary and other theft and so on. More work needs to be done on the profiles of different categories of crime to provide insights into crime prevention.

Repeat Victimisation

Several of the findings relating to the pattern of crime in the report have implications for crime prevention. One set of findings concerns the extent of repeat victimisation, particularly for institutional crime victims. Repeat victimisation has become an international focus of criminological research in recent years. It offers the tantalising possibility of alleviating undue suffering on the part of a small cohort of victims, increasing detection rates and reducing crime levels, all at the same time.

Pease (1994) has pointed to the importance of taking note of the frequency and timing of repeat victimisation in devising strategies to prevent crime. A good deal of the research on the timing of repeat victimisation has focused on burglary. It has consistently been found that those who have been victimised by burglary are very likely to be repeat victims of the same offence; and that the repeat incident is likely to occur very soon after the initial incident; with the probability of a repeat declining exponentially with time (Bowers et al., 1998; Johnson et al., 1997; Ratcliffe and McCullagh, 1998; Robinson, 1998).

The results from the 1998 QNHS crime module suggested that repeat victimisation within crime category may be marginally higher in Ireland than in Britain, and the results in Chapter 3 of this report showed that the extent of repeat victimisation, taking account of all crime categories, is marked. Half of the individual victims and four-fifths of the institutional victims of crime recorded in 1994/95 experienced at least one other criminal incident in the three-year period from mid-1993 to mid-1996.

Crime prevention strategies directed towards helping victims of reported crime could be a very good use of Garda resources. Contact with the victim following the incident could be used to improve the level of information provided on the status or outcome of the case (something which the victims in the survey were not satisfied with); to assess the need of victims for help in coping with the effects of the crime; and to target crime prevention measures onto those whose risk of re-victimisation is greatest. As well as alleviating the victim's suffering, a focus on repeat victims can provide a pay-off in terms of reduced crime and increased detection.

There are already some moves towards taking account of repeat victimisation in crime prevention in Ireland. It is targeted for specific action in the Garda Policing Plan 1998/1999, which aims to "identify, target and reduce repeat victimisation" (Garda Síochána, 1998b, p. 22). Repeat calls to the same address can be identified by examining computerised crime reports. Specific actions designed to reduce repeat victimisation include targeting prolific offenders, improved response to burglary victims, and further analysis and action on the drugs–crime relationship.

Young Offenders

From the results in Chapter 4, it was clear that a substantial proportion of identified offenders were children or teenagers: 44 per cent where the target was an individual or private household and 39 per cent where the target was a business or other organisation. It is not clear how representative these figures may be of all offenders: young offenders may be more likely to be seen, or apprehended and identified. They may, for instance, be more likely to rely on speed than on stealth to evade being caught. However, there were two categories of violent crime where most victims could estimate the age of the offender: assault and aggravated theft from the person. In over one-fifth of assault cases and nearly half of the incidents of aggravated theft from the person, where the victim could provide an estimate, the offender was a teenager. These estimates may be subject to error on the part of the victims, and the offenders may not meet the usual definition of "young offenders", since they could be age 18 or 19. Nevertheless, it does suggest that a substantial fraction of violent crime is attributable to "relatively young" offenders.

The link between illegal drug use and crime, discussed below, may account for the youth of offenders in many instances of aggravated theft from the person. O'Hare and O'Brien, for instance, found that nearly half of those treated for drug misuse in the Greater Dublin Area in 1990 were under the age of 25 (O'Hare and O'Brien, 1992). In assault cases, alcohol is more likely than illegal drugs to be implicated. This points to the need for education in the management of the use of the legal drug, alcohol, both on the part of users and on the part of those who provide the context in which it can be an enjoyable part of social life. Since these assaults rarely occur in isolated circumstances, a greater understanding and awareness of the role of bystanders in defusing or escalating an argument would also be important. It is also worth emphasising the unintended consequences that can result, such as long-term or recurring physical injuries to the victim.

In general, it would be useful to emphasise education on the effects of crime, while endeavouring not to over-dramatise the problem. The unintended consequences can go well beyond the impact on those directly victimised. In the case of vandalism, for instance, where victims estimated that two-fifths of offenders were teenagers or children, unintended consequences include the increased sense of apprehension and insecurity on the part of neighbourhood residents that can arise from the cumulation of several small acts of vandalism. Such "signs of crime", while minor in themselves, can lead to increased fears for personal safety, particularly on the part of the more vulnerable members of the community.

Drugs and Crime or Opportunity, Crime and Drugs?

The concentration of certain types of recorded crime in the Dublin area — particularly theft from the person, aggravated theft from the person, and aggravated burglary of institutions — is bound to raise the question of the link between drug use and crime. The abuse of heroin is particularly concentrated in Dublin: of the 296 prosecutions associated with this drug in 1995, only six were outside the Dublin Metropolitan Area.[1] Despite a good deal of public discussion regarding the link between crime and drugs, it is a topic that has received very little research attention in the Irish context (but see Medico-Social Research Board, 1984; Keogh, 1998). Admittedly, it is a difficult area to address. Most of the information available on the link between drug use and crime comes from data on apprehended offenders. The problem with drawing inferences from this is that offenders who are heavy drug users are probably more likely to be caught; and we know little about the drug habits (or lack thereof) of offenders who are not caught, or about the offending habits of drug users who do not present themselves for treatment. Despite the difficulty in specifying precisely how much crime can be attributed to drug users, there is general agreement on the link between certain categories of crime and heroin addiction in the Dublin area (e.g. Rottman, 1989; Keogh, 1998; Medico-Social Research Board, 1984; Korf and Wiersma, 1996).

Keogh (1998) conducted a survey of 352 known drug abusers in the Dublin area. The two principal sources of income were crime and social welfare, with 91 per cent obtaining income from crime — generally burglary, shoplifting and drug-dealing (Keogh, 1998, p. 21). A second aspect of Keogh's research involved matching the names of offenders identified on the crime report forms for detected crimes to the names of those identified by the Gardaí as drug users in the Dublin area, in order to ascertain what proportion of detected crime was committed by drug users. He found that 85 per cent of detected aggravated burglaries, 84 per

---

[1] Use of, or dealing in, illegal drugs was not included as a specific category of crime in the present study because of the absence of a clearly defined victim; in fact, the "victim" and offender may often be regarded as one and the same.

cent of detected larceny from unattended cars, and 82 per cent of detected burglaries and muggings were committed by known drug users. Notwithstanding the caveats noted above regarding the danger of generalising from detected offences to all offences, the findings are indicative of a strong link between drug use and these types of crime in the Dublin area (Keogh, 1998).

Although there is some indirect evidence of such a link in the present study in the "Dublin concentration" of much opportunistic or "snatch" theft, the only direct data on this issue comes from a set of questions to respondents as to whether they believed the issue was drug-related or alcohol-related. The perception of a link between drugs and crime is not shared — or at least not shared to the same extent — by the crime victims themselves. Most individual victims (62 per cent) and nearly half of the institutional victims (46 per cent) did not know whether drugs were a factor in the incident. Those victims with an opinion were more inclined to think that drugs were *not* a factor (22 and 30 per cent for individuals and institutions, respectively) than to think that they were (16 and 24 per cent). Aggravated theft from the person (42 per cent) and aggravated burglary directed against institutions (56 per cent) were the two categories where the victim was most inclined to think that the incident was drug-related.

If we accept that a substantial fraction of certain types of crime in the Dublin area is drugs-related, what implication does this have for prevention strategies? This depends on how we interpret the nature of the causal chain. Is drug abuse taken as a given — with causes outside the realm of direct crime prevention? In this scenario, the main "causes" of drug addiction would lie in aspects of the lives of the addicts that are outside the realm of what we usually think of as "crime prevention" — low levels of education, poor employment opportunities, low levels of family support. If we believe this to be the case, then the central component of the solution would be the treatment of drug offenders and programmes to improve their levels of education and training, and job prospects. Efforts at "target hardening" would be virtually useless, until rehabilitation had been accomplished, as they would be likely to lead to a displacement of crime to other areas, other victims, or to other types of incident.

Alternatively, are both drug abuse and crime in Dublin jointly determined by the criminal opportunity structure of the city? In this scenario, drug abuse and crime are both more common in Dublin because of the availability of drugs, the availability of "targets" from whom (or from which in the case of businesses) cash can be obtained, and the reduced informal social control associated with the anonymity of the city. If both drug abuse and "street crime" are seen as jointly determined by the opportunity structure of the city, then equal emphasis should be placed on making crime more difficult and on the rehabilitation of offenders. Offenders would then have more incentive to make real use of drug treatment programmes to overcome addiction. Bennett's work, referred to in Chapter 1, pointed to the role of choices and decision-making in drug addiction, a phenomenon we are accustomed to think of as compulsive and impulsive in nature (Bennett 1986).

Displacement of opportunistic thefts — the shift in time, place or type of offending — has been cited as a particular concern in the context of drugs-related crime. The fear is that to the extent that drug abusers steal in order to "feed the habit", efforts at crime prevention through "target hardening" — such as making it more difficult to steal cash from shops — may be associated with an increase in thefts from a vehicle or thefts from the person. In Chapter 2, we noted the strong similarity between aggravated theft from the person and aggravated burglary of institutions in terms of their "Dublin concentration", and their concentration in the business hours. The same is true, although to a lesser extent, of theft from a vehicle. If displacement were to occur, it could well be from one to another crime of these types.

However, there is a growing body of evidence to suggest that the problem of displacement may be over-emphasised in discussions of crime prevention (see review by Felson, 1998, pp. 140–142; Mativat and Tremblay, 1997). As evidence that displacement is not inevitable, Clarke (1980) cites a study of suicide in Birmingham. The study showed a marked drop in the rates of suicide between 1962 and 1970 as a result of the reduction in the poisonous content of the gas supply to householders for cooking and heating, so that it became much more difficult for people to kill themselves by turning on the gas taps. Displacement — an increase in suicide by other methods — did not occur in this context. If displacement does not occur in the case of suicide, then there is promise that it may not occur — or not occur to the extent it is feared — in the case of drugs-related crime.

What this implies in terms of crime prevention is that a combination of strategies is needed: treatment programmes, training to increase the job opportunities of former drug abusers, "target hardening" to make crime more difficult, and a direct attack on the supply of drugs. To the extent to which obtaining drugs, or the money to buy them, can be made more difficult, we would simultaneously increase the enthusiasm with which (former) drug abusers take advantage of treatment and training schemes. An acknowledgement of the need for a multi-faceted strategy and the involvement of specialist agencies in dealing with drugs-related crime is contained in the Policing Plan 1998/99 (Garda Síochána, 1998b, p. 23).

Other Strategies

Other crime prevention strategies are simpler, more obvious and depend on action taken by individuals and organisations themselves, rather then the Gardaí. For instance, one of the interesting findings in Chapter 2 regarding the timing of domestic burglaries was that more than two out of five took place during the daytime on weekdays — times when the home is likely to be empty when residents are at work, school or shopping. One strategy for preventing daytime burglaries might be to reduce signs that the home is empty, such as empty rubbish bins left outside all day, uncollected post or leaflets stuck in a letterbox or visible inside a glass porch door. A development of Neighbourhood Watch schemes might involve neighbours working jointly to ensure that such "signs of vacancy" are minimised, such as enlisting the help of neighbours to take in the empty rubbish bin, or to mow the lawn while a household is away on summer holidays. Actions such as these, which can be taken by individuals and households themselves, depend on the dissemination of information on the patterning of crime.

Crime Statistics and The Study of Crime in Ireland

It was clear from the comparison of the results from the 1998 QNHS crime module and the Garda statistics on crime that the two sources can provide a very different picture of the extent of crime in Ireland (Chapter 1). This points to the risk involved in drawing conclusions about trends over time from the recorded crime statistics when we do not know how reporting rates or recording practices may be changing. Further, the clear suggestion emerging from the present study that several types of crime against institutions tend to be reported only when the offender is caught, point to the need for a fuller understanding of the range of factors affecting the reporting of crime. Such an understanding can only come from regular victimisation surveys.

Regular crime victimisation surveys are needed to provide an independent source of information against which to assess crime levels and patterns and to evaluate progress in crime prevention. These surveys would provide ongoing information on crime levels and patterns which is independent of changes in reporting rates, or changes in the recording, classification and counting practices of the Gardaí.

Apart from crime victimisation surveys, the production of more detailed statistics on recorded crime has the potential to provide a large increment in value-added in terms of our understanding of crime in Ireland, with a relatively small additional cost. Moreover, given the difficulties involved in designing victimisation surveys which provide comprehensive cover of crimes against businesses or other organisations, the Garda statistics are likely to remain the primary source of information on crimes against institutional targets. Developments in the computerisation of the Garda records should simplify the process of producing additional breakdowns which would greatly enhance the usefulness of the crime statistics. The following provides an outline of the additional information that would be most useful.

Categories used in the Presentation of Statistics

The published Garda crime statistics provide a high level of detail for the country as a whole, but the criminal incidents in each Garda Division and in the five major cities (Dublin, Cork, Galway, Limerick and Waterford) are broken down only into the four major groups: offences against the person, offences against property, larcenies, and other offences. In the first chapter, it was noted that these groups are very broad — particularly the second and third groups — and fail to distinguish property crimes involving violence or threat to the victim.

Throughout this report, we have presented analyses that attempted to clarify the content of the crime statistics, by presenting results separately for ten different categories of crime, and for crimes against individuals and institutions. The analysis has shown the importance of maintaining this type of distinction. While there is no guarantee that the categories chosen here are the optimum ones, they do illustrate clearly that criminal incidents differ in important ways with respect to the characteristics of the target, the circumstances in which they occur and the impact on the victim. In particular, grouping all violent crime together can

be misleading: assault is very different in terms of the circumstances in which it occurs and the characteristics of the victims
from aggravated theft from the person, which, in turn, differs in
important respects from aggravated burglary — the only category
of violent crime that is primarily directed against institutions.

The first chapter outlined the logic underlying the selection of
the ten categories of crime used in sample selection and throughout the analysis. The categories were devised so as to distinguish
between crimes according to two main dimensions, to the extent
that this could be accomplished using the crime codes used by the
Gardaí. The dimensions were (a) whether the crime involved theft
of property; (b) whether the crime involved the use or threat of
violence against the victim; and (c) within the block of crimes involving theft, a further distinction was made according to the
major context in which the incident took place — theft of or from
a vehicle, burglary, theft from the person, and the residual category "other theft".

As noted in the first chapter, an overall index of crime would
be useful in perspectives emphasising a single major causative
factor underlying overall crime trends, such as unemployment,
the level of consumption, or a breakdown in social order. However, attempts at explaining the overall crime rate, or even the
overall property crime rate, in terms of such factors have not been
very successful. Moreover, the sheer diversity of types of incidents in terms of the setting, the characteristics of the victim, and
the type of property involved reduces the utility of a single index
for crime prevention purposes. It was also noted in Chapter 1 that
an overall index of indictable crimes would mask some important
differences in the trends over the last 17 years. In particular, recorded vandalism and crimes involving violence have tended to
increase over that period, while property crime without violence
has tended to decrease.

The specific categories of crime that are most useful are likely
to vary depending on the purpose. It is clear from the results of

this study that the crucial factor in predicting the level of psychological distress experienced by crime victims is whether the incident involved assault or threat. On the other hand, for crime prevention purposes, or to understand the situational factors influencing changes in the pattern of crime, we would want to distinguish incidents on the basis of their major situational characteristics: burglary, theft of vehicle, theft from a vehicle, assault and vandalism. The present classification of crimes into four major groups for the breakdowns by region in the Garda Síochána Annual Reports serves neither of these purposes adequately. An alternative classification, perhaps along the lines of the ten categories used in this report, would be more informative.

Individuals and Institutions as Victims

The published statistics do not distinguish crimes targeted against individuals from those targeted against institutions. This can sometimes be inferred from the crime type (e.g. larceny from shops and stalls, or malicious damage to schools), and the breakdown was provided for burglary in the 1998 statistics. However, this information remains unavailable for the other major crime types. Further progress in this area is needed, given the reliance on Garda statistics for policy and planning in the area of crime. The nature of the target of crime may change over time, as revealed by the switch since the 1960s from a preponderance of non-domestic to domestic premises as targets in recorded burglaries, noted in Chapter 2. Whether the target is an individual or private household, on the one hand, or a business or other organisation, on the other, has implications for the design of crime prevention strategies, and for the nature of the impact of the crime on the victim.

A More Comprehensive Count of all Reported Incidents

The sample for the present study was drawn from Garda records of victims of crime. Records of indictable crime are computerised and therefore readily available. They included detected and undetected crime and provided all necessary information to locate the victim. The sample also included the non-indictable crimes of common assault, criminal damage and unauthorised takings of vehicles. "Unauthorised takings" were also computerised, but it was necessary to seek details of common assault and criminal damage from manual records at Garda station level. The lack of a central record of all non-indictable crimes reported makes it difficult to provide figures on the total number of incidents reported.

It is expected that the current major upgrading of the Garda computer systems (the PULSE project) will make it easier in future to access information on all reported incidents. This should greatly enhance the information available on formerly unpublished numbers of non-indictable assaults, vandalism incidents and crimes such as "unauthorised taking of bicycles". With the exception of unauthorised vehicle takings, the total number of reported incidents was hitherto not available, and the published numbers for non-indictable incidents referred only to the subset where proceedings were taken. The total number of reported incidents of crimes in these categories, even where no proceedings are taken, should be routinely included in the Garda publications.

Greater Transparency with respect to the Counting and Classification of Incidents

The survey showed up a high level of mismatch between Garda records and victim details (see Chapters 1 and 2), which point to the difficulties inherent in comparing results from crime victimisation surveys with the Garda figures for recorded crime. They also point to the need for greater clarity in the presentation of Garda statistics as to the meaning of the categories used. Of particular concern is the proportion of respondents who were identified as victims in the Garda records but who claimed not to have reported a crime (5 per cent overall but 19 per cent for vehicle theft). There are several plausible reasons for this mismatch, including respondent error or, in the case of vehicle theft, a change of ownership that was not yet updated on the central registers, but we can present no clear explanation. The 7 per cent of respondents who claimed to have reported a different crime to that in the Garda records (Chapter 1) could be explained by differences in Garda recording procedures and the way the respondent understands the incident.

A related area where a "mismatch" was evident was in the disagreement regarding the meaning of "aggravation". A sizeable minority of victims of aggravated burglary and aggravated theft from the person (30 per cent) did not feel that threat or violence had been used. On the other hand, nearly one-fifth of cases of theft from the person, and more than one in ten cases of other theft targeting institution and non-residential burglaries were perceived to have involved assault or threats. A number of factors may underlie these differences between the respondent perception and official classification of the incident, including the classification of a crime as "aggravated" if the offender was carrying a weapon, even though it was not used or explicitly threatened during the incident, and differences between the respondent and Garda interpretation of what constitutes "threat" or assault. It appears that "snatch thefts" such as a handbag snatch may be classified by the Gardaí as "larceny from the person (muggings)", but not necessarily be seen as involving "aggravation" by the victims. In addition, the amount of detail provided by the respondent to the Garda or elicited by the Garda at the time of reporting the crime, could affect whether a crime is classified as aggravated or not. Moreover, the time-lag between the survey interview and the incident may have led the respondent to "forget" some of the details if the threat or assault itself was not perceived as severe by the victim.

The published statistics should include a clear account of how incidents are counted and classified. This would include information on the counting of complex incidents involving violation of several different laws, the counting of a series of incidents in-volving a single victim or of a single incident involving multiple victims, and the classification of incidents into the indictable or non-indictable categories for assault, vehicle theft, vandalism and bicycle theft. Also, in this regard, Rottman (1980) noted that:

> . . . the classifying and counting conventions employed for of-fences that are "detected" can differ from those for which no suspect is found. . . . If a suspect has been identified, the choice of offence categories will be made in terms of strategy for fu-ture court proceedings. The general tendency is to specify more but less serious offences when suspects are available than when they are not. (Rottman, 1980, p. 44)

A fuller understanding of the counting of incidents is needed if we are to draw conclusions about crime patterns from the pub-lished statistics on recorded crime.

Conclusion

The present study had its origins in a concern to assess and im-prove the level of service provided by the Gardaí to victims of crime. Steps have already been taken to improve services, notably by keeping victims better informed about progress and outcomes, and in facilitating contact with Victim Support. The study also examined crime details, the impact on victims, repeat victimisa-tion and reporting rates. Interpreting and contextualising the findings showed up the scarcity of relevant Irish research and evaluation in areas such as crime prevention and the impact of crime on victims. This lack has been evident for some time and is beginning to be addressed (see, for example, Department of Jus-tice, 1997).

Much will be learned from further analyses of the QNHS data. Victimisation surveys are not just an additional source of data to complement the police crime statistics, but are essential in placing the recorded crime figures in context. Without the information on reporting and recording of crime that can be derived from victimisation surveys, we have no way of knowing whether changes over time, or differences between jurisdictions, in police crime figures are artefacts of differences in reporting rates or recording practices. There remains, therefore, a need for greater research activity and provision of basic statistics, including a series of national victim surveys, similar to the regular sweeps of crime surveys in other countries, and public evaluations of crime prevention measures. To quote from the National Crime Forum Report 1998 (pp. 177, 178):

> There is a dearth of relevant, up-to-date information on which to base judgements and decisions in the criminal justice area in Ireland. The need for more and better quality information covers all levels from statistics within the administration to research into the causes and possible responses to crime. . . . That means that we do not have the evidence-based understanding on which to build planning and policy decisions, or to evaluate policies in action.

Appendix A

Sample Weighting
and Other Technical Issues

Victims and Incidents: Sample Weights

The unit of analysis in Garda crime statistics is the incident — a burglary, mugging, car theft, etc. A complex incident may include several offences, in which case the most serious is normally counted and becomes the reference crime. However, some individuals or institutions can be targeted several times in a given year. If an individual has a wallet or handbag snatched several times in a given year, we have one victim but several incidents. This happens much more frequently in the case of shops, which may experience several shoplifting incidents in a given period. In contrast, the unit of analysis in the classic crime victim survey is the victim. In the present study, we begin with a sample drawn on the basis of incidents, and devise two sets of sample weights (the incident weight and the victim weight) so that either the incident or the victim can be the unit of analysis, depending on the requirements of the discussion.

The "incident" weight weights the sample cases up to the population frame of all crimes in the included categories that were recorded in the target period (November 1994 to October 1995.) This weight incorporates a non-response weight that controls for response differences by type of victim (individual or institution), crime reported, and by type of area where the crime was reported; a sampling fraction weight, to control for the different sampling fractions used by crime category; and an "area" weight, to ensure representativeness according to whether the crime was committed in the Dublin Metropolitan Area or elsewhere in the country. This is the appropriate weight to use if we are interested in the crime itself as the unit.

The second weight (the "victim" weight) weights the sample cases up to the population of crime victims. As well as incorporating the non-response, sampling fraction, and area weights, this weight controls for the different probabilities of being selected into the sample associated with the number of crimes reported in a given period. This is the appropriate weight to use in analyses comparing the characteristics of crime victims to those of the general population. It approximates the kinds of totals that would be achieved in the classic victimisation survey results, where the victim is the unit of analysis.

The estimated number of victims of recorded crime needs to be interpreted with caution. A number of assumptions were made in calculating these weights, as detailed below. In particular, we assumed that variations in the number of crimes the victims claim to have reported accurately reflect variations in the number of crimes recorded in the Garda records for the victims. A second assumption made was that taking one-third of the incidents respondents claim to have reported in a three-year period will accurately reflect variations in reporting over one year. Finally, where information was missing or incomplete, the values were imputed so that victim weights could be calculated for all cases.[1]

---

[1] See Table 1.7 in Chapter 1 for an illustration of the difference between the incident and victim weights.

Non-Response Weights

In constructing the sample weights, we began by assessing whether there were response differences by crime type, type of area where the crime was reported (Dublin city, other towns with a population over 10,000 according to the 1991 census, or the remainder of the country), and by type of victim (individual or institution). This assessment involved comparing the completed sample to the original random sample (including the "reserve" sample cases, those who indicated to the Garda Research Unit that they did not wish to participate, and the survey non-respondents) in terms of these three characteristics.

Crime type was identified for the total sample and for the completed sample based on the code in the Garda records.[2] The area where the crime was reported was identified from the Garda records on the basis of the location of the station that recorded the crime.[3] The nature of the victim, whether an individual or an institution, was identified from the Garda records on the basis of the name and address. A separate measure was available for the completed sample which allowed us to more accurately distinguish between individual and institutional victims, but this was not available from the Garda records for cases not included in the survey sample or for non-respondents. As it turned out, there was a reasonably close relationship between the measure based on the address and that based on the survey data item: 94 per cent of those with an organisation name or address were institutions; and 84 per cent of those with names and addresses which did not mention an organisation were private. Using the address-based

---

[2] For the purpose of assessing non-response we used the crime type as coded in the Garda records, since this was available for respondents as well as those who did not participate in the survey. In weighting up to the population totals, however, we used the actual crime as reported by the respondent.

[3] This gives only an approximate breakdown by urban–rural location, however, since some crimes committed in rural locations may have been reported in the nearest (possibly large) town.

measure, then, means that some institutions are not identified as such because there is no mention of the organisation name or address in the Garda records. It was important to use the same measure in constructing the weights, however, since using the address-based measure for non-respondents and the survey based measure for respondents would have confounded differences in response rate with measurement-error in the address-based measure.

The non-response weights were constructed by dividing the completed sample and the total sample into 56 cells;[4] comparing the distribution of cases for the total and completed sample and constructing weights for the completed sample so that the distribution matched that of the total sample. The resulting weights adjust the "completed sample distribution" to the "total sample distribution" as shown in Table A.1.

The total sample figures include those cases excluded from the sample by the Garda Research Unit because they could not be located or declined to participate; the "reserve sample" of cases not selected for the survey sample; the survey non-respondents; and the survey respondents. Although the reserve sample cases, which were not included in the survey sample, are not "non-respondents", it was important to include them in the total since the size of the reserve sample was affected by the number of individuals who declined to participate prior to the field phase at the ESRI. If a particular crime category, for instance, had a high refusal or non-contact rate at the first stage conducted by the Garda Research Unit, there would be fewer of them in the reserve sample.

---

[4] The cells result from the cross-classification of crime type by type of area by type of victim. A small number of cells were empty for the total sample — mainly for crime types which tend to specifically affect either individuals (e.g. assault) or institutions (e.g. fraud); and three cells which were empty for the completed sample were combined with neighbouring cells.

Table A.1: Weighting Completed Sample for Non-Response and Sampling Error

Variable	Total Sample Distribution (including "reserve")	Unweighted Completed Sample Distribution
Crime Type		
Vehicle Theft	13.2	10.1
Theft from Vehicle	6.4	8.4
Fraud etc.	7.3	9.4
Assault	9.2	9.6
Burglary	8.9	10.9
Aggravated Burglary	7.7	8.8
Theft from Person	9.6	9.2
Theft from person, aggravated	15.4*	10.4
Other Theft	12.7	13.5
Vandalism	9.6	9.7
Type of Area		
Dublin	56.2	52.2
Other Large town	20.2	22.0
Remainder of country	23.6	25.8
*Type of Victim (based on name & address)***		
Individual	78.3	77.4
Institution	21.7	22.6
Number of Cases	*2,534*	*959*

* Note that the lower representation in the completed sample than in the total sample of aggravated theft from the person is due to the use of different sampling fractions for this group in the initial sample selection and in the survey sample selection. More cases than were needed were selected in the initial sample, and these cases are over-represented in the reserve sample of cases that were not approached at the survey stage.

** The breakdown based on name and address (which is the only one available for cases where the interview was not conducted) tends to understate the true proportion of incidents targeting institutions.

There were small variations between the total and completed sample in terms of crime type, particularly with respect to victims of vehicle theft who were more likely to be non-respondents. The higher proportion of victims of theft from person in the total sample than in the completed sample is not due to non-response: it arose because a smaller sampling fraction was used for this group in selecting the survey sample, so that they are over-represented in the reserve sample. The differences by type of area reflect a lower response rate in the Dublin region, as is commonly found in sample surveys. The differences by type of victim were very minor, with individual victims slightly under-represented in the completed sample.

The second step in constructing the crime weights involved weighting the completed sample to the population totals for crimes of a particular type. This takes account of the fact that different sampling fractions were used for the different crimes, and also incorporates a control for whether the crime occurred in the Dublin area or elsewhere. The survey data was weighted by the non-response weights, and the resulting distribution was compared to a special breakdown of the total number of crimes reported in 1995 in each of the categories, by area. Table A.2 shows the population totals and the weights applied to each crime category, by area. The non-indictable crimes and the indictable crimes within the vehicle theft, assault and vandalism categories were weighted separately. In weighting up to the population totals, the crime actually discussed in the first part of the questionnaire was used in those cases where this differed from the crime recorded in the Garda records.[5]

---

[5] See Table 1.6 in Chapter 1.

Table A.2: Incident Weights by Crime Type

	Total Number Recorded in 1995			Mean Weight		
	Dublin	*Elsewhere*	*Total*	*Dublin*	*Elsewhere*	*Total*
Theft of Vehicle, indictable	1,573	571	2,144	65.5	57.1	63.1
Theft of Vehicle, non-indictable	8,147	3,607	11,754	339.5	144.3	239.9
Theft From Vehicle	13,372	5,466	18,838	215.7	165.6	198.3
Fraud etc.	888	2,690	3,578	68.3	40.8	45.3
Other theft	13,095	10,625	23,720	211.2	168.7	189.8
Assault, indictable	193	326	519	24.1	13.0	15.7
Assault, non-indictable	2,245	4,282	6,527	187.1	84.0	103.6
Burglary	16,099	14,894	30,993	315.7	198.6	246.0
Aggravated burglary	1,157	332	1,489	18.7	13.3	17.1
Theft from person, aggravated	5,871	779	6,650	66.7	77.9	67.9
Theft from person	2,677	406	3,083	40.0	22.6	36.3
Vandalism, indictable	1,915	6,093	8,008	136.8	129.6	131.3
Vandalism, non-indictable	1,253	938	2,191	156.6	58.6	91.3

Victim Weights

Some individuals or institutions may report several crimes in a given year. The victim weights are designed to weight the sample up to the total population of victims reporting a crime in the target period, giving "equal representation" to victims reporting one and those reporting several crimes. Those reporting several crimes have a greater probability of being selected into the sample. The "victim" weights adjust for this so that victims reporting different numbers of crimes are equally represented.

In calculating the victim weights, the first step was to estimate the total number of incidents reported in the target period, including the "target" incident (the one on the basis of which the respondent was selected into the sample). The questionnaire contained a set of items dealing with the number of *other* incidents (apart from the one discussed in the main body of the questionnaire) that occurred and were reported over the last three years. This was adjusted to a one-year figure by dividing by three, and the crime on the basis of which the victim was selected was added back into the total.

In calculating the victim weights, we would ideally like to know the number of incidents that were *recorded* in each category for each victim in the target period. Since we do not have this information, we used the number the victim claims to have reported as a proxy. It is not necessary for the number reported to be *equal* to the number recorded in order for this proxy to fulfil its role in the weighting scheme: just that the relationship between reporting and recording is consistent across victims. Given this consistency, variations across respondents in the number reported would accurately reflect variations in the number recorded.

The use of number reported as a proxy for number recorded is flawed to the extent that (a) respondents forget having reported incidents and (b) recording of reported incidents varies according to characteristics of the victim. Respondents, especially those who have been victimised several times, may not only forget certain less serious incidents which occurred over the previous three years, but may also forget having reported them. We saw in Chapter 1 that there may be a considerable gap between the number of reported incidents and the police counts of crime. There are a number of reasons why a reported crime may not be recorded, notably if there is not sufficient evidence to indicate that an offence took place. In addition, counting procedures for a series of related incidents may mean that every reported incident, even when it is accepted that an offence has occurred, does not necessarily appear in the police totals as a separate incident. In the absence of individual-level information on the recording of reported incidents, however, the number the victim claims to have reported is the best estimate available.

The following strategies were adopted in dealing with incomplete or missing information:

- If the number of times an incident occurred was coded as "numerous" or "too many to count", the 90th percentile or next lowest non-outlying value for number of times (where an incident did occur) was assigned. This affected only a small number of cases, and only occurred for institutions. The number of cases involved was 14, and ranged from none — for the number of times an item kept outside was stolen — to 10 for property stolen by someone who had a right to be on the premises (including shoplifting).

- Where the number of times was missing, but the incident did occur, the median number for cases where an incident occurred was assigned, differentiating individual and institutional victims. For individuals, the median was 1 for all types of incidents. For institutions, the median ranged from 1 for vehicle theft to 6 for theft by someone who had a right to be on the premises. The number of cases affected was 174 across all types of incident, ranging from 5 for "something stolen by someone who had a right to be in your home" to 26 for "attempted break-in", for individual victims; and from 1 for vehicle theft to 26 for attempted break-in for institutional victims.

- If information on whether or not an incident occurred was missing, the number of incidents was imputed as the probable number of incidents that occurred (calculated as the proportion of non-missing cases where the incident did occur multiplied by the median number of incidents where it did occur). This was done separately for individual and institutional victims. Since the median for all types of incident is 1 in the case of individual victims, the imputed number of incidents reduces to the probability that an incident of this type would occur for an individual victim. The number of cases affected was 89 across all types of incidents, and ranged from 5 for assault to 27 for attempted break-in, for individual victims; and from 5 for assault to 15 for attempted break-in for institutional victims.

- The next step was to calculate the number of incidents reported to the Gardaí in the three-year period. The questionnaire item asked, for each type of incident that occurred, whether all, some, or none were reported. Where all incidents were reported, the number reported equals the number that occurred for that incident. Where none was reported, the number reported equals zero for that incident. Where some were reported, we made an attempt to calculate the most likely number reported by examining the probability that all would be reported versus the probability that none would be reported. For instance, in cases of individual victims of burglary, where either "all" or "none" of the incidents were reported, 96 per cent reported all incidents and 4 per cent reported none. Therefore, for cases of burglary where the victim was an individual who reported "some" of the incidents, we assumed that 96 per cent were reported. Again, this resulted in a non-integer "probable" number reported. The number of cases affected by this imputation was 106 across all types of incident, and ranged from 2 for vehicle theft to 32 for theft by someone who had a right to be on the premises for institutions. The number affected was smaller for individual victims, since the median number of incidents of all types was 1, so that either "all" or "none" would be reported. The number where some were reported ranged from 0 for burglary with theft to 9 for vandalism for individual victims.

- The next step was to categorise the type of incident using the ten crime categories that were used in the sample. This was done using the items in Section E of the questionnaire, as shown in Figure 3.1 in Chapter 3.

We were not able to distinguish indictable from non-indictable crimes within the assault, vehicle theft or vandalism cases (although we are able to do so for the incident about which the victim was interviewed). The published statistics clearly indicate that non-indictable cases are more common than indictable cases in the assault and vehicle theft categories, however, while the reverse is true for the vandalism cases recorded in the Garda published statistics. In order to take account of this difference in constructing the victim weights, we calculated the probable number of indictable and non-indictable incidents in each of these three categories by multiplying each reported incident by the ratio from the published statistics. For instance, each reported assault had a 7.4 per cent probability of being an indictable assault and a 92.6 per cent probability of being a non-indictable assault.

- The total number of other incidents reported in each category was then divided by three to get a one-year estimate; and the incident on the basis of which the individual was selected into the sample was added (since this incident was not included in the section of the questionnaire that discussed "other incidents that occurred in the last three years"). This provided an estimate of the number of incidents likely to be reported by each victim in the sample in a one-year period.

- The final step in constructing the victim weights was to calculate the probability that each victim would be randomly selected in the crime category that was the subject of the interview, given the sampling fraction used and given the number of incidents of that type they had reported. Victims in the sample with a lower probability of selection must "represent" a larger number of victims in the population.

The sampling fraction was taken as the number of incidents of each type in the completed sample divided by the total number of incidents of each type reported in 1995 (from the Garda Síochána

Annual Report 1995). When the sampling fraction for each crime category is multiplied by the number of crimes in that category reported by the victim, this gives the probability that the victim's name will be selected into the sample.[6]

The data were weighted by the inverse of the probability of selection into the actual crime category on which the interview was based, multiplied by the non-response weight; and the total number of crimes in each category was weighted to the total number reported in 1995. The victim weights gross the *total* crimes in the target category reported by victims to the population total number of incidents. This differs from the incident weights, which gross the crimes on which the interviews were based (counting one crime per victim) up to the total number of incidents.

Table A.3 shows the result of the rather complex weighting procedure. The averages in the first column indicate that "other theft" is a clear outlier, with the sample members reporting an average of 22 such incidents in 1995, compared with figures ranging from 1.01 to 2.32 for the other crime categories. The weighted results, which control for the fact that those reporting a greater number of crimes have a higher probability of selection into the sample, indicate that of all the victims of "other theft" in 1995, the average number of such incidents reported is 1.42. The weighted results allow us to assess the number of victims affected by the crimes in each category. For instance, the 2,144 indictable vehicle thefts in 1995 affected an estimated 2,122 different victims. "Other theft", which includes shoplifting, is much more likely to occur repeatedly to the same set of victims; the total of 23,720 such crimes in 1995 affected an estimated 16,665 victims.

---

[6] In a small number of cases, this probable number was greater than one. This tended to occur for large retail stores that reported a very high number of shoplifting incidents. If a particular victim (such as a branch of a large retail outlet) was selected more than once, we randomly selected the most recent incident for the purpose of the survey, and replaced the duplicate with another case from the reserve sample involving the same crime type and victim type (individual or institution).

Table A.3: Weighting for Analysis of Crime Victims (Victim Weights)

	Unweighted Figures			With Victim Weights		
	Mean N reported	Total N reported	N of victims	Mean N reported	Total N reported	N. of victims
Theft of Vehicle, indictable	1.01	35	34	1.01	2,144	2,122
Theft of Vehicle, non-indictable	1.06	52	49	1.05	11,754	11,180
Theft From Vehicle	1.20	114	95	1.10	18,838	17,142
Fraud etc.	2.27	179	79	1.28	3,578	2,785
Assault, indictable	1.01	33	33	1.01	519	516
Assault, non-indictable	1.57	99	63	1.07	6,527	6,075
Burglary, not aggravated	1.69	213	126	1.25	30,993	24,739
Aggravated burglary	1.45	126	87	1.22	1,489	1,222
Theft from person	1.02	87	85	1.02	3,083	3,032
Theft from person, aggravated	1.03	101	98	1.02	6,650	6,489
Other theft	22.20	2,775	125	1.42	23,720	16,655
Vandalism, indictable	2.32	142	61	1.20	8,008	6,675
Vandalism, non-indictable	1.02	25	24	1.02	2,191	2,146
Total	*4.15*	*3,979*	*959*	*1.60*	*119,494*	*74,564**

Note: * this figure is based on the separate "total victim weight" described in the text, and is less than the sum of victims across categories, since some individuals may have experienced several types of crime in the target period.

A separate weight is needed for the "total" column in tables where the victim weight is used. This is because the victim weights within category do not take account of the fact that a victim may have reported crimes in more than one category. For instance, an organisation may report several incidents of vandalism and several incidents of other theft. The victim weights gross the number of victims in each category up to the total number of victims of that type of crime in 1995. One consequence of this strategy is that the figure for the total number of victims across categories would overstate the total number of distinct victims of crime in 1995. This arises because the sum across categories double-counts those individuals or institutions that reported crimes in more than one category. The "total victim weight" was constructed in order to take account of the fact that a victim may report crimes in several different categories. The sum of the estimated number of victims in each category, then, will be greater than the total number of victims of *any* crime to the extent that individuals or organisations are victims of several different types of crime in a given period.

To construct the total victim weights, the data were weighted by the inverse of the probability of selection into *any* of the ten crime categories, multiplied by the non-response weight.

The probability of selection into a crime category is a function of the number of crimes reported in that category (r) and the sampling fraction (f) for that incident. The sampling fraction is the sample size for incidents of a particular type, divided by the total number of incidents of that type.

The probability of selection into any one category, then, is given by r*f. The probability of selection into any of the ten categories is given by the sum of the probabilities for all ten categories,[7] minus the sum of the products of all the joint probabilities. If there were three categories, for instance, the probability of selection would be:

---

[7] Since indictable and non-indictable incidents were separated for vehicle theft, assault and vandalism the number of categories used in the calculation of probability of selection was actually 13.

$$r_1f_1 + r_2f_2 + r_3f_3 - (r_1f_1{*}r_2f_2 + r_1f_1{*}r_3f_3 + r_2f_2{*}r_3f_3) - (r_1f_1{*}r_2f_2{*}r_3f_3)$$

(sum of probabilities) – (sum of two-way joint probabilities) – (sum of three-way joint probabilities).

With ten categories of crime, the number of joint probabilities becomes very large. Checks on the values of the joint probabilities indicated that there was very little change in the probability between the subtraction of the three-way and four-way joint probabilities, so the calculations were stopped after subtracting the four-way joint probabilities.

The Gross program developed by Johanna Gomulka (1992, 1994) was used to adjust the final weights so that the total number of incidents reported in each category matched the population totals for incidents, and the estimated number of victims in each category matched the estimated total victims using the within-category victim weights. The "total victim weights" differ from the within-category victim weights since they gross the total crimes reported by victims in *any* category to the population total incidents, rather than weighting the crimes on which the interviews were based up to the population total incidents. Since the total weights are particularly sensitive to the measures of the total number of incidents reported, the total figure of about 75,000 different victims of the 120,000 crimes should be treated with caution.

In general, the estimated total number of victims of recorded crime needs to be interpreted with care. A number of assumptions were made in calculating these weights. In particular, we assumed that variations in the number of crimes the victims claim to have reported accurately reflect variations in the number of crimes recorded in the Garda records for the victims. If some victims tend to report a large number of incidents that are not recorded by the Gardaí, then these victims will be under-represented in the victim weights. On the other hand, if victims forget that they have reported an incident (or even that it occurred), they will tend to be over-represented when the victim weights are used. A second assumption made was that taking one-third of the incidents that respondents claim to have reported in a three-year period will accurately reflect variations in reporting over one year. This might be problematic if, for instance, there was a crime wave in the year immediately prior to the target period with a drop in crime during the target period itself. Those victims who experienced crime during the crime wave would have their victim weights adjusted downwards, and would tend to be under-represented in the figures using these weights. Finally, where information was missing or incomplete,[8] the values were imputed so that victim weights could be calculated for all cases. In general, the imputations took the form of assigning a median value, distinguishing between individual and institutional victims. These imputations would not have distorted the overall distribution of reporting, but if the cases where information was imputed differed systematically in some way from those for whom all information was available (such as being at particularly high or low risk of victimisation), this could have introduced a bias into the victim weights.

Estimating the Number of Recorded Incidents Against Individuals and Private Households, 1997–1998

This section provides further details on how the number of crimes against individuals and private households from the last quarter of 1997 to the third quarter of 1998 was estimated. These figures were used in Chapter 1, in conjunction with figures from the QNHS crime and victimisation module, to estimate the percentage of reported crimes that were recorded by the police.

---

[8] Incomplete information resulted from the coding of the question on the number of incidents that were reported into three categories "All", "Some", or "None".

Columns A and B of Table A.4 show the total number of recorded incidents in each category, from the Garda Annual reports for 1997 and 1998.

The crimes included in each category are as follows:

- *Theft of Vehicle*: larceny of MPV and unauthorised takings of MPV (including cases where no proceedings taken);

- *Theft from Vehicle*: larceny from unattended vehicles;

- *Burglary (including aggravated)*: burglary, armed attack on house, armed aggravated burglary, aggravated burglary other;

- *Vandalism*: arson, killing/maiming of cattle; malicious damage to schools;[9] other malicious injury to property, non-indictable criminal damage;

- *Non-violent Theft*: larceny from person (pickpocket);

- *Theft with Violence*: larceny from person (muggings), robbery, armed robbery;

- *Theft of Bicycle*: larceny of pedal cycle, taking possession of pedal cycle without consent (non-indictable).

Column C provides an estimate of the number of incidents taking place between the fourth quarter of 1997 and the third quarter of 1998 — the reference period of the QNHS crime and victimisation module (Central Statistics Office, 1999a). This figure is obtained by adding three-quarters of the 1998 figure to one-quarter of the 1997 figure.

---

[9] "Malicious damage to schools" clearly does not target private households. However, it is included in the totals in Columns A and B because the estimate of the percentage of incidents targeting individuals or households (Column D) is based on a total figure that includes this type of incident.

Table A.4: Estimating Number of Crimes Recorded by Type of Incident in 1997–98

	A	B	C	D	E
	Total Recorded 1997	Total Recorded 1998	Estimated One-year 1997/98	Estimated % Individual/ Household	Estimated Recorded Cases
Theft of Vehicle	16,039	15,293	15,480	93.2%	14,427
Theft from Vehicle	13,441	12,377	12,643	87.6%	11,080
Burglary (including aggravated)	28,663	26,565	27,090	(60.4)%	16,363
Vandalism	11,955	11,262	11,435	55.7%	6,369
Non-violent Theft	3,652	3,202	3,315	100.0%	3,315
Theft with Violence	5,078	3,878	4,178	92.1%	3,847
Theft of bicycle	347	336	339	100.0%	339
Total	79,175	72,913	74,479		55,740

Source: Garda Síochána Annual Reports 1997 and 1998; Table 2.1 in Chapter 2 of the present study.

Column D shows the estimated percentage of incidents in each category that targeted individuals or private households rather than businesses or other organisations. These figures come from Table 2.1 in Chapter 2 of this report. In the case of burglary, the 1998 Garda Síochána Annual Report provides a breakdown between burglaries of dwellings and other burglaries for both years. These figures were used for burglary, and the estimated number of aggravated burglaries against individuals or private households was added to this total.

Column E shows the estimated number of incidents in the period from the last quarter of 1997 to the third quarter of 1998 that targeted individuals or private households. Apart from burglary, as noted above, the figure is calculated as Column C multiplied by Column D.

Appendix B

Survey Questionnaire

ECONOMIC AND SOCIAL RESEARCH INSTITUTE

Limited Company No. 18269 CHY 5337   **4 Burlington Road   Dublin 4   Ireland**

Tel: (01) 667-1525   Fax: (01) 668-6231

SURVEY OF VICTIMS OF CRIME, JULY 1996

CONFIDENTIAL

	For Office Use Only

H1 **Respondent ID** _____

H2 Crime (quota sheet) _____

H3 Date of Interview _____Day _____ Month _____ Year

H4 Interviewer ID _____

H5 Interviewer Name _____

For Office Use Only

H1
H2
H3
H4
H5

I'm from the Economic and Social Research Institute [show identity]. The Institute is carrying out a national survey of victims of crime on behalf of the Research Unit of the Garda Síochána. You should have received a letter about the survey some weeks ago. [Show respondent copy of letter.] You have been selected at random to participate in the survey.

The purpose of the survey is to learn about the experiences of victims of crime in order to help ensure the best possible service to them. It will also provide information of value in crime prevention.

It is very important to collect information from all of those included in the sample, so that the study can accurately reflect the full range of problems and needs of crime victims.

Any information you provide will be treated in the strictest confidence and no information will be published or released to the Gardaí or anyone else which would reveal your identity.

[Interviewer: Go to A1 on p.2]

****

INTERVIEWER ITEMS
[To be completed at END of interview without reference to Respondent]

H6 **Sex of respondent** $\Box_1$ Male $\Box_2$ Female   H6

H7 Victim is a $\Box_1$ private household/individual or $\Box_2$ business or other institution?   H7

H8   **Where did the interview take place . . .**
    [✔ here if crime committed elsewhere $\Box_{99}$]

a. Type of building
$\Box_1$ apartment / flat
$\Box_2$ maisonette
$\Box_3$ terraced house, end
$\Box_4$ terraced house, other
$\Box_5$ semi-detached house
$\Box_6$ detached house
$\Box_7$ place of business
$\Box_8$ mobile home, caravan
$\Box_9$ other, please specify

b. Affluence of Area
$\Box_1$ rather well-off residential / business
$\Box_2$ average residential / business area
$\Box_3$ run down area
$\Box_4$ other, please specify .

c. Urban-Rural Location
$\Box_1$ centre of city, town
$\Box_2$ elsewhere in city, town
$\Box_3$ village
$\Box_4$ open country

H8
H8a
H8b
H8c

H9 **Respondent was interviewed . . .**

$\Box_1$ alone
$\Box_2$ only small children present
$\Box_3$ other teenagers/ adults present some of time
$\Box_4$ other teenagers/ adults present most of time
$\Box_5$ other, please specify

H10 **How much confidence do you have in the accuracy /completeness of the responses?**

$\Box_1$ very high level of confidence
$\Box_2$ fairly high level of confidence
$\Box_3$ don't know / unsure
$\Box_4$ fairly low level of confidence
$\Box_5$ very low level of confidence

H9
H10

[Interviewer: enter name/date of crime in space below only if different from that on quota sheet]

I understand that over the last 12 months or so, you were the victim of [_____].
I'd like to begin by asking you some questions about the incident which took place in
{ _____ month/year }. We will come back to any other criminal incidents later.

For Office Use Only
Crime_____
Mo/yr _ _ _ _

A1. **Did the incident take place in this area or elsewhere?** ☐₁ Here ☐₂ Elsewhere

A1

A2 **Please give the name of the town/city or rural area where the incident took place.**

A2 _ _ . _ _ _

Place/city/town/village name _____ County _____

A3 **Was this in . . .** ☐₁ town/city centre ☐₂ town/city-elsewhere ☐₃ Village ☐₄ open country

A3

FRAUD /EMBEZZLEMENT: **Go to A20 , top of Page 6**

ASSAULT THEFT FROM PERSON OTHER THEFT *	BURGLARY VANDALISM	THEFT OF VEHICLE THEFT FROM VEHICLE
A4a **Did the assault/theft take place:** ☐₁ in your home ☐₂ in vicinity of home (garden, garage etc.)* ☐₃ near home ☐₄ at work ☐₅ near workplace ☐₆ at school/college ☐₇ near school/college ☐₈ in/near pub / dance hall / disco ☐₉ at/near other public place (shopping area, church etc.) ☐₁₀ elsewhere, please specify _____ *Other Theft and 'vicinity of home' , = Theft from Vicinity of Premises	A4b. **Could you tell me whether the burglary / vandalism was at . .** ☐₁ your home ☐₂ garden, shed, outbuildings ☐₃ farm ☐₄ other business premises ☐₅ other non-business premises (school, church, etc.) ☐₆ other, please specify _____	A4c. **Was the vehicle a . . .** ☐₁ car → Year of reg ____ ☐₂ van ☐₅ truck ☐₃ motorcycle ☐₆ tractor ☐₄ moped ☐₇ other, please specify _____ A4d. **Where was the vehicle parked at the time?** ☐₁ garage ☐₂ driveway ☐₃ on street near home ☐₄ public car park ☐₅ private car park ☐₆ on street, elsewhere ☐₇ other, specify _____

A4a
A4b
A4c
A4c.1reg

A4d

ALL (except Fraud / Embezzlement)

A5. **When did the incident take place, was it . . . ?** [tick one box on each line]
a. → ☐₁ daytime [8 am to 8pm], or ☐₂ night-time [8 pm to 8 am] ☐₃ D.K.
b. → ☐₁ Weekday [8am Mon. to 8pm Fri.] ☐₂ Weekend [8pm Fri. to 8am Mon.] ☐₃ D.K.

A5a
A5b

A5c. **Was there any special event on at the time that drew large numbers of people to the area, such as a match, concert or Féile?** ☐₁ Yes ☐₂ No ☐₃ don't know

A5c.

A6a. **Were you yourself present at the time of the incident?** ☐₁ Yes ☐₂ No

A6a.

A6b. **Was anyone else present at the time [apart from the offender(s) and respondent]?**

A6b.

☐₁ Yes→A6c ☐₂ No→A8 ☐₃ DK →A8

A6c. [If OTHERS present, apart from offender(s)] **Were they . . .**
☐₁ Household/family members
☐₂ Others known to R (e.g. friends, neighbours, co-workers, boss etc.) [tick all that apply]
☐₃ Bystanders, strangers

A6c1,
A6c2
A6c3

A7. [**Apart from yourself**] **Were the other people present . . . ?** [✓ all that apply. Do not include R]
☐₁ children, number____ ☐₂ teenagers, number ___ ☐₃ adult(s), number ___
 (under age 12) (age 12-17) (age 18 and over)

A7.1
A7.2
A7.3

A8. [If nobody at all present at the time] **Who discovered the crime?**
☐₁ respondent ☐₃ child(ren) ☐₅ neighbour ☐₇ Garda
☐₂ spouse/partner ☐₄ caretaker ☐₆ employee ☐₈ other

A8

		For Office Use Only
ASSAULT: Go to A10a		
OTHERS: A9 **Were you assaulted or threatened during the incident?**		
☐₁ Yes, Go to A10a ☐₂ No Go to A11a		A9
A10a. What was the nature of the assault? Were you . . . [tick all that apply]		A10a1
☐₁ punched ☐₃ bitten ☐₅ hit with blunt object ☐₇ threatened with weapon		A10a2
☐₂ kicked ☐₄ pushed ☐₆ hit/stabbed with sharp object ☐₈ other, please specify to the ground _____		A10a3
A10b. [If weapon used/threatened] **Was it a** ..[tick all that apply]		A10b1
☐₁ knife ☐₃ gun or rifle ☐₅ syringe		A10b2
☐₂ club or stick ☐₄ bottle / glass ☐₆ other, please specify		A10b3
		A10c
A10c. **Were you physically injured?** ☐₁ Yes [Go to A10d] ☐₂ No [Go to A10g]		
A10d. **If yes, what kind of treatment did your injuries require?**		A10d
☐₁ cuts/ bruises, not requiring medical attn. ☐₃ injuries requiring overnight hospital stay		
☐₂ needed medical treatment, but not hospital stay ☐₄ hospitalisation for more than 1 night		
☐₅ other, please specify _____		
A10e. **As a result of the attack, do you suffer any permanent or recurring physical injury or disability?** ☐₁ Yes Go to A10f ☐₂ No Go to A10g		A10e
A10f. [If yes] **Can you describe the nature of the physical injury or disability?**		
_____		A10f (text,30)
A10g. **Was there any element of sexual assault in the attack?** ☐₁ Yes ☐₂ No		A10g
A11a. Was anyone else (accompanying you or in your household / in the business or institution) **assaulted or threatened during the incident?**		A11a
☐₁ Yes ☐₂ No→ A13. ☐₃ Nobody with R / Nobody else present → A13		
[If more than one: **Thinking of the other person who was most affected . . .**]		A11b
A11b. **Was this person** ☐₁ Male or ☐₂ Female.		A11c
A11c **What was this person's approximate age?** _____ years		
A12a. **Was this person . . .** [tick all that apply]		A12a1
☐₁ punched ☐₃ bitten ☐₅ hit with blunt object ☐₇ threatened with weapon		A12a2
☐₂ kicked ☐₄ pushed ☐₆ hit/stabbed with sharp object ☐₈ other, please specify to the ground _____		A12a3
A12b. [If weapon used/threatened], **Was it a** . . .[tick all that apply]		A12b1
☐₁ knife ☐₃ gun or rifle ☐₅ syringe		A12b2
☐₂ club or stick ☐₄ bottle / glass ☐₆ other, please specify		A12b3
A12c. **Was the other person physically injured?** ☐₁ Yes ☐₂ No → A12g		A12c
A12d. **If yes, what kind of treatment did their injuries require?**		A12d
☐₁ cuts/ bruises, not requiring medical attn. ☐₃ injuries requiring overnight hospital stay		
☐₂ needed medical treatment, but not hospital stay ☐₄ hospitalisation for more than 1 night		
☐₅ other, please specify _____		
A12e. **As a result of the attack, does this person suffer any permanent or recurring physical injury or disability?** ☐₁ Yes Go to A12f ☐₂ No Go to A12g		A12e
A12f. **If yes, can you describe the nature of the injury or disability?**		A12f (text 30)
_____		A12g
A12g. **Was there any element of sexual assault in the attack, as regards this other person?** ☐₁ Yes ☐₂ No		

ASSAULT: A13a. **Was any of your property (including clothes) stolen or damaged during the incident?**
☐₁ Something stolen →A14a
☐₂ Damaged, nothing stolen →A14f
☐₃ No → Section B (p. 6)

VANDALISM: A13b. **Was any property stolen during the incident?**
☐₁ Yes, → A14a   ☐₂ No → A14f

THEFT OF VEHICLE: A13c **Apart from the vehicle [✓ in col 1], was any other property stolen?**
☐₁ Yes → A14a   ☐₂ No → A14b

OTHERS: Go to A14a

A14a. **What property was stolen?** [✓ all that apply in Col. 1]   ☐₉₉ Nothing stolen → A14 e
A14b. **Was (any of) the stolen property recovered?**
☐₁ Yes, **What was recovered?** [✓ in Col 2]   ☐₉₉ None recovered → A14 e
A14c. **Was [any of] the recovered property damaged?**
☐₁ Yes, **What property?** [✓ in Col 3]   ☐₉₉ None damaged → A14e
A14d. **What was the extent of the damage to the recovered property?** [Column 4]

A14e. **Was any property damaged (other than any property stolen) during the incident?**
☐₁ Yes, → A14f   ☐₉₉ No property damaged (Go to Next page)
A14f. **What property was damaged?** [✓ all that apply in Column 3 and go to A14g]
A14g. **Was the damage minor or substantial?** [✓ for all property damaged in Column 4]

(✓ all that apply) in appropriate column	Property stolen			3 Property Damaged? A14c, A14e	4 Extent of Damage A14d or A14g	
	1 Stolen A14a	2 Recovered A14b				
	✓ all that apply	Some	All	✓ all that apply	Minor	Sub-stantial
1. cash	☐₁	☐₁	☐₂			
2. cheques	☐₁	☐₁	☐₂	☐₁	☐₁	☐₂
3. credit / ATM cards	☐₁	☐₁	☐₂	☐₁	☐₁	☐₂
4. jewellery / silverware	☐₁	☐₁	☐₂	☐₁	☐₁	☐₂
5. handbag/wallet/purse	☐₁	☐₁	☐₂	☐₁	☐₁	☐₂
6. other personal accessories (e.g. shopping bag, clothing)	☐₁	☐₁	☐₂	☐₁	☐₁	☐₂
7. camera/video camera	☐₁	☐₁	☐₂	☐₁	☐₁	☐₂
8. television /video recorder	☐₁	☐₁	☐₂	☐₁	☐₁	☐₂
9. hi-fi equipment /stereo	☐₁	☐₁	☐₂	☐₁	☐₁	☐₂
10. computer	☐₁	☐₁	☐₂	☐₁	☐₁	☐₂
11. other household appliance	☐₁	☐₁	☐₂	☐₁	☐₁	☐₂
12. furniture	☐₁	☐₁	☐₂	☐₁	☐₁	☐₂
13. car radio	☐₁	☐₁	☐₂	☐₁	☐₁	☐₂
14. car appliance	☐₁	☐₁	☐₂	☐₁	☐₁	☐₂
15. firearm(s)	☐₁	☐₁	☐₂	☐₁	☐₁	☐₂
16. cigarettes, alcohol, drugs	☐₁	☐₁	☐₂	☐₁	☐₁	☐₂
17. livestock	☐₁	☐₁	☐₂	☐₁	☐₁	☐₂
18. bicycle	☐₁	☐₁	☐₂	☐₁	☐₁	☐₂
19. Other , please specify _____ _____	☐₁	☐₁	☐₂	☐₁	☐₁	☐₂
20. Vehicle	☐₁	☐₁	☐₂	☐₁	☐₁	☐₂
21. Premises : tick in Col 3 if damaged; and extent in col 4.				☐₁	☐₁	☐₂

A13a

A13b

A13c

A14a

A14b

A14c

A14e
A14f
A14g

[codes a-e, g for each item, as appropriate]

CASHa,CASHb
CHEKa.. CHEKg
CREDa ... CREDg
JEWLa ... JEWLg
BAGa .... BAGg
OTHPa ... OTHPg

CAMa... CAMg
TVIDa ... TVIDg
HIFIa ... HIFIg
COMPa ...COMPg
OTHHa ...OTHHg
FURNa ... FURNg

CARRa ... CARRg
CARAa ...CARAg

GUNSa ... GUNSg
CIGSa ... CIGSg
LIVSa ... LIVSg
BIKEa ... BIKEg

OTH1a ... OTH1g
OTH2a ... OTH1g
OTH3a ... OTH3g

VEHa ... VEHg
PRMe, PRMg

THEFT OF VEHICLE/ THEFT FROM VEHICLE: GO TO A15A

PREMISES CRIMES (BURGLARY, VANDALISM, THEFT FROM VICINITY of PREMISES):
GO TO A16, A 17 OR A18 as appropriate

OTHERS: Go To Section B (next page)

For Office Use Only

A15a. Was the vehicle damaged during the incident?

☐$_1$ Yes → A15b   ☐$_2$ No→ A15c   ☐$_3$ DK or NA → A15c

A15a

A15b   How was the vehicle damaged? [✓ all that apply]

☐$_1$ door locks   ☐$_4$ ignition   ☐$_7$ other, please specify _____

☐$_2$ window(s)   ☐$_5$ crash damage   _____

☐$_3$ steering column ☐$_6$ burnt out

[code up to 3]
A15b.1
A15b.2
A15b.3

A15c. Was the vehicle protected by any of the following at the time?   Yes   No

A15d. Have any of these been added or improved since the incident?

	Yes	No	Added	Improved	No
1. car alarm	☐$_1$	☐$_2$	☐$_1$	☐$_2$	☐$_3$
2. steering lock	☐$_1$	☐$_2$	☐$_1$	☐$_2$	☐$_3$
3. registration no. etched on windows	☐$_1$	☐$_2$	☐$_1$	☐$_2$	☐$_3$
4. other device, specify _____	☐$_1$	☐$_2$	☐$_1$	☐$_2$	☐$_3$

A15c1...c4

A15d1...d4

A15e. How did the thieves gain entry to the vehicle? [✓ all that apply]

☐$_1$ broke window   ☐$_3$ vehicle was unlocked   ☐$_5$ don't know

☐$_2$ forced door locks ☐$_4$ Other, specify _____

[code up to 3
A15e.1
A15e.2
A15e.3

VANDALISM OR OTHER PREMISES DAMAGED→ A16

A16. What was the nature of the damage to the premises? [✓ all that apply]

☐$_1$ property ransacked ☐$_3$ broken window(s) /door(s) ☐$_5$ damaged garden furniture, plants

☐$_2$ graffiti   ☐$_4$ damaged fences   ☐$_6$ other, please specify

[code up to 3]
A16.1
A16.2
A16.3

BURGLARY → A17 and A18 _____

A17. How did the burglar(s) gain entry?

☐$_1$ front door   ☐$_3$ ground-flr window ☐$_5$ via garage   ☐$_7$ other, please specify

☐$_2$ back door   ☐$_4$ upstairs window   ☐$_6$ Skylight   ☐$_8$ don't know

A17

A18. Is the house / premises normally empty . . . [✓ one box on each line)

a. **for at least 2 hours a day?**   ☐$_1$ Yes   ☐$_2$ No [normally = 4+ days a wk.]   A18a

b. **on weekends**   ☐$_1$ Yes   ☐$_2$ No [normally = most weekends]   A18b

c. **at the same time each day**   ☐$_1$ Yes   ☐$_2$ No   A18c

d. **at the same time each night**   ☐$_1$ Yes   ☐$_2$ No   A18d

ALL PREMISES CRIMES (BURGLARY, VANDALISM, THEFT FROM VICINITY of PREMISES)

A19a. Were the premises protected by any of the following at the time of the incident?
[✓ all that apply]

A19b. Have any of these been added or improved since the incident?

	Added	Improved	No	
☐$_1$ Alarm linked to Gardai	☐$_1$	☐$_2$	☐$_3$	A19a1,A19b1
☐$_2$ Monitored alarm (e.g. Telecom Phonewatch)	☐$_1$	☐$_2$	☐$_3$	A19a2,A19b2
☐$_3$ Other alarm	☐$_1$	☐$_2$	☐$_3$	A19a3,A19b3
☐$_4$ Reinforced door locks	☐$_1$	☐$_2$	☐$_3$	A19a4,A19b4
☐$_5$ Window locks	☐$_1$	☐$_2$	☐$_3$	A19a5,A19b5
☐$_6$ Window grills or shutters	☐$_1$	☐$_2$	☐$_3$	A19a6,A19b6
☐$_7$ Security chain or peephole (on door)	☐$_1$	☐$_2$	☐$_3$	A19a7,A19b7
☐$_8$ Automatic light switches (timer or sensor)	☐$_1$	☐$_2$	☐$_3$	A19a8,A19b8
☐$_9$ Dog	☐$_1$	☐$_2$	☐$_3$	A19a9,A19b9
☐$_{10}$ Defensive perimeter wall or fence	☐$_1$	☐$_2$	☐$_3$	A19a10,A19b10
☐$_{11}$ Caretaker or security guard	☐$_1$	☐$_2$	☐$_3$	A19a11,A19b11
☐$_{12}$ Other, please specify	☐$_1$	☐$_2$	☐$_3$	A19a12,A19b12

A20

A20. Was the victim of this fraud or embezzlement
　　❑₁ An individual or private household　　　❑₂ A business or institution

A21a. **What kind of fraud or embezzlement took place?** Please✓ all that apply in connection with this particular reported fraud/ embezzlement	A21b. **Was this a single incident, or did it take place over a period of time?** [Please ✓ one box on each line for all that apply]					
	single incident	over several days	over several weeks	over several months	over several years	other (specify)
Culprit(s) . . .						
❑₁ cashed cheque made out to someone else	❑₁	❑₂	❑₃	❑₄	❑₅	❑₆ ____
❑₂ lodged cash/cheques to own account	❑₁	❑₂	❑₃	❑₄	❑₅	❑₆ ____
❑₃ forged accounts and took cash	❑₁	❑₂	❑₃	❑₄	❑₅	❑₆ ____
❑₄ obtained cash under false pretences	❑₁	❑₂	❑₃	❑₄	❑₅	❑₆ ____
❑₅ used stolen cheque or credit card	❑₁	❑₂	❑₃	❑₄	❑₅	❑₆ ____
❑₆ used forged bank notes	❑₁	❑₂	❑₃	❑₄	❑₅	❑₆ ____
❑₇ absconded without paying bills	❑₁	❑₂	❑₃	❑₄	❑₅	❑₆ ____
❑₈ made a false claim	❑₁	❑₂	❑₃	❑₄	❑₅	❑₆ ____
❑₉ Other , please specify	❑₁	❑₂	❑₃	❑₄	❑₅	❑₆ ____
_____						
_____						

A21a1,A21b1
A21a2,A21b2
A21a3,A21b3
A21a4,A21b4
A21a5,A21b5
A21a6,A21b6
A21a7,A21b7
A21a8,A21b8
A21a9,A21b9

A21c

A21c Did you recover any of the money defrauded or embezzled?
　　❑₁ Yes, all　　　❑₂ Yes, most　　　❑₃ Yes, some　　　❑₄ No

****

Section B: IMPACT -- ALL

Now I would like to ask you about the financial costs and other effects the incident may have had.

FINANCIAL COSTS (ALL)	B1a.	**Were you insured against the loss or damage [including medical costs, if any] involved in the incident?** ❑₁ Yes → Go to B1b　　❑₂ No → B1c	B1a
	B1b.	**Has your insurance premium increased since the incident?** ❑₁ Yes, increased or will increase　❑₂ No　　❑₃ Don't know	B1b
	B1c.	**Have you taken out [additional] such insurance since the incident?** ❑₁ Yes　　　　　　❑₂ No	B1c
	B1d.	**What was the total financial cost to you and your insurance company of the incident, [including medical costs, if any] ?** ❑₁ Less than £300　　❑₄ £1,000 - under £5,000 ❑₂ £300-under £500　　❑₅ £5,000 - under £10,000 ❑₃ £500 - under £1000　❑₆ £10,000 or more ❑₇ No financial costs	B1d
	B1e.	**What was the financial cost to you personally [this business /institution] (after taking account of any insurance receipts)?** ❑₁ Less than £300　　❑₄ £1,000 - under £5,000 ❑₂ £300-under £500　　❑₅ £5,000 - under £10,000 ❑₃ £500 - under £1000　❑₆ £10,000 or more ❑₇ No financial costs	B1e

PERSONAL IMPACT - ALL

Now I would like to ask you more about some of the non-financial effects the incident may have had on you.

B2a. **As a result of the incident did you at any stage . . . ?** [Show card and tick all that apply in Column A; If yes, ask B2b before going to next item. If no to all, ✓ here $\square_{99}$]

B2b [If yes to any] **Are you still affected in this way?** [✓ all that apply Col B If no to all, ✓ here $\square_{99}$]

B3a. **Has the incident affected anyone else [in your household /who works here/ who was present at the time] in any of these ways?**
$\square_1$ Yes → B3b $\square_2$ No → B4 $\square_3$ No-one else present/in HH /works here → B4

B3b **Thinking of the person most affected, is this person** $\square_1$ **male or** $\square_2$ **female?**

B3c **What is their approximate age?** _____ [Age in years]

B3d. **What effect did the incident have on this person, did [he / she] . . . ?** [Show card and ✓ all that apply in Col D. If no to all, ✓ here $\square_{99}$]

		RESPONDENT	OTHER PERSON MOST AFFECTED
A B2a Effects	B B2b Still affected?	C	D. B3d
$\square_1$	$\square_1$	1. . . become more anxious or fearful	$\square_1$
$\square_2$	$\square_2$	2. . . have trouble sleeping	$\square_2$
$\square_3$	$\square_3$	3. . . go out less often or become reluctant to go out alone	$\square_3$
$\square_4$	$\square_4$	4. . . have trouble concentrating	$\square_4$
$\square_5$	$\square_5$	5. . . become more suspicious of people	$\square_5$
$\square_6$	$\square_6$	6. . . blame yourself in any way for the incident	$\square_6$
$\square_7$	$\square_7$	7. . . move (or intend to move) residence	$\square_7$
$\square_8$	$\square_8$	8. . . lose time at work. How much? _____ days	$\square_8$
$\square_9$	$\square_9$	9. . . lose or have to leave your job	$\square_9$
$\square_{10}$	$\square_{10}$	10. . . have to close your business	$\square_{10}$
$\square_{11}$	$\square_{11}$	11. . . strengthen security at home[or business/institution]	$\square_{11}$
$\square_{12}$	$\square_{12}$	12. . . strengthen vehicle security	$\square_{12}$
$\square_{13}$	$\square_{13}$	13. . . suffer other non-financial effects? please specify _____	$\square_{13}$

B2a
B2b
B3a
B3b
B3c
B3d
B2a1,B2b1, B3d1
B2a2,B2b2, B3d2
B2a3,B2b3, B3d3
. . . .
B2a13,B2b13, B3d13

B4 **Were you given support to cope with the effects of the crime by any of the following?**
[tick all that apply]
$\square_1$ family $\square_4$ Women's Aid $\square_7$ Gardaí
$\square_2$ friends/neighbours $\square_5$ other voluntary group $\square_8$ other, please specify
$\square_3$ Victim Support $\square_6$ clergy   _____
$\square_9$ no support wanted / needed

B5 **Did you have any contact with Victim Support following the incident?** $\square_1$ Yes $\square_2$ No

B5a. [If yes] **What was the nature of this contact?** [tick all that apply]
$\square_1$ you contacted them (e.g. by telephone) $\square_5$ you were left a leaflet/note saying they called
$\square_2$ you received a telephone call $\square_6$ can't recall
$\square_3$ you had a personal visit $\square_7$ other, please specify
$\square_4$ you received a letter   _____

B6 **Do you feel that the services of a specialised agency to help victims of crime were/ would have been useful to you?** $\square_1$ Yes $\square_2$ No $\square_3$ Not Sure

B7 **Taking everything into consideration, how serious was the incident for you?**
$\square_1$ very serious $\square_2$ fairly serious $\square_3$ not very serious

[code up to 3 items]
B4.1
B4.2
B4.3

B5

(code up to 3 items)

B5a1,B5a2,B5a3

B6

B7

Section C: Offender and Outcome -- All

C1a. How many offenders were involved in the incident?

☐₁ one ☐₃ three or more

☐₂ two ☐₄ offender(s) not identified → Go to C2a

C1a

C1b. Was/ were the offender[s] ... ☐₁ male(s) ☐₂ female(s) ☐₃ both ☐₉ DK

C1b

C1c Was/were the offender[s] ... ☐₁ child(ren) ☐₂ teenager(s) ☐₃ adult(s) ☐₉ DK

☐₄ other, please specify _____

C1c

C1d. Did you know the offender(s)?

☐₁ Yes (all known) ☐₂ at least one known, other(s) not known

☐₃ not known → Go to C2a

C1d

C1e. How did you know the offender(s) ? [✓ all that apply, if more than 1 offender]

☐₁ spouse(partner) or ex-spouse(partner) ☐₇ friend / acquaintance

☐₂ relative ☐₈ neighbour

☐₃ business partner ☐₉ none of the above, but known by name

☐₄ co-worker ☐₁₀ none of the above, but known by sight

☐₅ employer ☐₁₁ Other, specify _____

☐₆ employee ☐₁₂ no answer

(code up to 3)
C1e1
C1e2
C1e3

C1f. Did you give this information to the Gardaí?

☐₁ Yes → C2a ☐₂ No → C1g

C1f

C1g. Why not? [tick all that apply]

☐₁ fear of reprisal ☐₂ did not want to get person in trouble

☐₃ other, please specify _____

(code up to 3)
C1g1
C1g2
C1g3

C2a Were you subject to intimidation by the offender(s) or their associates at any stage?

☐₁ Yes ☐₂ No → C2c

C2a

C2b [If yes] When was this? [tick all that apply]

☐₁ when reporting to the Gardaí ☐₄ after sentencing/ acquittal

☐₂ after crime was reported ☐₅ other, please specify

☐₃ as a witness _____

(code up to 3)
C2b1
C2b2
C2b3

C2c Did you receive adequate protection ...

from the Gardaí?	☐₁ Yes	☐₂ No	☐₃ Not wanted/needed
in court?	☐₁ Yes	☐₂ No	☐₃ Not wanted/needed ☐₄ NA
elsewhere?	☐₁ Yes	☐₂ No	☐₃ Not wanted/needed

C2cGardai
C2cCourt
C2cElse

C2d [If "No" to any] How might this have been improved? _____

C2d (text 30)

C3a Did you receive adequate encouragement and support ...

from the Gardaí?	☐₁ Yes	☐₂ No	☐₃ Not wanted/needed
in court?	☐₁ Yes	☐₂ No	☐₃ Not wanted/needed ☐₄ NA
elsewhere?	☐₁ Yes	☐₂ No	☐₃ Not wanted/needed

C3aGardai
C3aCourt
C3aElse

C3b [If 'No' to any] How might this have been improved? _____

C3b (text 30)

C4 Do you feel that the services of a specialised service to help witnesses before, during and after court proceedings were/would have been useful to you?

☐₁ yes, very helpful ☐₃ not of much help ☐₅ not sure

☐₂ yes, of some help ☐₄ of no help ☐₆ NA

C4

C5a. In your opinion, was the incident drug-related in any way? Are you . . .

- $\square_1$ certain it was
- $\square_2$ fairly certain it was
- $\square_3$ don't know
- $\square_4$ fairly certain it wasn't
- $\square_5$ certain it wasn't

C5b. What makes you think so? [tick all that apply]

- $\square_1$ offender was known to Gardaí as an addict
- $\square_2$ offender known to respondent as an addict
- $\square_3$ offender was known generally as an addict
- $\square_4$ offender admitted addiction to Gardaí or in court
- $\square_5$ offender had previous convictions in which drugs were a factor
- $\square_6$ weapon used (syringe)
- $\square_7$ general behaviour or appearance
- $\square_8$ other, please specify

_____

C6a. In your opinion, was the consumption of alcohol a factor in the incident? Are you . . .

- $\square_1$ certain it was
- $\square_2$ fairly certain it was
- $\square_3$ don't know
- $\square_4$ fairly certain it wasn't

$\square_5$ certain it wasn't

C6b. What makes you think so? [tick all that apply]

- $\square_1$ offence took place in (or just outside) pub or club
- $\square_2$ offender seen drinking prior to incident
- $\square_3$ statement by offender to Gardaí
- $\square_4$ evidence in court
- $\square_5$ general behaviour or appearance

C7   Was (were) the offender(s) apprehended?

- $\square_1$ Yes, at least one apprehended → C7a
- $\square_9$ don't know [Go to D1, page 10]
- $\square_2$ No →C7b

[If at least one offender aprehended]
C7a. What was the outcome as regards the offender(s)?

- $\square_4$ case being processed
- $\square_5$ offender(s) cautioned only
- $\square_6$ diverted under juvenile justice scheme
- $\square_7$ case not proceeded with (other reason)
- $\square_8$ prosecuted but acquitted
- $\square_9$ convicted & given custodial sentence (e.g. prison)
- $\square_{10}$ convicted and given probation, community service or other non-custodial sentence
- $\square_{11}$ Other: Please specify _____
- $\square_{12}$ don't know outcome

[If offender NOT apprehended]
C7b. Is the case still open or has it been closed?

- $\square_1$ case still open
- $\square_2$ case closed
- $\square_3$ don't know whether case open / closed

C8a: Overall, as regards the outcome of the case, were you . . .

- $\square_1$ Very satisfied
- $\square_2$ Fairly satisfied
- $\square_3$ Neither satisfied nor dissatisfied → D1 (next page)
- $\square_4$ Fairly Dissatisfied
- $\square_5$ Very Dissatisfied

C8b. What satisfied you the most? [tick 1 box]

- $\square_1$ arrest of offender
- $\square_2$ conviction of offender
- $\square_3$ recovery of property
- $\square_4$ don't know
- $\square_5$ other, please specify

_____

C8c. What dissatisfied you the most? [tick 1 box]

- $\square_1$ failure to arrest
- $\square_2$ property not recovered
- $\square_3$ failure to proceed with case
- $\square_4$ failure to convict
- $\square_5$ sentence too lenient
- $\square_6$ don't know
- $\square_7$ other, specify

_____

Section D - Satisfaction with Garda Service -- ALL

I would now like to ask you some questions about the service provided by the Gardaí.

D1   How was the crime reported to the Gardaí? [tick one box only]

☐₁ you called 999   ☐₆ monitored alarm alerted Gardaí
☐₂ you telephoned local station   ☐₇ discovered by Gardaí
☐₃ you informed Garda on patrol   ☐₈ other, please specify
☐₄ you called to station   _____
☐₅ call made by someone else
                                       ☐₉ can't recall/don't know

D1

D2   How many gardaí first attended the scene?

☐₁ none   ☐₄ more than two
☐₂ one   ☐₅ can't recall/don't know
☐₃ two   ☐₆ not relevant (e.g. R went to station)

D2

D3   Did the Garda(í) who first dealt with you give you any of the following information?

	Yes	No	Can't Recall	
a. His/her/their name(s)	☐₁	☐₂	☐₃	D3a
b. Garda contact telephone number	☐₁	☐₂	☐₃	D3b
c. advice on procedures, whom to contact	☐₁	☐₂	☐₃	D3c
d. information on Victim Support	☐₁	☐₂	☐₃	D3d
e. other information (please specify)	☐₁	☐₂	☐₃	D3e

_____

D4

D4   Was a written statement taken from you?   ☐₁ Yes   ☐₂ No   ☐₃ Can't Recall

D5:   Could you tell me how satisfied or dissatisfied you were with each of the following aspects of your first contact with the Gardaí?

	Very Satisfied	Satisfied	Neither Satisfied nor Dissatisfied	Dissatisfied	Very Dissatisfied	Don't know or NA	
a. Speed with which initial call was answered	☐₁	☐₂	☐₃	☐₄	☐₅	☐₆	D5a
b. Speed with which Gardaí came to the scene	☐₁	☐₂	☐₃	☐₄	☐₅	☐₆	D5b
c. Thoroughness of Gardaí	☐₁	☐₂	☐₃	☐₄	☐₅	☐₆	D5c
d. Politeness of Gardaí	☐₁	☐₂	☐₃	☐₄	☐₅	☐₆	D5d
e. Understanding of problem shown by Gardaí	☐₁	☐₂	☐₃	☐₄	☐₅	☐₆	D5e
f. Answers by Gardaí to your questions	☐₁	☐₂	☐₃	☐₄	☐₅	☐₆	D5f
g. other (please specify)	☐₁	☐₂	☐₃	☐₄	☐₅	☐₆	D5g

_____

D6

D6   Overall, how would you rate the performance of the Garda(í) who first dealt with your case? Were you ...

☐₁ very satisfied
☐₂ satisfied
☐₃ neither satisfied or dissatisfied
☐₄ dissatisfied
☐₅ very dissatisfied

10

	For Office Use Only

BURGLARY   <u>Others go to D10</u>

D7   Were you advised that specialist officers (such as fingerprint or photograph experts) would call on you?   ❑₁ Yes ❑₂ No ❑₃ Can't Recall

D7

D8   Did specialist Gardaí actually call?   ❑₁ Yes ❑₂ No ❑₃ Can't Recall

D8

D9   [If yes] How would you rate the performance of the specialist Garda(í) who dealt with your case?   Were you ...
     ❑₁ very satisfied
     ❑₂ satisfied
     ❑₃ neither satisfied nor dissatisfied
     ❑₄ dissatisfied
     ❑₅ very dissatisfied

D9

ALL

D10   Since reporting the incident, were you contacted, either personally or on the telephone, by any of the following?
     a. the first Garda(í) who visited you   ❑₁ Yes ❑₂ No ❑₃ Can't Recall
     b. anyone else from the Garda Síochána   ❑₁ Yes ❑₂ No ❑₃ Can't Recall

D10a
D10b

How satisfied are/were you about <u>being kept informed</u> of the

	Very Satisfied	Satisfied	Neither Satisfied nor Dissatisfied	Dissatisfied	Very Dissatisfied	Case not yet concluded
D11 <u>progress</u> of your case?	❑₁	❑₂	❑₃	❑₄	❑₅	
D12 the <u>outcome</u> of your case?	❑₁	❑₂	❑₃	❑₄	❑₅	❑₆

D11
D12

D13   All in all, how good a job do the gardaí do in your area in controlling crime?
     ❑₁ very good
     ❑₂ fairly good
     ❑₃ neither good nor poor
     ❑₄ fairly poor
     ❑₅ very poor

D13

D14   If you were the victim of a similar crime on a future occasion, would you, as a result of this incident, be more inclined or less likely to report the matter to the Gardaí ?
     ❑₁ more likely
     ❑₂ about as likely / no difference
     ❑₃ less likely
     ❑₄ depends, please specify _____

D14

D15   Do you have any further comments regarding the service provided by the Gardaí?
     _____
     _____
     _____
     _____
     _____
     _____

D15

Now I'd like to ask you some questions about <u>other incidents</u> (apart from the crime we discussed earlier) that may have happened to you or other members of your household over the <u>last 3 years</u> in the Republic of Ireland.

E1   **Over the last three years** . . . [For each item ✓ Yes or No in Col 1. If yes, ask E2-E4 before going to next item]

E2   [If Yes] **How many times did this happen during the past 3 years?** [Record N times Col A; 1=once]

E3   [If Yes] **Did you report the incident [all of these incidents] to the Gardai?** [Tick one box in Col. B]

E4   [If any not reported] **Could you tell me the main reason this incident was not reported?** [Enter one number from LIST OF REASONS CRIME NOT REPORTED below, in Column B]

[Note: Record each incident under one heading only Do NOT include crime discussed in Section A Record number of times in Col A; 1=once] **Over the last three years [since June 1 1993]** . . .	E1 A E2 How Yes No many times?	E3 B E4 Reported? Yes Some No Why (all) not?	For Office Use Only
A. . . . Were you or any member of your household assaulted — that is, punched, kicked or pushed to the ground etc., or injured or threatened with a weapon?	☐₁ ☐₂ ___	☐₁ ☐₂ ☐₃ ___	E1A,E2A, E3A,E4A
A1. . . .Did this assault [any of these assaults] occur as part of a ☐₁ burglary/robbery or ☐₂ mugging/theft from person?	☐₁ ☐₂ ___	☐₁ ☐₂ ☐₃ ___	E1A1type, E1A1,E2A1, E3A1,E4A1
B. . . . Did anyone illegally enter your home, that is, by breaking in or gain entry without your permission? [No→C below]	☐₁ ☐₂ ___	☐₁ ☐₂ ☐₃ ___	E1B,E2B, E3B,E4B
B1. Was anything stolen during this [any one of these] illegal entry [entries] that occurred during the last 3 years?	☐₁ ☐₂ ___	☐₁ ☐₂ ☐₃	E1B1,E2B1, E3B1,E4B1
C. . . . Was there evidence [e.g. broken window, door locks etc.] that someone <u>attempted</u> to illegally enter your home?	☐₁ ☐₂ ___	☐₁ ☐₂ ☐₃ ___	E1C,E2C, E3C,E4C
D. . . . Was anything stolen by someone who had a right to be in your home? (e.g. salesperson, acquaintance, repairman)	☐₁ ☐₂ ___	☐₁ ☐₂ ☐₃ ___	E1D,E2D, E3D,E4D
E. Did anyone in this household own or have the use of a car, truck, van or motorbike in the last 3 years? ☐₁ Yes ☐₂ No →H below			E1E
F. . . . Did anyone steal (or use without permission) a car, truck, van or motorbike belonging to you or to someone in your household ?	Yes No Number Times ☐₁ ☐₂ ___	Yes Some No Why not? ☐₁ ☐₂ ☐₃ ___	E1F,E2F, E3F,E4F
G. . . .Was anything stolen <u>from inside</u> a car, van or truck belonging to you or someone in this household?	☐₁ ☐₂ ___	☐₁ ☐₂ ☐₃ ___	E1G,E2G, E3G,E4G
H. . . . Was any item that is <u>kept outside</u> — like a bicycle, garden furniture, tools, farm machinery or equipment etc. — stolen? [Exclude if already entered above]	☐₁ ☐₂ ___	☐₁ ☐₂ ☐₃ ___	E1H,E2H, E3H,E4H
J. . . . Was there any other occasion when a valuable item was <u>stolen from you or someone who lives in your household</u>, such as in the street, a shop, on holidays in Ireland etc. [eg. handbag snatch / pocket picked. Exclude if entered above].	☐₁ ☐₂ ___	☐₁ ☐₂ ☐₃ ___	E1J,E2J, E3J,E4J
K. . . . Was the outside of your home or any property attached to the home (such as the garden, outbuildings or a car parked outside) <u>damaged or vandalised</u>?	☐₁ ☐₂ ___	☐₁ ☐₂ ☐₃ ___	E1K,E2K, E3K,E4K
L. . . . Has anyone absconded without paying money owed, or defrauded or embezzled money from you or anyone in your household?	☐₁ ☐₂ ___	☐₁ ☐₂ ☐₃ ___	E1L,E2L, E3L,E4L
M. Have you or any member of your household been the victim of any other crime over the last three years? Please specify	☐₁ ☐₂ ___	☐₁ ☐₂ ☐₃ ___	E1M,E2M, E3M,E4M

LIST OF REASONS CRIME NOT REPORTED [choose MAIN reason]

1. Not important /serious enough to R
2. Gardaí could do nothing
3. Gardaí would not be interested
4. Fear of reprisal

5. Did not want to get person responsible (or his/her family) in trouble
6. Made private arrangement for compensation with person responsible
7. Reported incident to another authority (eg. local authority)
8. Respondent felt (partly) responsible for incident
9. Other, please specify _____

Now I'd like to ask you some questions about <u>other incidents</u> (apart from the crime we discussed earlier) that may have happened <u>within this establishment</u> (that is on the premises, or to someone working here while on duty) over the <u>last three years</u>. Please only tell us about crimes that occurred in the Republic of Ireland.

E5 **Over the last three years** . . . [For each item ✓ Yes or No in Col A. If yes, ask E6-E8 before going to next item]

E6 [If Yes] **How many times did this happen during the past 3 years?** [Record N times Col A; 1=once]

E7 [If Yes] **Did you report the incident/all of these incidents to the Gardai?** [✓ one box in Col. B]

E8 [If any not reported] **Could you tell me the main reason this incident was not reported?**
[Enter one number from LIST OF REASONS CRIME NOT REPORTED, in Column B]

[Record each incident under one heading only Do NOT include crime discussed in Section A Record number of times in Col A; 1=once] **Over the last three years [since June 1 1993]** . . .	E5 **A** E6 How Yes No many times?	E7 **B** E8 Reported? Yes Some No Why (all) not?	**For Office Use Only**
A. . . . Was anyone within this establishment assaulted — that is, punched, kicked or pushed to the ground etc., or injured or threatened with a weapon?	□₁ □₂ ___	□₁ □₂ □₃ ___	E5A,E6A, E7A,E8A
A1. Did this [any of these] assault(s) occur as part of a □₁ burglary/robbery or □₂ mugging /theft from someone in the establishment?	□₁ □₂ ___	□₁ □₂ □₃ ___	E5A1type, E5A1,E6A1, E7A1,E8A1
B. . . . Did anyone illegally enter the premises, that is, by breaking in or gaining entry without permission? [No→C below]	□₁ □₂ ___	□₁ □₂ □₃ ___	E5B,E6B, E7B,E8B
B2. Was anything stolen during this [any one of these] illegal entry [entries] that occurred during the last 3 years?	□₁ □₂ ___	□₁ □₂ □₃ ___	E5B2,E6B2, E7B2,E8B2
C. . . . Was there evidence (e.g. broken windows, door locks) that someone <u>attempted</u> to illegally enter the premises?	□₁ □₂ ___	□₁ □₂ □₃ ___	E5C,E6C, E7C,E8C
D. . . . Was anything stolen by someone who had a right to be on the premises? (e.g. employee, customer, repairman)	□₁ □₂ ___	□₁ □₂ □₃ ___	E5D,E6D, E7D,E8D
E. Did this establishment own or have the use of a car, truck, van or motorbike in the last 3 years (not including private cars of people working here)? □₁ Yes □₂ No →H below			E5E
	Yes No Number Times	Yes Some No Why not?	
F. . . . Did anyone steal (or use without permission) a car, truck, van or motorbike belonging to this establishment ?	□₁ □₂ ___	□₁ □₂ □₃ ___	E5F,E6F, E7F,E8F
G. . . .Was anything stolen from inside a car, van or truck belonging to this establishment?	□₁ □₂ ___	□₁ □₂ □₃ ___	E5G,E6G, E7G,E8G
H. . . . Was any item that is <u>kept outside</u> — like tools, machinery or equipment etc. — stolen? [Exclude motor vehicles which should be entered under G]	□₁ □₂ ___	□₁ □₂ □₃ ___	E5H,E6H, E7H,E8H
J. . . . Was there any other occasion when a valuable item was stolen from you or someone within this establishment? [eg. shoplifting / handbag snatched / pocket picked etc. Exclude if already entered above].	□₁ □₂ ___	□₁ □₂ □₃ ___	E5J,E6J, E7J,E8J
K. . . . Was the outside of the premises or any property attached to the premises (such as outbuildings or a car parked outside) <u>damaged or vandalised</u>?	□₁ □₂ ___	□₁ □₂ □₃ ___	E5K,E6K, E7K,E8K
L. . . . Has anyone absconded without paying money owed or defrauded or embezzled money from this establishment?	□₁ □₂ ___	□₁ □₂ □₃ ___	E5L,E6L, E7L,E8L
M. Has this establishment been the victim of any other crime over the last three years? Please specify	□₁ □₂ ___	□₁ □₂ □₃ ___	E5M,E6M, E7M,E8M

LIST OF REASONS CRIME NOT REPORTED

1. Not important /serious enough to R
2. Gardai could do nothing
3. Gardai would not be interested
4. Fear of reprisal
5. Did not want to get person responsible (or his/her family) in trouble
6. Made private arrangement for compensation with person responsible
7. Reported incident to another authority (eg. local authority)
8. Respondent felt (partly) responsible for incident
9. Other, please specify _____

Section F - Perceptions of Crime ALL

I'd like to ask some more general questions about law and order in the area you live in.

F1   How likely would you say it is that <u>over the next 12 months</u> any of the following will happen to you? [tick one box on each line]

	Very Unlikely	Unlikely	Likely	Very Likely	Don't Know	
a. your home broken into & property stolen or damaged	□₁	□₂	□₃	□₄	□₅	F1a
b. your home damaged or defaced by vandals	□₁	□₂	□₃	□₄	□₅	F1b
c. your vehicle stolen □₆ NA	□₁	□₂	□₃	□₄	□₅	F1c
d. having property stolen from your vehicle □₆ NA	□₁	□₂	□₃	□₄	□₅	F1d
e. being mugged or robbed in a public place (including pick-pocketing and bag -snatching)	□₁	□₂	□₃	□₄	□₅	F1e
f. being sexually assaulted or molested	□₁	□₂	□₃	□₄	□₅	F1f
g. being assaulted or hit . . . at home	□₁	□₂	□₃	□₄	□₅	F1g
h. . . . outside your home	□₁	□₂	□₃	□₄	□₅	F1h
j. being threatened, insulted, or harassed by strangers	□₁	□₂	□₃	□₄	□₅	F1j

F2   How common would you say that each of the following is in your neighbourhood? For each item listed please say whether or not you think it is very common; fairly common; not very common; or not at all common . [Int. Read list and tick 1,2,3 or 4 on each line]

	Very common	Fairly common	Not very common	Not at all common	
a. graffiti on walls or buildings	□₁	□₂	□₃	□₄	F2a
b. teenagers hanging around on the streets	□₁	□₂	□₃	□₄	F2b
c. rubbish and litter lying about	□₁	□₂	□₃	□₄	F2c
d. Homes and gardens in bad condition	□₁	□₂	□₃	□₄	F2d
e. Vandalism and deliberate damage to property	□₁	□₂	□₃	□₄	F2e
f. People being drunk in public	□₁	□₂	□₃	□₄	F2f
g. drug use	□₁	□₂	□₃	□₄	F2g

F3   Compared with the rest of Ireland how much crime would you say is in your area?

□₁ A lot more   □₂ A bit more   □₃ About the same   □₄ A bit less   □₅ A lot less   F3

F4.	How safe do you feel walking alone in the area around your home . . .	Very safe	Fairly Safe	Unsafe	Very unsafe	Don't know	
	a. during day-time?	□₁	□₂	□₃	□₄	□₅	F4a
	b. after dark?	□₁	□₂	□₃	□₄	□₅	F4b
F5.	How safe do you feel alone in your home ...						
	a. during day-time?	□₁	□₂	□₃	□₄	□₅	F5a
	b. after dark?	□₁	□₂	□₃	□₄	□₅	F5b

F6.   Do you live in a Neighbourhood Watch or Community Alert Area?

a. Neighbourhood Watch	□₁ Yes →F7& F8	□₂ No → p. 15	□₃ DK.→ p. 15	F6a
b. Community Alert	□₁ Yes →F7& F8	□₂ No → p. 15	□₃ DK.→ p. 15	F6b

F7. When was it set up?   □₁ Within the last 12 months □₂ More than 12 months ago □₃ DK   F7

F8. Do you feel the scheme is effective in

a. . . . preventing crime?	□₁ Yes	□₂ No	□₃ D.K.	F8a
b. . . . helping you feel more secure?	□₁ Yes	□₂ No	□₃ D.K.	F8b

14

G(i) Classification Details - Individual/ Household   [Institutions -- go to G(ii) p. 16]

I'd like to ask you now some questions about you and your household. These details are required for purposes of classification and analysis only, and, as is the case for all other questions, will remain confidential and anonymous.

G1   **How many people live in this household altogether** (including Respondent)? _____

G2   **How many of these are . . . ?** [including Respondent; record actual number for each]
a. ____ Children under 12   d. ____ Elderly men (65+)
b. ____ Children 13-18   e. ____ Elderly women (65+)
c. Age of youngest child ____ yrs   f. ____ Adult men (age 18-64)
g. ____ Adult women (age 18-64)

G3   [If more than one person in HH] **Does the household consist of a . . .** [tick one box only]

Family Household	Non-Family Household
❑₁ Couple, with no children	With or without other persons
❑₂ Couple, at least one child under 18	❑₆ Other related individuals
❑₃ Couple, adult children (all over 18)	❑₇ Unrelated persons
❑₄ Lone parent, at least one child under 18	❑₈ Other, specify
❑₅ Lone parent, adult children (all over 18)	

G4   **What is your date of birth?** ____Day _____ Mon _____ Year
[Int: Enter approximate age in years if refused: _____]

G5   **Which of the following best describes your marital status?** [tick one box only]

❑₁ Single, never married	❑₅ Separated
❑₂ Married, living with spouse	❑₆ Divorced
❑₃ Married, living apart from spouse	❑₇ Widowed
❑₄ Living Together	

G6.   **Which of the following best describes your situation at present?** [Please tick one box only]

Working for Pay	Not Working for Pay
	❑₅ Unemployed
❑₁ Working (Full-time)	❑₆ On FÁS course or scheme
❑₂ Working (Part-time)	❑₇ At school /college
❑₃ Self Employed (Alone)	❑₈ Engaged in home duties
❑₄ Self Employed (Employing others)	❑₉ Unable to work due to illness/disability
	❑₁₀ Retired
	❑₁₁ Other (Specify) _____

G7a.   [If not working] **Have you ever worked in paid employment since leaving school ?**
❑₁ Yes   ❑₂ No

G7b.   [If working or ever worked] **What kind of work do/did you do?**
[If never worked] **What kind of work does/did the main earner in the household do?**

Please give the name or title of the job [Int: For farmers, ask how many acres]
_____

G7c.   **What is main business of the company or organisation you [main earner] work[ed] for?**
_____

G7d.   **Please give a description of your [main earner's] duties in this company or organisation.**
_____
_____

G8.   **What is the highest level of education you achieved** (Tick one box only)

❑₁ Left before Group, Inter or Junior Cert	❑₄ Third Level diploma or certificate
❑₂ Group, Inter or Junior Cert	❑₅ Third Level degree (Bachelors or above)
❑₃ Leaving Cert (or 'O' or 'A' Levels)	❑₆ Other, specify _____

G9 As regards housing tenure, is your house/flat ... [tick one box]

- $\square_1$ owned outright
- $\square_2$ being purchased under tenant purchase scheme
- $\square_3$ being purchased on a mortgage
- $\square_4$ rented from the local authority
- $\square_5$ rented otherwise (e.g. private landlord)
- $\square_6$ provided rent free
- $\square_7$ other, please specify

G9

G10a **Which of the following sources of income does the household receive?** [Column A]

G10b **And of these sources of income which is the largest source of income at present?** [Col B]

A. Receive? G10a		B. Largest Source G10b	
$\square_1$ Yes $\square_2$ No	1. Wages or salaries	$\square_1$	G10a1
$\square_1$ Yes $\square_2$ No	2. Income from self-employment	$\square_2$	G10a2
$\square_1$ Yes $\square_2$ No	3. Income from agriculture	$\square_3$	G10a3
$\square_1$ Yes $\square_2$ No	4. Private Pensions	$\square_4$	G10a4
$\square_1$ Yes $\square_2$ No	5. Social Welfare Payments	$\square_5$	G10a5
$\square_1$ Yes $\square_2$ No	6. Income from Investments, Savings, or Property	$\square_6$	G10a6
$\square_1$ Yes $\square_2$ No	7. Children's Allowance (Child Benefit)	$\square_7$	G10a7
$\square_1$ Yes $\square_2$ No	8. FAS course or scheme allowance	$\square_8$	G10a8
$\square_1$ Yes $\square_2$ No	9. Other Sources (specify) _____	$\square_9$	G10a9_1
			G10a9_2
			G10a9_3

Section G(ii) - Classification Details - Institutions (Business or Other Organisation)

G10b

I'd like to ask you now some questions about the organisation which was victimised. These details are required for purposes of classification and analysis only, and, as is the case for all other questions, will remain confidential and anonymous.

G11 **What is the nature of this organisation?**

- $\square_1$ manufacturing company
- $\square_2$ public house or restaurant
- $\square_3$ bank
- $\square_4$ shop /retail company
- $\square_5$ other private sector services company
- $\square_6$ post office
- $\square_7$ school/college
- $\square_8$ local authority
- $\square_9$ other public sector _____
- $\square_{10}$ church
- $\square_{11}$ social or sport club
- $\square_{12}$ other, please specify _____

G11

G12 **What is the size of the establishment in terms of the number employed? [this branch only]**

- $\square_1$ Self only
- $\square_2$ 1-5 employees
- $\square_3$ 6-10 employees
- $\square_4$ 11- 30 employees
- $\square_5$ 31-50 employees
- $\square_6$ over 50 employees

G12

G13 **What is your position in the organisation?**

- $\square_1$ owner
- $\square_2$ part-owner or partner
- $\square_3$ manager /principal
- $\square_4$ employee
- $\square_5$ client/customer/club member
- $\square_6$ other, please specify

G13

****

This brings us to the end of the Survey. Thank you very much for your time and co-operation. I would like to reassure you once more that the information you have provided will be treated in the strictest confidence.

****

INTERVIEWER: Please complete Interviewer Items on Page 1 immediately after leaving respondent

References

Adler, F. (1983), *Nations Not Obsessed with Crime*, Littleton, CO: Rothman.

Alvazzi Del Frate, A. (1998), *Victims of Crime in the Developing World*, United Nations Interregional Crime and Justice Research Institute, Publication No. 57, Rome: United Nations Publications.

Bayley, D.H. (1996), *Police for the Future*, New York: Oxford University Press.

Beavon, D.J., P.L. Brantingham and P.J. Brantingham (1994), "The Influence of Street Networks on the Patterning of Property Offences" in R.V. Clarke (ed.), *Crime Prevention Studies*, Vol. 2, Monsey, NY: Criminal Justice Press.

Bennett, T. (1986), "A Decision-making Approach to Opioid Addiction" in D.B. Cornish and R.V. Clarke (eds.), *The Reasoning Criminal: Rational Choice Perspectives on Offending*, New York: Springer-Verlag, pp. 83–102.

Block, R.L. (ed.) (1984), *Victimisation and Fear of Crime: World Perspectives*, Washington DC: US Government Printing Office.

Borooah, V.K. and C.A. Carcach (1997), "Crime and Fear: Evidence from Australia", *The British Journal of Criminology*, Vol. 37, No. 4, Autumn.

Bowers, K.J., A. Hirschfield and S.D. Johnson (1998), "Victimisation Revisited: A Case Study of Non-residential Repeat Burglary on Merseyside", *The British Journal of Criminology*, Vol. 38, No. 3, Summer.

Box, S. (1987), *Recession, Crime and Punishment*, London: Macmillan.

Boyle, M. and T. Haire (1996), *Fear of Crime and Likelihood of Victimisation in Northern Ireland: Research Findings*, Belfast: Northern Ireland Office, Statistics and Research Branch.

Brantingham, P.J. and P.L. Brantingham (1990), "Situational Crime Prevention in Practice", *Canadian Journal of Criminology*, January, pp. 17–40.

Breen, R. (1995), "Attitudes towards the Security Forces" in R. Breen, P. Devine and G. Robinson (eds.), *Social Attitudes in Northern Ireland: The Fourth Report*, Belfast: Blackstaff Press.

Breen, R. and D. Rottman (1985), *Crime Victimisation in the Republic of Ireland*, Dublin: Economic and Social Research Institute.

Brewer, J.D., B. Lockhart and P. Rodgers (1997), *Crime in Ireland, 1945-95: Here Be Dragons*, Oxford: Clarendon Press.

Callan, T., B. Nolan, B.J. Whelan, C.T. Whelan and J. Williams (1996), *Poverty in the 1990s: Evidence from the 1994 Living in Ireland Survey*, Dublin: Oak Tree Press.

Callan, T., R. Layte, B. Nolan, D. Watson, C.T. Whelan, J. Williams and B. Maître (1999), *Monitoring Poverty Trends: Data from the 1997 Living in Ireland Survey*, Dublin: Stationery Office and Combat Poverty Agency.

Central Statistics Office (1999a), *Quarterly National Household Survey: Crime and Victimisation, September–November 1998*, Dublin: Stationery Office.

Central Statistics Office (1999b), *Vital Statistics: Fourth Quarter and Yearly Summary 1998*, Dublin: Stationery Office.

Clarke, R.V. and P. Mayhew (1998), "Preventing Crime in Parking Lots: What We Need to Know" in R.B. Peiser (ed.), *Reducing Crime Through Real Estate Development and Management*, Washington, DC: Urban Land Institute.

Clarke, R.V. (1980), "Situational Crime Prevention: Theory and Practice", *British Journal of Criminology*, Vol. 20, pp. 136–147.

Clarke, R.V. (ed.) (1994), *Crime Prevention Studies*, Vol. 2, Monsey, NY: Criminal Justice Press.

Clarke, R.V. and D. Weisburd (1994), "Diffusion of Crime Control Benefits: Observations on the Reverse of Displacement", *Crime Prevention Studies*, Vol. 2, Monsey, NY: Criminal Justice Press, pp. 165–184.

Cohen, R.L. and M. Felson (1979), "Social Change and Crime Rate Trends: A Routine Activity Approach", *American Sociological Review*, Vol. 44, August, pp. 588–608.

Cornish, D.B. and R.V. Clarke (eds.) (1986), *The Reasoning Criminal: Rational Choice Perspectives on Offending*, New York: Springer-Verlag.

Deadman, D. and D. Pyle (1997), "Forecasting Recorded Property Crime Using a Time-Series Econometric Model", *The British Journal of Criminology*, Vol. 37, Issue 3, Summer.

Department of Justice (1997), *Tackling Crime: Discussion Paper*, Department of Justice Strategic Management Initiative, May 1997, Dublin: Stationery Office.

Department of Justice, Equality and Law Reform (1999), *Victim's Charter and Guide to the Criminal Justice System*, Dublin: Department of Justice, Equality and Law Reform.

Dooley, E. (1995), *Homicide in Ireland, 1972–1991*, Dublin: Stationery Office.

Durkheim, E. (1984), *The Division of Labour in Society*, London: Macmillan Press. (First published in 1893.)

Fahey, T. and D. Watson (1995), *An Analysis of Social Housing Need.* General Research Series, Paper No. 168, Dublin: The Economic and Social Research Institute.

Farrall, S., J. Bannister, J. Ditton and E. Gilchrist (1997), "Questioning the Measurement of the 'Fear of Crime': Findings from a Major Methodological Study", *The British Journal of Criminology*, Volume 37, No. 4, Autumn.

Farraro, K.F. and R. LaGrange (1987), "The Measurement of the Fear of Crime", *Sociological Inquiry*, Vol. 57, No. 1, pp. 70–101.

Farrell, G. and K. Pease (1993), *Once Bitten, Twice Bitten: Repeat Victimisation and its Implications for Crime Prevention*, Crime Prevention Unit Series, Paper 46, London: Home Office.

Felson, M. (1998), *Crime and Everyday Life*, Second Edition, London: Pine Forge Press.

Felson, M. and L.E. Cohen (1980), "Human Ecology and Crime: A Routine Activity Approach" in M. Maguire, R. Morgan and R. Reiner (eds.) (1994), *The Oxford Handbook of Criminology*, Oxford: Oxford University Press.

Felson, M. and L.E. Cohen (1981), "Modelling Crime Rate Trends: A Criminal Opportunity Perspective", *Journal of Research in Crime and Delinquency*, Vol. 18, pp. 138–164 (as corrected, 1982, Vol. 19, No. 1).

Felson, M. and R.V. Clarke (1997), *Business and Crime Prevention*, Monsey, NY: Criminal Justice Press.

Field, S. (1990), *Trends in Crime and Their Interpretation*, London: Home Office Research Study, No. 119.

Garda Síochána, An (1996), *Annual Report 1995,* Dublin: Government Publications Office (also other years).

Garda Síochána, An (1998a), *Annual Report 1997*, Dublin: Government Publications Office.

Garda Síochána, An (1998b), *Policing Plan 1998/99*, Dublin: Government Publications Office.

Garda Síochána, An (1999), *Annual Report of An Garda Síochána 1998*. Dublin: Government Publications Office.

Gilchrist, E., J. Bannister, J. Ditton and S. Farrall (1998), "Women and the 'Fear of Crime': Challenging the Accepted Stereotype", *The British Journal of Criminology*, Vol. 38, No. 2, Spring.

Gomulka, J. (1992), "Grossing-up Revisited" in R. Hancock and H. Sutherland (eds.), "Microsimulation Models for Public Policy Analysis: New Frontiers", STICERD, Occasional Paper No. 17, London School of Economics.

Gomulka, J. (1994), "Grossing-up: A Note on Calculating Household Weights from Family Composition Totals", Microsimulation Unit Research Note No. MU/RN/4, University of Cambridge.

Hale, C. (1996), "Fear of Crime: A Review of the Literature", *International Review of Victimology*, Vol. 4, pp. 79–150.

Hale, C. (1998), "Crime and the Business Cycle in Post-war Britain Revisited", *The British Journal of Criminology*, Vol. 38, No. 4, Autumn.

Hale, C. and D. Sabbagh (1991), "Testing the Relationship between Unemployment and Crime: A Methodological Comment and Empirical Analysis Using Time Series Data for England and Wales", *Journal of Research in Crime and Delinquency*, Vol. 28, pp. 400–417.

Hirschi, T. (1969), *Causes of Delinquency*, Berkeley, CA: University of California Press.

Hirschi, T. (1983), "Crime and the Family" in James Q. Wilson (ed.), *Crime and Public Policy*, San Francisco, CA: Institute for Contemporary Studies, pp. 53–68.

Hough, M. (1995), *Anxiety about Crime: Findings from the 1994 British Crime Survey*, Home Office Research Bulletin, No. 147, London: HMSO.

Hough, M. and P. Mayhew (1983), *The British Crime Survey: First Report*, Home Office Research Study, No. 76, London: HMSO.

Johnson, S.D., K. Bowers and A. Hirschfield (1997), "New Insights into the Spatial and Temporal Distribution of Repeat Victimisation", *The British Journal of Criminology*, Vol. 37, Issue 2, Spring.

Jones, T., B. MacClean, and J. Young (1986), *The Islington Crime Survey: Crime, Victimisation and Policing in Inner-city London*, Aldershot, England: Gower Publishing Company.

Kelleher and Associates with M. O'Connor (1995), *Making the Links: Towards an Integrated Strategy for the Elimination of Violence against Women in Intimate Relationships with Men*, Dublin: Women's Aid.

Keogh, E. (1998), "Illicit Drug Use and Related Criminal Activity in Dublin Metropolitan Region", *Communiqué: Management Journal of the Garda Síochána*, March, pp. 18-23.

Kevlin, R. (1998), "Quality of Service to Victims of Domestic Burglary", *Communiqué: Management Journal of the Garda Síochána*, March, pp. 12-17.

Korf, Dirk J. and N. Wiersma (1996), *Drug-Related Petty Crime: Preliminary Report of Pilot Project on Drug-Related Petty Crime for the EU Commission European Monitoring Centre for Drugs and Drug Addiction*, Dublin, 18 October 1996.

Maguire, M. (1994), "Crime Statistics, Patterns and Trends: Changing Perceptions and their Implications" in M. Maguire, R. Morgan and R. Reiner (eds.), *The Oxford Handbook of Criminology*, Oxford: Oxford University Press, pp. 233-291.

Maguire, M. in collaboration with T. Bennett (1982), *Burglary in a Dwelling: The Offence, the Offender and the Victim*, London: Heinemann Educational.

Maguire, M., R. Morgan and R. Reiner (1994), *The Oxford Handbook of Criminology*, Oxford: Oxford University Press.

Maltz, M.D. (1999), *Bridging Gaps in Police Crime Data*, Washington, DC: Bureau of Justice Statistics.

Mativat, F. and P. Tremblay (1997), "Counterfeiting Credit Cards: Displacement Effects, Suitable Offenders and Crime Wave Patterns", *The British Journal of Criminology*, Volume 37, Issue 2: Spring.

Mayhew, P. and J.J.M. van Dijk (1997), *Criminal Victimisation in Eleven Industrialised Countries: Key Findings from the 1996 International Crime Victims Survey*, The Hague, Netherlands: Ministry of Justice, WODC (Research and Documentation Centre of the Ministry of Justice).

Mayhew, P. and N. Aye Maung (1992), *Surveying Crime: Findings from the 1992 British Crime Survey*, Home Office Research and Statistics Department, Research Findings, No. 2, London: HMSO.

Mayhew, P., N. Aye Maung and C. Mirrlees-Black (1993), *The 1992 British Crime Survey, First Report*, Home Office Research Study, No. 76, London: HMSO.

Mayhew, P., R.V. Clarke, A. Sturman and J.M. Hough (1976), *Crime as Opportunity*, London: HMSO.

McCullagh, C. (1996), *Crime in Ireland*, Cork: Cork University Press.

McKeown, K. and M. Brosnan (1998), "Police and Community: An Evaluation of Neighbourhood Watch and Community Alert in Ireland", Unpublished report to An Garda Síochána.

Medico-Social Research Board (1984), *Heroin Use in the Dun Laoghaire Borough Area, 1983–84.* Dublin: Medico-Social Research Board.

Merton, R.K. (1968), *Social Theory and Social Structure*, New York: Free Press. (First published in 1957.)

Miller, T.R., M.A. Cohen and B. Wiersema (1996), *Victim Costs and Consequences: A New Look*, Washington, DC: National Institute of Justice.

Mirrlees-Black, C. (1993), *The 1992 British Crime Survey*, Home Office Research Study, No. 132, London: HMSO.

Mirrlees-Black, C. and C. Byron (1999), *Domestic Violence: Findings from the BCS Self-Completion Questionnaire*, London: Home Office Research Development and Statistics Directorate, Research Findings, No. 86.

Mirrlees-Black, C., P. Mayhew and A. Percy (1996), *The 1996 British Crime Survey, England and Wales*, Home Office Statistical Bulletin Issue 19/96, London: Home Office Research and Statistics.

Mirrlees-Black, C., T. Budd, S. Partridge and P. Mayhew (1998), *The 1998 British Crime Survey: England and Wales*, London: Home Office Research, Development and Statistics Division, Issue 21/98.

Morris, T. (1989), *Crime and Criminal Justice since 1945*, Oxford, UK: Basil Blackwell.

Murphy, M. and B.J. Whelan (1995), "Public Attitudes to the Gardaí" *Communiqué*, Dublin: An Garda Síochána.

National Crime Forum (1998), *National Crime Forum Report*, Dublin: Institute of Public Administration.

National Economic and Social Council (1996), *Strategy Into the 21st Century*, Dublin: The National Economic and Social Council, Report No. 99.

Nee, C. and M. Taylor (1988), "Residential Burglary in the Republic of Ireland: Some Support for the Situational Approach" in M. Tomlinson, T. Varley and C. McCullagh (eds.) (1988), *Whose Law and Order: Aspects of Crime and Social Control in Irish Society*, Belfast: The Sociological Association of Ireland, pp. 143–154.

Nettler, G. (1978), *Explaining Crime*, New York: McGraw-Hill.

O'Connell, M. and A. Whelan (1994), "Crime Victimisation in Ireland", *Irish Criminal Law Journal*, Vol. 4, pp. 85–112.

O'Connell, M. and A. Whelan (1996), "Taking Wrongs Seriously. Public Perceptions of Crime Seriousness", *The British Journal of Criminology*, Volume 36, Issue 2: Spring.

O'Hare, A. and M. O'Brien (1992), *Treated Drug Misuse in the Greater Dublin Area*, Dublin: The Health Research Board.

O'Mahony, D., K. McEvoy, R. Geary, J. Morison and M. Brogden (1997), *The Northern Ireland Communities Crime Survey*, Belfast: Queen's University.

O'Mahony, P. (1993), *Crime and Punishment in Ireland*, Dublin: Round Hall Press.

O'Mahony, P. (1997), *Mountjoy Prisoners: A Sociological and Criminological Profile*, Dublin: Stationery Office.

Pease, K. (1994), "Crime Prevention" in M. Maguire, R. Morgan and R. Reiner, *The Oxford Handbook of Criminology*, Oxford: Oxford University Press, pp. 659–704.

Pease, K. (1998), *Repeat Victimisation: Taking Stock*, Crime Detection and Prevention Series Paper, No. 90, London: Home Office.

Pease, K. and G. Laycock (1996), "Revictimization: Reducing the Heat on Hot Victims" US Department of Justice, National Institute for Justice, Research in Action Series.

Pyle, D. and D.F. Deadman (1994), "Crime and the Business Cycle in Post-war Britain", *British Journal of Criminology*, Vol. 34, pp. 399–57.

Rand, M. (1999), *Criminal Victimization 1997: Changes 1996–97 with Trends 1993-97, A National Crime Victimization Survey Report*, January, NCJ 173385, US Department of Justice: Bureau of Justice Statistics.

Ratcliffe, J.H. and M.J. McCullagh (1998), "Identifying Repeat Victimisation with GIS", *The British Journal of Criminology*, Vol. 38, No. 4, Autumn.

Rengert, G. (1996), *The Geography of Illegal Drugs*, Boulder, CO: Westview Press.

Report to the Lord Mayor's Commission on Crime (1994), Dublin.

Robinson, M.B. (1998), "Burglary Revictimisation: The Time Period of Heightened Risk", *The British Journal of Criminology*, Vol. 38, No. 1, Winter.

Rottman, D.B. (1980), *Crime in the Republic of Ireland: Statistical Trends and their Interpretation*, ESRI Paper No. 102, Dublin: The Economic and Social Research Institute.

Rottman, D.B. (1984), *The Criminal Justice System: Policy And Performance*, NESC Report, No. 77, Dublin: The National Economic and Social Council.

Rottman, D.B. (1989), "Crime in Geographical Perspective" in W. Parker and A. Carter (eds.), *Ireland: Contemporary Perspectives on the Land and its People*, London: Routledge.

Shelley, L.I. (1981), *Crime and Modernization: The Impact of Industrialization and Urbanization on Crime*, Carbondale, IL: Southern Illinois University Press (Science and International Affairs Series).

Skogan, W. (1986), "Fear of Crime and Neighbourhood Change" in A.J. Reiss and M. Tonry (eds.), *Communities and Crime*. Chicago: University of Chicago Press.

Skogan, W. (1994), *Contacts between Police and Public*, London: HMSO. Home Office Research Study, No. 134.

Smith, W.R. and M. Torstensson (1997), "Fear of Crime: Gender Differences in Risk Perception and Neutralising Fear of Crime. Toward Resolving the Paradoxes", *The British Journal of Criminology*, Vol. 37, No. 4, Autumn.

Sutherland, E. (1961), *White Collar Crime*, New York: Holt, Rinehart and Winston. (Originally published in 1949)

Tedeschi, J. and R.B. Felson (1994), *Violence, Aggression and Coercive Action*, Washington DC: American Psychological Association Books.

Toby, J. (1979), "Delinquency in Cross-Cultural Perspective" in Lamar T. Empey (ed.), *Juvenile Justice: The Progressive Legacy and Current Reforms*, Charlottesville, VA: The University Press of Virginia, pp. 104–149.

Tomlinson, M., T. Varley and C. McCullagh (eds.) (1988), *Whose Law and Order: Aspects of Crime and Social Control in Irish Society*, The Sociological Association of Ireland.

van Dijk, J.J.M. and P. Mayhew (1992), *Criminal Victimisation in the Industrialised World: Key Findings from the 1989 and 1992 International Crime Surveys*, The Hague, Netherlands: Directorate of Crime Prevention, Ministry of Justice.

van Dijk, J.J.M., P. Mayhew and M. Killias (1991), *Experiences of Crime across the World: Key Findings from the 1989 International Crime Survey*, Deventer, Holland: Kluwer Law and Taxation Publishers.

van Koppen, P.J. and R.W.J. Jansen (1998), "The Road to the Robbery. Travel Patterns in Commercial Robberies", *The British Journal of Criminology*, Vol. 38, No. 2: Spring.

Weisburd, D. (1997), "Reorienting Crime Prevention Research and Policy: From the Causes of Criminality to the Context of Crime", (Paper presented at the 1996 Conference on Criminal Justice Research and Evaluation), US Government Printing Office: National Institute of Justice Paper, June 1997.

Wilson, J.Q. (1975), *Thinking about Crime*, New York: Vintage Books.

Winkel, F.W. (1998), "Fear of Crime and Criminal Victimisation: Testing a Theory of Psychological Incapacitation of the 'Stressor' Based on Downward Comparison Processes", *The British Journal of Criminology*, Vol. 38, No. 3, Summer.

Wolpin, K. (1978), "An Economic Model of Crime and Punishment in England and Wales, 1894–1967", *Journal of Political Economy*, Vol. 86, pp. 815–840.

Young, J. (1994), "Incessant Chatter: Recent Paradigms in Criminology" in Mike Maguire, Rod Morgan and Robert Reiner (eds.), *The Oxford Handbook of Criminology*, Oxford: Clarendon Press, pp. 69–124.

Zimring, F.E. and G. Hawkins (1997), *Crime Is Not the Problem: Lethal Violence in America*, New York: Oxford University Press.